C# Core Language
Little Black Book

Bill Wagner

President and CEO
Roland Elgey

Publisher
Al Valvano

Associate Publisher
Katherine R. Hartlove

Acquisitions Editor
Jawahara Saidullah

Product Marketing Managers
Tracy Rooney
Jeff Johnson

Project Editors
Don Eamon
Sally M. Scott

Technical Reviewer
Eric Kinateder
Keith Lynch

Production Coordinator
Todd Halvorsen

Cover Designer
Laura Wellander

C# Core Language Little Black Book

The Coriolis Group, LLC
14455 North Hayden Road
Suite 220
Scottsdale, Arizona 85260

(480) 483-0192
FAX (480) 483-0193
www.coriolis.com

Library of Congress Cataloging-in-Publication Data
Wagner, Bill.
   C# core language little black book / by Bill Wagner.
      p. cm.
   Includes index.
   ISBN 1-58880-058-X
   1. C# (Computer program language)   2. Computer programming.   I. Title.
QA76.73.C154 W34 2001
005.13'3–dc21

2001047678

Printed in the United States of America
10 9 8 7 6 5 4 3 2 1

The Coriolis Group, LLC • 14455 North Hayden Road, Suite 220 • Scottsdale, Arizona 85260

A Note from Coriolis

Coriolis Technology Press was founded to create a very elite group of books: the ones you keep closest to your machine. In the real world, you have to choose the books you rely on every day *very* carefully, and we understand that.

To win a place for our books on that coveted shelf beside your PC, we guarantee several important qualities in every book we publish. These qualities are:

- *Technical accuracy*—It's no good if it doesn't work. Every Coriolis Technology Press book is reviewed by technical experts in the topic field, and it is sent through several editing and proofreading passes in order to create the piece of work you now hold in your hands.

- *Innovative editorial design*—We've put years of research and refinement into the ways we present information in our books. Our books' editorial approach is uniquely designed to reflect the way people learn new technologies and search for solutions to technology problems.

- *Practical focus*—We put only pertinent information into our books and avoid any fluff. Every fact included between these two covers must serve the mission of the book as a whole.

- *Accessibility*—The information in a book is worthless unless you can find it quickly when you need it. We put a lot of effort into our indexes, and heavily cross-reference our chapters, to make it easy for you to move right to the information you need.

Here at The Coriolis Group we have been publishing and packaging books, technical journals, and training materials since 1989. We have put a lot of thought into our books; please write to us at **ctp@coriolis.com** and let us know what you think. We hope that you're happy with the book in your hands, and that in the future, when you reach for software development and networking information, you'll turn to one of our books first.

Coriolis Technology Press
The Coriolis Group
14455 N. Hayden Road, Suite 220
Scottsdale, Arizona
85260

Email: ctp@coriolis.com
Phone: (480) 483-0192
Toll free: (800) 410-0192

To Lara, Sarah, and Scott.
But most of all, to Marlene, my lifelong love.

&

About the Author

Bill Wagner spends his days designing and writing software, as well as teaching others to do the same. He cofounded SRT Solutions so that he could continue to mentor software developers, design and develop software, and help new and emerging companies leverage technology effectively to grow their businesses.

Bill enjoys learning new software development tools and techniques and then teaching others to use them effectively. He has been a columnist for *Visual C++ Developers Journal* and has written for *Visual Studio Magazine* for more than a year, writing about C++, C#, and VisualStudio. NET. He has also been published in *Microsoft Systems Journal* (now, *MSDN Magazine*). He has written two eBooks on STL programming, available at **www.mightywords.com**. Bill has also given talks on exception safety and STL programming at Visual C++ developers conferences. He has given several talks at the Ann Arbor Computing Society and has taught week-long seminars for software developers. Topics have ranged from graphics programming, to the C++ programming language, to MFC and COM programming, Windows NT systems programming, DirectX, and OpenGL. In addition to training and mentoring, Bill still actively designs applications and developers software.

Bill has more than 15 years of experience writing software, designing applications, and mentoring software developers; he has been writing software for Windows for 10 years. He has worked in many different application domains, ranging from decision support systems and interactive Web sites to children's games. Bill has also developed software for genomic and proteomic research systems, document management systems, and networking software. Bill has written software using Pascal, C, C++, Java, and C#, and he also has written software for a variety of Unix systems. He is always looking for the next big innovation in software development and can't wait to use it.

Acknowledgments

Writing a book involves so many people. First of all, I need to thank my business partners, Dianne Marsh and Bob Rasmussen, who helped keep our business running while I was writing this book. I want to thank acquisitions editors Jawahara Saidullah and Kevin Weeks, both of whom helped me to begin the process. Jessica Choi helped convert my original drafts of the first chapters into the far-more-useful text you are now holding. Don Eamon, the project editor, stewarded the project to its completion. Eric Kinateder did a fantastic job of technical editing. He deserves special accommodation for tech reviewing text based on .NET Beta 1 and for finding all the changes for Beta 2. Darren Meiss did the content editing in order to make the prose far more readable. Keith Lynch made sure all the notations were consistent. I also want to thank all the participants in C# newsgroups who faithfully answered my queries when the behavior of my samples did not match my original interpretation of the documents.

Finally, I need to thank my family for all the sacrifices they made so I could write this book. There were countless hours spent writing instead of having more enjoyable family time.

Contents at a Glance

Table of Contents

Introduction

Thanks for buying *C# Core Language Little Black Book*. I enjoyed writing it, having the opportunity to delve so deeply into C# in this way.

Over the course of writing this book, I became firmly convinced that C# will be an important language for future development. I find that I can write, correct, and complete programs more quickly in C# than in C++ or Java. I also find that I get better performance with C# than with either Visual Basic or Java. C# lets me program at a higher level of abstraction when I want to by using properties, indexers, and other RAD tools. It also lets me program at a lower level using unsafe techniques, such as pointer manipulation, when I need to for better performance. Finally, C# attributes let me replace entire repetitive blocks of code with a single keyword. This feature saves me time developing and understanding code that has already been written.

Read this book, and experiment with your own C# applications. I think you will agree that developing great applications just got easier and more fun.

Is This Book for You?

C# Core Language Little Black Book was written with the intermediate or advanced user in mind. Among the topics that are covered are:

- New C# syntax elements, such as properties and indexers
- How to write .NET compliant components in C#
- How C# integrates with the .NET framework, including ASP.NET and Web Services
- C# Exception support
- C# Multithreading support

How to Use This Book

This book is loosely divided into three sections. The first four chapters introduce the basic elements of the C# language. Readers who have experience with C, C++, or Java can skim these chapters. C# has some new subtle syntax differences, so I would recommend browsing these chapters.

Chapters 5 through 13 cover the new elements of the C# language and the more advanced C# language topics. These chapters build on each other, and you should try to read them in order. However, if you are looking for a specific solution, go ahead and leap to it. I have tried to make each chapter independent; because of the complex nature of C#, however, that is a bit difficult.

Chapters 14 through 21 cover how C# fits into the .NET framework as a whole. You will learn the ways in which C# integrates with the framework and how to create components that can be used in .NET programs written in other languages. You also learn techniques for reducing testing-cycle time and benchmarking C# code. These chapters are independent of each other, but you should rely on the information found in preceding chapters as a "knowledge base."

Finally, the appendices of the book provide a quick reference to the C# preprocessor directives and XML documentation keywords. I wrote these appendices not as a complete guide but as a quick page that you could use to find how to use these tools when you are creating programs. I can never remember all the keywords for these tools, so a quick reference organized by the task is helpful to me. I hope it is as helpful to you as well.

The *Little Black Book* Philosophy

Written by experienced professionals, Coriolis *Little Black Books* are terse, easily "thumb-able" question-answerers and problem solvers. The *Little Black Book*'s unique two-part chapter format—brief technical overviews followed by practical immediate solutions—is structured to help you use your knowledge, solve problems, and quickly master complex technical issues to become an expert. By breaking down complex topics into easily manageable components, this format helps you quickly find what you're looking for, with the diagrams and code you need to make it happen.

Each chapter contains samples that demonstrate the techniques involved, in concise format that you can reuse in your own work. Later chapters demonstrate larger programs that show you how different techniques work together to solve larger problems.

I welcome your feedback on this book. You can either email The Coriolis Group at **ctp@coriolis.com** or email me directly at **wwagner@ SRTsolutions.com**. Errata, updates, and more are available at **www. SRTsolutions.com/cslbb.htm**.

Chapter 1

Hello C#

In Brief

This book is a combination of a programmer's guide and a reference for the C# language. You will learn each feature of the C# language and why the features are designed the way they are. This new knowledge will help you create more correct and robust C# programs and components by leveraging the best C# feature for each task.

The C# language is similar to the C, C++, and Java languages, which makes it easy for you to learn C# if you have experience in one or more of these languages. However, some of the syntax elements are slightly different in C# compared to these other languages. If you are not careful, these differences can trip you up. Throughout this book, whenever there are syntax changes from one of these languages that might be confusing, those changes will be marked as follows:

NOTE (C++ Users): *This note would mark a change from the C++ syntax.*

NOTE (Java Users): *This note would mark a change from the Java syntax.*

You do not need to have C++ or Java experience to read this book because I have included a discussion of all the elements of the language, even those that are unchanged from C/C++. However, you should have some object-oriented programming experience because this book doesn't cover object-oriented programming techniques in depth, but it does show how C# embraces object-oriented programming idioms.

This chapter introduces you to the major topics that are covered in this book—the C# language, the Common Language Runtime (CLR), the .NET Base Class Libraries (BCL), and the Visual Studio .NET IDE. The first three are very interdependent, with the C# language having been designed to be the most natural language a person could use to implement .NET programs. In fact, many of the new features in C# make it easier to create and maintain .NET programs. The Visual Studio .NET IDE contains many features that make it a powerful tool to use when you develop C# programs.

Let's begin with a brief description of C#. C# is a new object-oriented language. Some have also called it a "component-oriented language." It is in the C/C++/Java family of languages, and most of its syntax elements are probably familiar to anyone who has used these languages, especially C++ and Java. But C# is not a clone of any of those languages—it has new elements that are innovative and provide some great ways to express high-level constructs. These new constructs make it easier to express your design intent inside your classes and also to programmers using your classes.

Although I will not spend the entire book comparing C# to C++ and Java, these comparisons *are* a good way to get you started with C#. C# is a pure object-oriented language in the sense that you must define all functions and variables inside the scope of a class. C#, unlike C++, doesn't have global functions. C# is similar to Java in that the definition of methods is inline in the class definition and unlike C++ where *include files* declare classes and *source files* define them. C# has some operator overloading capabilities, like C++. However, the techniques for overloading operators in C# is different than the techniques in C++.

New Syntax in C#

As mentioned in the preceding section, C# adds some new syntax elements that are not available in either C++ or Java: properties, indexers, and attributes. *Properties* are syntactic support for **get( )** and **set( )** methods commonly found in C++ and Java. In fact, properties are a unique syntax for the bean properties in a Java bean. They act like data fields to clients of your class but yet are implemented as functions inside the class.

Indexers are a way to treat an object as an array. They are similar to overloading the [] operator in C++. C# indexers can have multiple parameters because C# supports multidimensional arrays.

The other significant difference between C# and C++ and Java is attributes. *Attributes* are the C# way of supporting declarative programming. You add attributes to your code, and the compiler injects code into your source stream based on the attribute. C# has attributes that help with database programming, Web programming, and classes and methods that help you define your own attributes.

Assemblies

After you write all the code, you will need to deploy it. All .NET components are deployed as an assembly. The C# compiler builds an assembly from your source file(s), which can be either an executable or a dynamic-link library (DLL). An assembly contains the following:

- All the Microsoft Intermediate Language (MSIL) code for your component
- The manifest that describes the assembly
- Any other resources needed by the assembly

Microsoft Intermediate Language

The MSIL code is the binary intermediate form for a .NET program. MSIL is analogous to P-CODE in Visual Basic, or Java BYTE-CODE format in Java programs. You can examine the MSIL code in any assembly by using the MSIL Disassembler. When your assembly gets loaded into the managed environment, the MSIL is compiled using just-in-time (JIT) compilation to convert the MSIL into machine instructions. The Common Language Runtime keeps the machine code cached to increase performance.

Manifest

The manifest contains information about the assembly. This includes versioning information, a list of all types and methods in the assembly, and the access levels of all the types and methods in the assembly. An assembly can be packaged in either a DLL file for a class library, or an EXE file for an executable program.

The assembly format is a significant improvement over COM delivery methods. In COM, component information was distributed across three different locations. The DLL file contained the executable code to run when your COM object was accessed. A TLB file contained the interface description for the component. The Registry contained information about the component, such as its name, CLSID, executable file, and version. This multiple installation caused numerous problems. It was very common for these three pieces of information to get out of synch with each other. When creating a component, you might update the code, but not the type library. Or, you might forget to re-register a component when a new interface was added. The .NET assembly format fixes these problems. All the information that describes a component is stored in the assembly. This information includes the executable code and the metadata that describes the component. Version information, interface descriptions, and code are all stored in one neat package. The component cannot get out of synch with itself. Later, I explain how you can make sure that your application works with the correct version of the components it uses and how you can correctly update versions of any shared components you create.

Common Language Runtime

The CLR is a managed environment that executes your programs and functions as an execution engine. The CLR has many responsibilities, including the following:

- Loading .NET assemblies
- JIT compiling MSIL to create machine code
- Running the JIT-compiled executable
- Providing memory management and garbage collection

The CLR improves on the component management strategies available in the Windows operating system or with COM components. You can install components as either global components that can be shared by many programs, or you can install components as local, for use in only one program. Every assembly contains version information that helps ensure that programs always use a compatible version of every component. The CLR can even handle multiple versions of the same component on the same machine.

The .NET Base Class Libraries

The Base Class Libraries encompass all the .NET classes that you can access in your C# program. Unlike many other high-level languages, C# doesn't have a standard library; the standard C# library is the .NET BCL. The BCL provides all the capabilities you would expect from a runtime environment and contains classes for common data structures, Windows UI elements, Web UI elements, database access, file I/O, and other common programming tasks. Covering the entire BCL—more than 1,400 classes—is outside the scope of this book, but the BCL and C# are very closely linked. I use many of the major parts of the BCL throughout the book, and you will become familiar with the BCL classes. This chapter shows a few of the BCL classes in the System namespace. Throughout the book, you will learn about the more common BCL classes.

The Visual Studio .NET IDE

The Visual Studio .NET IDE (VS .NET) is, in my opinion, the most effective tool for developing C# programs. Although you do not technically need to use Visual Studio .NET to create C# programs, you probably will choose to use it anyway. All the samples I created for this book were written using Visual Studio .NET. You will learn about the tools and productivity aids in both Visual Studio .NET and the .NET framework SDK. You will also learn how Visual Studio .NET automates many common programming tasks, such as creating classes and files, adding methods, and including BCL assemblies. You will also learn about the debugger and how to create XML documentation for your classes.

Using the C# Language

Writing a book covering a language is a bit tricky. Once you get beyond the simple "Hello World" sample, it gets very difficult to limit the code in samples to only those features of the language being examined. Often, the end result is samples that are inefficient and somewhat incorrect in an effort to avoid having to use elements of the language that have not been covered. I have tried to avoid that in this book and have written samples that use the features of the language that I would use in an actual production program.

When I use features that have not yet been covered, I point to the later section of the book where that particular feature is covered. Any piece of code you find in this book is complete as it stands. After finishing the entire book, you can reference the samples in previous chapters and use them as reference material when you need example code. You need not worry that earlier samples are avoiding language features that are pertinent to your problem. When I describe the code in each chapter, I concentrate only on the syntax elements being covered. The elements that have not yet been described are not covered, but I briefly mention what they are and where I cover them. Finally, Chapter 17 contains a few large case studies that show you how some typical .NET programs are organized. You can use those samples as a starting point for different types of programs: console applications, windows applications, Web applications, and Web services. These samples are larger and more complex than earlier samples and are small applications in their own right.

Getting Started

It's time to dive into C# programming. A C# program contains a number of classes. One of those classes contains a method named **Main**, which has the following four valid definitions:

```
public static void Main ()
public static int Main ()
public static void Main (string [] args)
public static int Main (string [] args)
```

NOTE (Java Users): *The string class in C# is lower case, as opposed to Java's string class.*

The **Main** method is always *public*, meaning that a method can be accessed by any code, and any user of the class can access **Main**. The **Main** method is also always a *static* method in a class, meaning that it can be called before an object of that class type is created. Static methods are often referred to as class methods because they are associated with a class type rather than an instance of a class.

Main can return an integer return code, indicating the success or failure of the program. By convention, a return value of 0 indicates success, and any nonzero return value indicates the particular error code for the program. Or, you can choose to declare **Main** with a void return, and no success code gets returned.

The last two forms of **Main** show how to access command-line parameters. The command-line parameters are passed to the program as an array of string objects. The array of string objects is a C# built-in array.

Related solution:	*Found on page:*
Using Arrays	335

For the moment, think of this array as a C built-in array.

NOTE (C++ Users): *The first argument, args[0] is not the program name, as in C and C++. It is the first parameter after the program name.*

The C# *string* keyword is an alias for the **System.String** class, which illustrates an important C# concept: C# does not have a predefined language type as such. All types in C# are actually .NET types, a design that makes it much easier for C# programs to interact with programs and components written in other .NET-compliant languages (VB .NET, Managed C++, and others.) Similarly, the *int* type for the return type of the **Main** method is a synonym for **System.Int32**, another .NET type.

Moving Forward

This chapter gives a brief overview of the Visual Studio .NET environment and shows a simple Hello C# application. In the "Immediate Solutions" section, I will show some of the simpler tools in the debugger and give you a brief overview of the MISL Disassembler.

In reading this chapter, you are learning some of the features that make C# a new and unique language. It is familiar to those of you who use C++ or Java, but some of the syntax is new and different in the C# language. In the next chapter, I provide an overview of the language elements in the C# language.

Immediate Solutions

Using Visual Studio .NET

NOTE: *Although you may be familiar with previous versions of Visual C++, Visual Basic, or Visual J++, walk through this Immediate Solution. The new Visual Studio .NET IDE has many new and different features; also, many familiar features are accessed differently. To start Visual Studio .NET, perform the following steps:*

1. *Select File|Project|New. Visual Studio .NET displays the dialog box shown in Figure 1.1.*

2. *Choose the Visual C# Projects folder in Project Types.*

3. *Select the Console Application as the template.*

4. *Enter "helloCs" for the project type.* ~name~

I choose the C:\cslbb folder for the project location. All the projects for this book are under this folder.

5. *Click on OK.*

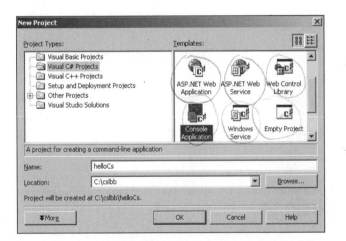

Figure 1.1   This is the Visual Studio .NET New Project dialog box. It shows the different types of projects you can create.

Visual Studio .NET creates a simple project.

Your project contains two source files: helloCs.cs and AssemblyInfo.cs. Let's go through helloCs.cs first (see Listing 1.1), which contains the source code for this simple application. Every Visual Studio .NET wizard generates code to place the application in a namespace. The namespace is the name of the application, in this case **helloCs**. It also generates one class, named **Class1**. Visual Studio .NET generates a public constructor for that class and a **Main** method. Visual Studio .NET generates the version of **Main** that returns an integer and gives you the command-line parameters.

Listing 1.1   The helloCs.cs file created by Visual Studio .NET.

```
using System;

namespace helloCs
{
  /// <summary>
  /// Summary description for Class1.
  /// </summary>
  class Class1
  {
    static void Main(string[] args)
    {
      //
      // TODO: Add code to start application here
      //
    }
  }
}
```

The remainder of the Immediate Solutions walk you through all the code in this listing and explain each part.

Writing Hello C#

This version of helloCs.cs runs but doesn't do anything. So, you can modify it to say "hello" (see Listing 1.2 later in this section to see the complete code). Let's go through this code piece by piece.

Using and Declaring Namespaces

A *namespace* is a way to organize code to avoid name collisions. Namespaces prevent multiple groups or companies from accidentally writing classes or functions that have the same name and are therefore incompatible. Visual Studio .NET creates a namespace for each project you create. Take a look at the following code:

```
namespace helloCs
{
```

All the code in this program is contained in the **helloCs** namespace. The last closing brace ends this namespace. You may declare the same namespace in multiple files.

Related solution:	Found on page:
Using a Namespace	162

Also notice the following:

```
using System;
```

The **using** directive promotes code from the namespace so that it can be used in the current file. In this example, the **Console** class is part of the **System** namespace. If this line were missing, you would need to write **System.Console** instead of **Console** in the later lines. Visual Studio .NET always includes the **using System** directive because almost every program will use the **System** namespace.

You will declare your own namespaces to prevent name collisions with other code. And you will include namespaces to tell the compiler which portions of the BCL should be assumed when you use other classes.

Declaring Classes

Your entire C# code must be contained inside a class. You declare a class by using an access modifier, the **class** keyword, and the name of the class, as in the following:

```
public class HelloCSharp
{
```

This line declares a new class, named **HelloCSharp**. I changed the name from **Class1** to a more descriptive name for this application's main class. The class is declared with **public** access. This means that there are no restrictions on what code can use this class.

Declaring Methods

The next piece of code contains the methods in the class. *Methods* define the functions that a class supports. Each method has an access modifier that defines what other code can call that particular method, as in the following:

```
private void SayHello (string name)
{
  Console.WriteLine ("Hello {0}", name);
}
```

The first method in this class is the **SayHello** method. This method is an instance member of the **HelloCSharp** class. It is also a private method, which only other members of the **HelloCSharp** class can access. The return type is void, meaning that there is no return value from this method. The **SayHello** method takes one string parameter that represents the name to use.

This method has only one executable line. The method calls a static method **WriteLine** in the **Console** class, which formats and prints a string to the system console. The system console is the command window for the program. The **WriteLine** method is an *overloaded* method, meaning that there are several different **WriteLine** methods in the **Console** class. Each is distinguished by a different set of parameters. The version called here takes a format string and an array of objects. The format string **"Hello {0}"** determines how to print the remaining arguments to the function. Any number of extra parameters can be added to this method. Any number inside brackets is interpreted as the index to these optional parameters. Here, {0} means to print the first optional argument using the default **Object.ToString( )** method; for the string class, it simply prints the contents of the string. So, this method prints "Hello" and the name to the command window.

Writing **Main**

All C# programs start execution in the **Main( )** method, which is a public static method in one of the classes in the program:

```
public static void Main(string[] args)
{
```

The next method in this class is the **Main** method. This method is public and static. I used the version of **Main** that VisualStudio generated. You may want to pick one of the other forms, depending on your needs. The following code creates a new **HelloCSharp** object:

```
HelloCSharp theAppObject — new HelloCSharp ();
```

The "new" keyword is the way to create a new object. The **HelloCSharp** object is assigned to a local variable named **theAppObject**.

NOTE (C++ Users): *You always use the "new" keyword to create a new object. In C#, class objects are always created on the managed heap. Notice that even if there are no parameters to the constructor, the parameters are necessary.*

The following block of code calls the **SayHello** method to print a message to the user:

```
if (args.Length > 0) {
  theAppObject.SayHello(args[0]);
} else {
  theAppObject.SayHello ("You");
}
```

If any arguments exist on the command line, the first argument is passed to the **SayHello** method. If not, the constant string **"You"** gets passed to the **SayHello** function. The **Length** property of an array returns the number of elements in the array. The valid array indices are from 0 to Length–1. And finally, the **Main** method calls the **ReadLine( )** static method to wait for user input:

```
  Console.ReadLine ();
}
```

This is merely a convenience when you run this program within Visual Studio .NET. Visual Studio .NET will create a new window when you launch the program within the IDE. This line keeps that window open until you press Enter. Take a look at Listing 1.2.

Listing 1.2   The finished Hello C# sample, showing the changes made.

```
namespace helloCs
{
  using System;

  /// <summary>
  ///     Summary description for HelloCSharp.
  /// </summary>
  public class HelloCSharp
  {
```

```
/// <summary>
/// Say Hello Method.
/// </summary>
/// <param name="name"> The Name of the user.</param>
/// <remarks>
/// This method prints a hello message to the user.
/// </remarks>
private void SayHello (string name)
{
  Console.WriteLine ("Hello {0}", name);
}


/// <summary>
/// Main entry point.
/// </summary>
/// <param name="args"> The command-line arguments.</param>
/// <remarks>
/// This is the entry point for the program. It examines
/// the command-line parameters and calls SayHello method
/// to print a message to the user. Because the console
/// window created by Visual Studio .NET closes when the
/// program exits, this method waits until the user presses
/// the "Enter" key before exiting.
/// </remarks>
public static void Main(string[] args)
{
  HelloCSharp theAppObject = new HelloCSharp ();
  if (args.Length > 0) {
    theAppObject.SayHello(args[0]);
  } else {
    theAppObject.SayHello ("You");
  }
  Console.ReadLine ();
}
}
}
```

Your program should look like Listing 1.2. Now examine the other items that Visual Studio .NET created. Figure 1.2 shows the Solution Explorer window. The References folder contains any namespaces that your project references. Visual Studio .NET adds three components to this folder. The **System** assembly contains all the classes defined in the **System** namespace. The **System.Data** assembly contains classes to work with ADO.NET, and the **System.XML** contains classes that work with standard XML.

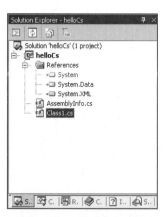

Figure 1.2 The Solution Explorer shows you the files in your project and the assemblies your project references.

The AssemblyInfo.cs information contains version and copyright information for the sample. See Chapters 18 and 19 for more details on this information.

Using the Visual Studio .NET Debugger

Now, all you have to do is build the program and run it, which you can do by following these steps:

1. Select Build|Build.

   The C# compiler creates your program. The compiler creates a single executable file and a program database file. The default configuration for Visual Studio .NET is the debug configuration.

2. Select Debug|Start to run the program, and you will see the following output:

   ```
   Hello You
   ```

You can set command-line parameters that Visual Studio .NET sends to your program when you debug it. You set these command-line properties by doing the following:

1. Add the command-line parameters in the Visual Studio .NET IDE so that you can see your own custom message from the sample.

2. Select Project|Properties.

3. Open the Configuration Properties folder on the left side of the dialog box (see Figure 1.3).

4. Select the Debugging location under the Configuration Properties folder.

5. Add a string to the Debug Arguments item in the list control on the right side of the control.

NOTE: *Notice that I have quoted the string. If you omit the quotes, you will see the message, "Hello new". By quoting the string, it gets passed to the program as a single argument. You get "Hello new C# Programmer".*

Now, let's explore a bit inside the debugger. The Visual Studio .NET debugger contains many of the same features as the Visual C++ Debugger. Use the F9 key to add a breakpoint in the current line.

1. Set a breakpoint at the first line of the **Main** function.

2. When the breakpoint hits, change the display to the Locals window.

You can modify the program arguments programmatically. However, you cannot add or remove elements from an array in the debugger. Figure 1.4 shows the Locals window in the debugger.

3. Cursor to the value of **args[0]**, and type the new value.

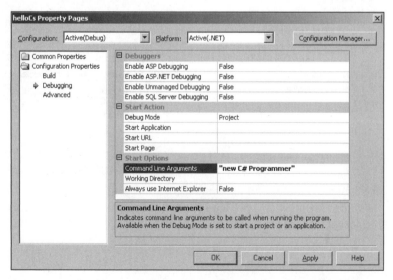

Figure 1.3   The debugger settings for your project; use this dialog box to modify the program arguments for your project.

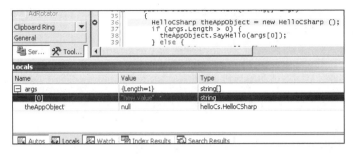

Figure 1.4   You can examine and change variable values in the debugger.

At the top of the figure, you can see the debugger showing you where execution of your program has stopped.

Using the Disassembler

The last tool you learn about in this chapter is the MSIL Disassembler. The MSIL Disassembler is a useful tool to examine the contents of an assembly and view the code and manifest in an assembly. It also shows the contents of any classes in an assembly, regardless of the permissions of those elements. In addition to all that, this tool helps you understand how the C# compiler turns your code into MSIL. The Disassembler comes as part of the Visual Studio .NET installation. You will find it in "C:\Program Files\Microsoft.Net\FrameworkSDK\ Bin\ildasm.exe". I added a menu item for the Disassembler in Visual Studio .NET's list of external tools. Figure 1.5 shows the External Tools configuration dialog. The $(TargetPath) parameter tells Visual Studio. NET to pass the current target to the Disassembler. Figure 1.6 shows the MSIL Disassembler window for the helloCs.exe assembler.

The executable contains one namespace (**helloCs**), one class (**HelloCSharp**), and the manifest. Namespaces are the blue shields. A class is the blue rectangle with the prongs coming off the right. There are three methods in the **HelloCSharp** class:

• A constructor

• **Main**

• **SayHello**

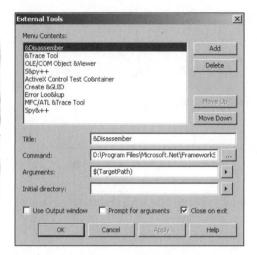

Figure 1.5   You can add the disassembler tool to the Visual Studio .NET by selecting Tools|External Tools.

Figure 1.6   The MSIL Disassembler shows the classes, methods, and variables inside your class.

Methods are denoted by the pink squares. If the square contains an *S*, it is a static method. Notice that even though I removed the constructor from the source code, it still exists in the object code. If you do not create any constructors for your class, the C# compiler creates a public default constructor. I prefer not writing the default constructor, unless you need to do something different than the compiler-generated version. The manifest contains the assembly information. Later in the book, I explain how to manipulate this information. For now, all you need to know is that the manifest describes the assembly, including the company that created the assembly, any copyright information, and any versioning information. If you double-click on the **Main** method, you see the window displayed in Figure 1.7.

```
HelloCSharp::Main : void(class System.String[])                          _□×
.method public hidebysig static void  Main(class System.String[] args) il managed
{
  .entrypoint
  // Code size       41 (0x29)
  .maxstack  3
  .locals (class helloCs.HelloCSharp V_0)
  IL_0000:  newobj      instance void helloCs.HelloCSharp::.ctor()
  IL_0005:  stloc.0
  IL_0006:  ldarg.0
  IL_0007:  ldlen
  IL_0008:  conv.i4
  IL_0009:  ldc.i4.0
  IL_000a:  ble.s       IL_0017
  IL_000c:  ldloc.0
  IL_000d:  ldarg.0
  IL_000e:  ldc.i4.0
  IL_000f:  ldelem.ref
  IL_0010:  call        instance void helloCs.HelloCSharp::SayHello(class System.String)
  IL_0015:  br.s        IL_0022
  IL_0017:  ldloc.0
  IL_0018:  ldstr       "You"
  IL_001d:  call        instance void helloCs.HelloCSharp::SayHello(class System.String)
  IL_0022:  call        class System.String [mscorlib]System.Console::ReadLine()
  IL_0027:  pop
  IL_0028:  ret
} // end of method HelloCSharp::Main
```

Figure 1.7   The Disassembler shows the source code along with the MSIL code when you examine a function.

This shows the disassembly for the **Main** method. MSIL looks very similar to assembler code. Look at the different calls in the assembler. Any calls to **new** are translated into the MSIL **newobj** statement. The MSIL tells you whether a method is an instance method or a class method. Remember that static methods and class methods are synonyms. Finally, MSIL **call** statements tell you in which assembly a particular method resides. In this case, the **System.Console. ReadLine** method is in the mscorlib.dll assembly.

The MSIL Disassembler is a powerful tool. If you open a debug assembly, you can view the source code along with the assembler code for the assembler. Be careful when you ship debug code: users with the Disassembler can see the source code. This is not possible, however, with a release build. I continue to use the Disassembler throughout the book to show you elements of C# and how they work inside .NET.

C# Statements and Control Flow

In Brief

This chapter introduces you to the statements and control structures in the C# language. Readers with extensive C and C++ experience can skim this chapter for notes on new features and changed syntax from those languages.

It is almost impossible to discuss the syntax of a language without introducing every programming concept supported by the language. On the other hand, when I discuss the more detailed programming concepts, I don't want you to get lost in new syntax. So, this chapter contains quite a few forward references to where programming topics get more detailed coverage.

I chose this order for three reasons. First, C/C++ programmers can skim this chapter looking for the syntactic differences and start reading again in Chapter 3. Second, I avoid any concerns that later samples will use only a limited subset of the language. Third, putting all the syntax elements in one chapter should serve as a reference for you after you read the entire book. So, each syntax element gets a very short description in this chapter.

Object Types

The C# language has three different object types:

- *Value types*—Small, lightweight objects that are created on the stack or inline in a reference object. Examples are integers and Boolean values. Enumeration values are also value types.

- *Reference types*—Objects of a user-defined class. These objects are typically larger and are always created on the managed heap. They are called reference types because they are always passed to methods by reference.

- *Pointer types*—Represent raw memory addresses. Pointer types are used with unsafe code.

Value Types

The built-in numeric types in C# are all value types. Also, the C# built-in types are actually aliases to the corresponding CLR types (see Table 2.1).

So, these two variable declarations are equivalent:

```
int i;
System.Int32 i2;
```

Because **int** and **System.Int32** are synonyms, any members of the **System.Int32** type can be called on an **int**:

```
int i;
System.Type t = i.GetType ();
```

Table 2.1 Corresponding C# intrinsic types and .NET CLR types.

C# Type	Corresponding CLR Type
bool	**System.Boolean** (true or false value)
sbyte	**System.SByte** (signed 8-bit integer)
byte	**System.Byte** (unsigned 8-bit integer)
short	**System.Int16** (signed 16-bit integer)
ushort	**System.Uint16** (unsigned 16-bit integer)
int	**System.Int32** (signed 32-bit integer)
uint	**System.Uint32** (unsigned 32-bit integer)
long	**System.Int64** (signed 64-bit integer)
ulong	**System.Uint64** (unsigned 64-bit integer)
char	**System.Char** (unsigned 16-bit integer)
decimal	**System.Decimal** (12-byte fixed point number)
float	**System.Float** (single precision floating point)
double	**System.Double** (double precision floating point)

Value types are lightweight quantities that are passed to functions by value. Value types do not have finalizers and are not garbage collected. Because they are allocated on the stack or inline, they cease to exist immediately when they go out of scope. Value types can be converted to reference types and back by a process known as *boxing*. They have a built-in default constructor that sets all the constituent fields to 0. Boolean values are initialized to false.

Any integral type can be implicitly converted to a larger integral type.

NOTE (C++ Users): *Unlike in C and C++, there are no implicit conversions from integral types to Boolean types in C#. The following code is not valid C#:*

```
int i = func ();
if (i) {
   func2 ();
}
```

This must be rewritten as the following:

```
int i = func ();
if (i != 0) {
   func2 ();
}
```

You can create your own lightweight value types by using the **struct** keyword.

Reference Types

Reference types are types that are managed by the CLR and declared using the **class**, **interface**, or **delegate** keywords. Reference types are always created on the managed heap. The CLR garbage collector is responsible for releasing memory resources acquired by reference types. When an object can no longer be referenced anywhere, the CLR garbage collector will return the memory to the managed heap. You create an instance of a class with the new operator:

```
System.Collections.Queue q = new System.Collections.Queue ();
```

Two of the C# built-in types are synonyms for CLR class types, as established in Table 2.2.

Table 2.2 C# reference types and corresponding CLR types.

C# Type	CLR Type
string	**System.String** (string object)
object	**System.Object** (the root object)

System.String is a *sealed* class, which means that you cannot derive a new class from **string** or **System.String**.

System.Object is the root class for all reference types. Any object in the system is derived from **System.Object**. Therefore, all reference types can access the methods in **System.Object**. **System.Object** is an *abstract* class. That means that you cannot create an instance of **object**. You may only create instances of concrete objects that are derived from **object**. This means that the following code will not compile:

```
System.Object o = new System.Object ();
```

Instead, you must create a concrete object that is derived from **System.Object** and implicitly access the **System.Object** reference or methods:

```
string s = new string ();
System.Object o = s; // Implicit conversion.
System.Type t = s.GetType (); // access System.Object method.
```

You create new reference types using the **class**, **interface**, or **delegate** keywords.

Related solutions:	Found on page:
Using Structs	98
Using Properties for Delegates	147
Creating Abstract Classes	178
Using Interfaces	196

Pointer Types

Pointer types are used exclusively with unsafe code. C# provides a mechanism to create and work with raw memory addresses. You will use this feature for performance reasons or when you need to interact with some COM objects or Win32 APIs. You declare a pointer using the **fixed** keyword in an **unsafe** code block:

```
unsafe {
  fixed (int* pInt = (int*)intArray) {
    // work with pInt here.
  } // Fixed block ends here.
} // unsafe block ends here.
```

The **unsafe** block marks this code as unmanaged. The CLR will run unmanaged code only in trusted situations. The **fixed** keyword marks a memory address as fixed. When the garbage collector runs, it can and does move objects around in memory, which will invalidate any pointer types. The **fixed** keyword tells the CLR not to move the object being referenced when a garbage collection occurs. For these reasons, you should make sure that you use pointer types judiciously and keep them for only short periods of time.

Defining Types

All object-oriented languages provide you with the capability of defining your own types and adding them to the language, and C# is no exception. C# provides several different kinds of new types you can create: classes, structs, interfaces, and enumerations. You can package related types in a namespace.

Namespaces

You will define your own namespaces as a way of organizing your code, so that if two different programmers inadvertently create types with the same name, they do not collide. A namespace simply declares that all the code inside that block must be accessed using that particular namespace. You can declare the same namespace multiple times to create namespaces that span multiple source code files.

```
namespace CsharpLittleBlackBook {
  // Some C# llb code here.
} // end of namespace.
```

Classes and Structs

You create a C# program by defining classes and structs that provide the functionality for your program. Classes represent references types, and structs represent value types. All the executable code in your program will be inside a class or a struct.

You can declare a class by using modifiers that limit access to the class or by limiting the uses of a class. You can place four different access modifiers on class declarations:

- *public*—Means that there are no access restrictions on this class.

- *internal*—Means that this class can be accessed only from within the same assembly. Note that namespaces have no bearing on internal access. There is no way to enforce namespace access to a single assembly.

- *protected*—Means that only the containing entity, or elements derived from the containing entity, can access this element. This can only be used with nested classes.

- *private*—Means that this element can be accessed only from the containing entity. This access can be used only with nested classes.

There is one other access modifier: *protected internal* combines protected access with internal access. This element can be accessed from any entity that could access protected or internal elements.

You can place two other modifiers on class declarations:

- *Abstract*—Defines a type that can be used only as a base class. No objects of this type can be created. This type can be used only as a base class.

- *Sealed*—Defines a type that cannot be used as a base class.

Sealed and abstract are mutually exclusive.

Inside a class you will place data declarations, nested types (other classes, structs, enums), method declarations, properties, indexers, and other C# elements. For now, understand that a class definition defines a new reference type, and all the elements inside the class define how that type behaves.

Structs are similar to classes with a few restrictions. Structs are always **public** and always **sealed**. You cannot add either of these modifiers to a struct; they are implicit.

Defining Interfaces

You use the **interface** keyword to create new interface types. An *interface* is a set of functions that logically form a group. Interfaces can inherit only from other interfaces, or from **System.Object**. Interfaces are limited to methods, properties, indexers, and events. In particular, interfaces cannot contain data members, constants, constructors, destructors, operators, static methods, or nested types.

All the methods in an interface are implicitly public. None of the methods are defined in the interface body. An interface defines only the function names, return value, and parameter lists. Any class that implements an interface must implement all the functions defined in that interface.

You can use interfaces to define callbacks, specify common behavior across disparate classes, or express a common programming idiom. Interface definitions do not contain the implementation of any of the methods in the interface; classes that implement an interface are required to do that.

Interfaces are by definition abstract, and all methods in an interface are by definition virtual. You do not specify either of these keywords when you create an interface; they are implicit.

Enumerations

Enumerations are a way to define a set of related constants. You will use them to specify a set of possible choices or options. Enumerations are better than a set of defined constants because an enumeration represents a type rather than a value. The compiler can ensure that a value of the correct type (an enumeration) is always passed to functions.

Statements

C# statements are derived from the C language. Whitespace is not significant in a C# program, nor are source code lines. The following are equivalent and equally valid:

```
for (int i=0;i<10;i++){Console.Write ("{0}: ", i);
  Console.WriteLine (args[i]);}

for (int i = 0; i < 10; i++) {
  Console.Write ("{0}: ", i);
  Console.WriteLine (args[I]);
}
```

All C# statements end in a semicolon (;). A single semicolon creates an empty statement. For example, the following block does nothing 10 times:

```
for ( int i = 0; i < 10; i++)
  ;
```

Braces ({ and }) denote code blocks. A code block can be used any-time a single statement is expected. Braces also delineate blocks that define namespaces, classes, and functions.

Comments

C# uses two forms of comments, plus one extra variant. A comment can start with /* and end with */. This style of comment can span multiple lines. A single line comment starts with //. All characters af-ter // until the next line break is a comment. A variant of the single line comment uses /// to denote a comment that contains XML source for building documentation. The C# compiler can create Web-based documentation from the source code when these /// comments are present.

Branching Statements

Branching statements are the programming equivalent of "do this, or do that, or do something else." They provide the means for you to select which "branch" of code to take. The C# language contains two different branching statements that you use to control the flow of execution in your C# programs: **if/else** and **switch/case/break**.

The **if/else** statement lets you pick one of two paths based on a Bool-ean expression. The **switch/case/break** statement lets you pick be-tween one of several values for a single variable. The **switch** statement can be used only with integral or string variables. The **if** statement can be used with any Boolean expression. You should use the **switch** statement when possible because it generates more efficient code.

Iterations

Iteration statements provide the means to execute a block of code multiple times. C# has four different iteration statements: the **for** loop, the **while** loop, the **do/while** loop, and the **foreach** loop.

The **while** loop and the **do/while** loop are closely related. They both execute a block of statements as long as a Boolean expression is true. The difference is that the **do/while** loop always executes the block of code at least once, and evaluates the condition at the end of the block of code. The **while** loop evaluates the condition before starting the block of code, and it may never execute the block of code.

The **for** loop and the **foreach** loop are ways to execute a block of code based on a number of iterations. The **for** loop contains a counter variable and executes until the counter has passed some condition. The **foreach** loop is a new C# statement that executes a block of code for each object in a collection or an array.

Exception Handling

C# provides an exception-handling mechanism similar to that of Java or C++. You signal an exception by throwing the exception. You place code that might throw exceptions inside a **try** block. You handle exceptions using a **catch** block. Multiple **catch** blocks can be chained to handle different types of exceptions. A **finally** block holds code that needs to be executed even if exceptions occur. It is where you place code that frees resources so that your code does not have resource leaks in the presence of exceptions.

C# also provides keywords you can use to turn on or off overflow exceptions generated by integer arithmetic. Code placed inside a checked block will generate an exception if it overflows or underflows. Code placed inside an unchecked block will ignore any overflows or underflows. The default behavior is controlled by a compiler switch that is normally set to *checked*.

Related solution:	*Found on page:*
Programming with Exceptions	234

Types and Reflection

C# provides mechanisms to query the actual type of an object at runtime. You use these keywords to load an object at runtime before using its actual capabilities. You can query an object to see if it is of a certain type or if it supports an interface. Other keywords and functions let you retrieve the type of the object and examine the methods and properties that are supported by that particular type.

This kind of late binding does break some of the tenets of object-oriented programming. In most cases, you should not need to know the runtime type of objects to use them. If you find that you need to query an object's runtime type, you should review your design to see if you can come up with a better way to create the solution.

Type information and reflection are most commonly used in application where you need to dynamically load an assembly and use it as an add-on.

Related solution:	Found on page:
Refining Type Information	387

Unsafe Programming

Because C# is a new language and .NET is a new environment, both the language and the runtime contain mechanisms that make it easier to interact with your existing codebase, whether you have COM objects, C++ classes, ActiveX controls, or if you need to call native Win32 elements. C# also provides ways to access raw memory on the managed heap. Unsafe programming techniques can also provide noticeable performance improvements when used correctly.

Related solution:	Found on page:
Using Unsafe Code	271

Expressions

Expressions define some kind of computation. They include variables or literal values, and some set of operators. They may be variable assignments, mathematical computations, or Boolean computations.

Arithmetic Operators

C# includes all of the mathematical operators from the C language. Here are the standard mathematical operators in C#:

- **+** is the addition operator.
- **–** is the subtraction operator.
- ***** is the multiplication operator.
- **/** is the division operator.
- **%** is the modulus operator. (This is the integer remainder for a division. For example, 5 % 3 is equal to 2.)

C# also contains two shortcuts (directly borrowed from C) for incrementing and decrementing a value. **++** increments a value, **--** decrements a value.

A single **=** assigns a value. C# also provides shortcuts for modifying a value. All the arithmetic operators can be used to provide a shortened form of an expression, called a compound operator. For example, look at this expression:

```
int i = 5;
i += 6;
```

The following expression is exactly the same:

```
int i = 5;
i = i + 6;
```

Any mathematical operator can be combined with the equals sign in the same way: *=, -=, and so on.

Get in the habit of using the compound operators whenever you can. The C# compiler can generate more efficient, faster code when you use the compound operators.

Boolean Operators

C# supports the usual logical operators:

- **&&** is the logical AND operator
- || is the logical OR operator
- ! is the logical NOT operator

C# also supports bitwise Boolean operators:

- **&** is the bitwise AND operator
- | is the bitwise OR operator
- ^ is the bitwise exclusive OR (XOR)
- ~ is the bitwise NOT operator

The logical operators support a concept known as "short circuit evaluation." Examine the following code:

```
if ((obj != null) && (obj->Func ()))
{
    // do something...
}
```

This will never cause an exception. If **obj** is null, the second operand—**obj->Func ()**—is never executed. As soon as the final result is known, the individual operands are no longer processed. The OR operator works the same:

```
if ((k > 5) || (Func (k))
{
    // Do something ...
}
```

The **Func (k)** will never be called for any value of **k** greater than 5. Short circuit works again.

None of the bitwise operators short-circuit; they can't short-circuit and still be correct. You can also use compound assignment versions of all the bitwise operators: **&=, |=, ^=**, and **~=**.

User-defined types can overload any of the following Boolean operators: **&, |, ^, ~**, and **!**.

Simply speaking, you can overload all the bitwise operators and the logical NOT operator.

You can also provide overloaded operators for "operator true" and "operator false." These let you write code of the following form:

```
if (x) {
  // do stuff...
}
```

Related solution:	Found on page:
Defining Comparison Operators	131

Casts and Conversions

The cast operators let you convert one type into another. There are two variants of casts: implicit and explicit. Implicit conversions are conversions that the compiler will make for you. Explicit conversions are conversions that you must explicitly request.

Conversions from a derived type to a base type are implicit.

```
string s;
object o = s; // implicitly convert string to object.
```

Conversions between value types where there is no chance of losing information are implicit:

```
int j;
long k = j; // implicitly convert from int to long.
```

Explicit conversions require that you specifically request them:

```
object o;
string s = o; // Does not compile.
```

```
string s = (string)o; // Compiles, but might throw exception.
long k;
int j = k; // will not compile.
int j = (int) k; // Compiles.  See checked / unchecked.
```

In the case of object type conversions, explicit conversions may throw an **InvalidCastException** if the conversion fails.

In the case of numeric conversions, the behavior depends on the value of the checked/unchecked flag. (See checked/unchecked statements later in this chapter.) In checked code, these throw an **OverflowException**. In unchecked code, the overflow is ignored.

User-defined types can create their own cast or conversion operators. You can control whether a conversion is explicit or implicit by using the implicit or explicit keywords.

Indirection

The indirection operators (**&**, *) are used with pointers in unsafe programming.

The **&** operator takes the address of an object:

```
long addr = &object;
```

The * operator returns the object referred to by a pointer:

```
object o = *addr;
```

A Few Words on Operator Precedence and Associativity

All operators have a defined precedence and order, which ensures that any statement containing multiple operators will always result in the same answer. This is just like in math, where you learned that multiplication and division always occur before subtraction and addition. Table 2.3 lists the relative precedence of all the C# operators.

Table 2.3   The precedence of different operators in the C# language.

Category	Operators
Primary	() . [], x++ x--
Unary	+ - ~ ! (cast) ++x --x
Multiplicative	* / %
Additive	+ -
Shift	<< >>
Relational	< > >= <= is
Equality	== !=
Logical AND	&
Logical OR	|
Conditional AND	&&
Conditional OR	||
Conditional	?:
Assignment	= += -= *= /= %= &= |= ^= <<= >>=

The second property that governs the order of evaluation is *associativity*. All binary operators except assignments are left-associative. This means that the following statement sets **j** to the value 5, not 9:

```
int j = 12 - 5 - 2;
```

Namely, it evaluates (12–5)–2, not 12–(5–2).

Assignment is right-associative. The following statement sets *a* and *b* to the value currently held by *c*:

```
a = b = c;
```

Namely, it evaluates a=(b=c), not (a=b)=c.

Associativity determines the order in which operators of equal precedence are evaluated.

Frankly, I don't remember the order of operators very well. I know the mathematical ones because they were drilled into my head repeatedly throughout my school years. Notice, however, that the highest-order precedence is parentheses. Whenever you write lengthy expressions, use them. The compiler may know exactly how to evaluate this statement:

```
a*++b-c/d+e%f>>2/g*i
```

But no one else will know that it should be this:

```
(((a * (++b)) - (c / d)) + (e % f)) >> ((2 / g) * i)
```

The second example isn't really readable, but you can figure it out if you take a bit of time. I recommend always using parentheses and whitespace whenever it will help other programmers understand your logic. Use Table 2.3 to understand when other programmers have avoided this rule.

Immediate Solutions

Declaring and Initializing Variables

You declare a variable by using its type and giving it a name:

```
int i;
```

To initialize the variable you must give it a value or use the **new** operator:

```
int i = 5;
int j = new int ();
```

The first declaration creates an integer and sets its value to 5. The second creates an integer by using the default constructor.

Declaring a reference type variable is exactly the same:

```
System.ArrayList 1; // declared, but not initialized.
1 = new System.ArrayList (); // initialized.
System.ArrayList 12 = new System.ArrayList ();
  // declared and initialized.
```

The new operator creates the actual object, either in the declaration or following it. You must initialize variables before you use them in C#.

You declare a pointer using the * operator as part of the variable declaration. You can only declare pointers inside **unsafe** code. Also, pointers are usually declared with the **fixed** keyword to prevent the garbage collector from moving the block of memory and invalidating the variable, as in the following:

```
unsafe { // Declare an unsafe block.
  fixed (int* pBits = (int*)memBlock) { // memBlock fixed.
    // Do any work with pInt here.
  } // Fixed block ends here. MemBlock can be moved.
} // unsafe code ends here.
```

Using Simple Statements

This section discusses the simplest statements in C#. These are the building blocks of the language.

Using the Empty Statement

The empty statement is a simple semicolon.

```
;
```

The empty statement doesn't do anything. An alternative to the empty statement is the empty block, shown as:

```
{}
```

Often, a null statement is a bug:

```
if (i != 0);
    Func ();
```

The bug can be more easily seen with a little different formatting:

```
if (i != 0)
    ;
Func ();
```

The compiler warns you about a possible null statement. There are times when you will use the empty statement in loops. Consider the following code:

```
while (func (this))
    ;
```

Here, **func ()** is a Boolean function. This loop calls **func ()** repeatedly as long as it returns true. The following code does the same thing:

```
bool b = true;
while (b)
    b = func (this);
```

Writing Comments

The single line comment does not have a terminator. It ends at the end of the current line:

```
int i; // Simple counter.
i++;
```

Multiline comments start with **/*** and end with ***/**:

```
/* This class is used to read
tables from a database. */
```

The multiline comments do not nest:

```
/* Comment out this code...
int i = 4;
for (i = 0; i <5; i++)
{
  someFunc (); /* Do some work. */
}
... End of commented out code */
```

This statement will cause an error because the comment **/* Do some work. */** ends the block of commented-out code. A good recommendation is to reserve the use of the multiline comments for commenting out code. Inline comments should be of the **//** variety.

There is one other variant in a C# comment—the XML documentation comment. Any comment that begins with **///** will be parsed as an API document by the C# compiler. You can use this feature to create code that contains its own documentation. (See Appendix B for a list of XML comment tags.)

Using Blocks { }

C# does not contain special keywords for the end of many control statements (**for**, **if**, **switch**, **foreach**, **do**, **while**, and others.). Instead, C# follows the example of C, C++, and Java where any group of statements placed inside a block can replace a single statement:

```
for (int i = 0; i < 50; i++)
{ // Start of compound statement
  func1 (i);
  func2 (i);
} // End of compound statement.
```

The opening brace { denotes the beginning of the block. The closing brace } denotes the end of the block.

Declaring Namespaces

Namespaces are declared using the **namespace** keyword, followed by the namespace, followed by the block of code in that namespace:

```
namespace CSLBB {
  // Code here...
} // end of namespace
```

Namespaces can be nested, as in this example:

```
namespace Coriolis {
  // Some code...
    namespace CSLBB {
    // More code...
    } // end of namespace Coriolis.CSLBB
} // end of namespace Coriolis.
```

Or, a compound namespace can be declared with one namespace statement:

```
namespace Coriolis.CSLBB {
  // Code here...
} // end of namespace Coriolis.CSLBB.
```

Namespaces are a way to organize code to avoid collisions when users integrate code from multiple third parties. I strongly recommend that the outermost namespace you declare be based on the company name (for example, Microsoft or Coriolis). Inner namespaces can be used to organize code based on product families, libraries, or features. There is no limit to how many namespaces can be nested.

Related solution:	*Found on page:*
Organizing Functionality Using Namespaces	165

Declaring Classes

You use the **class** keyword to create new reference types. You create a class by using an access modifier, the **class** keyword, the class name followed by at most one optional base class, followed by any number of interfaces your class implements, followed by the contents of the class in a block of code:

```
public class MyTimeZone : System.TimeZone, ICloneable {
  // A definition of my time zone class.
}
```

This statement defines a class named **MyTimeZone.** The **MyTimeZone** class is derived from the **System.TimeZone** class. It also implements the **ICloneable** interface.

If you do not declare a base class, your class implicitly derives from **object** or **System.Object**. All three of the following declarations are equivalent:

```
public class myClass {
  // Some code...
}
```

```
public class myClass : object {
  // Some code ...
}
```

```
public class myClass : System.Object {
  // Some code ...
}
```

Classes are "internal" by default. Only nested classes may be defined as "private" or "protected."

> **NOTE (C++ Users):** *Unlike in C++, C# class declarations do not need to end with a semicolon. Leaving them in, however, is valid.*

Related solutions:	Found on page:
Creating a Simple Class	76
Understanding Inheritance	180
Defining Interfaces	199

Declaring Interfaces

You declare an interface by using the **interface** keyword:

```
interface ImyNewInterface {
  // Some method declarations...
} // End of the ImyNewInterface declaration.
```

? ? CANNOT ?

By convention, interface names begin with an uppercase *I*. Interfaces are public by default. You can use any of the access modifiers to change the access level of an interface. Interfaces are implicitly public.

Related solution:	Found on page:
Defining Interfaces	199

Declaring Structs

The **struct** keyword declares a new value type. You declare a struct using any of the access modifiers, the keyword struct, the name of the struct, any optional interfaces that are being implemented, and the struct body.

NOTE (C++ Users): *C++ does not make any major distinction between struct and class. C# does. The difference between a struct and a class is where those objects are created. Struct objects are always created inline in other objects, or on the stack when they are local variables. Class objects are always created on the managed heap.*

Take a look at the following code:

```
public struct myStruct : ICloneable, IComparable {
  // struct body ...
  // include Clone () and Compare () methods.
}
```

This declares a value type named **myStruct** that implements the **ICloneable** and the **IComparable** interfaces. Structs cannot derive from any reference types, although they do implicitly derive from **System.Object**. Structs are implicitly sealed. No other type may derive from a struct.

Related solution:	Found on page:
Using Structs	98

Declaring Enumerations

An enumeration is a named set of constants. These are used, as in the
following example, to describe a set of choices:

```
public enum sizes : int {
  small = 0,
  medium,
  large,
  x_large
}
```

This example creates a public enumeration called sizes. The valid
values for sizes are "small", "medium", "large", and "x_large". Small
has the integral value 0, medium is 1, and so on. The **public** modifier
is optional—enumerations are public by default. You can create enumerations using any of the other access modifiers. The **int** base type
is also optional. Enumerations are stored using integers by default.
You can create enumerations that use any integral type to store values. The values in an enumeration start at 0 by default. You can create
an enumeration that starts at some other value. You can even define
enumerated values that specify all the values. This is most commonly
used for bit fields that can be combined using an OR operation:

```
public enum direction : byte {
     north = 0x01,
     east = 0x02,
     south = 0x04,
     west = 0x08
}
```

Now, you can create northeast by combining the values:

```
int dir = (int) direction.north | direction.east;
// dir has the value 3 (0x01 | 0x02).
```

Using Constants and Read-Only Values

Constants are declared using the **const** keyword:

```
const double pi = 3.1415;
```

43

You can also create a form of a constant using the **readonly** keyword:

```
readonly double pi = 3.1415;
```

So, what's the difference? Statements using **const** are evaluated at compile time, whereas **readonly** values are evaluated at runtime. This difference has important implications: **readonly** values can be initialized from a value that is not known until runtime, and **readonly** values change with new versions correctly. If you change a constant, the only way to update client code that uses a constant is to recompile it. Also, **const** values are implicitly static; **readonly** values can be either static or instance values.

You must initialize both **const** and **readonly** values when they are declared. You cannot initialize a constant after declaring it.

Declaring Variables

You declare local variables in C# using the type, the variable name, and an optional value:

```
int i; // i declared, but has no value.
int j = 5; // j declared, with an initial value.
```

The concept of initialization is very important in C#. The C# compiler enforces this simple rule: A variable *must* be initialized before it is accessed. For example, this code generates a compiler error:

```
int i;
foo (i); // i has not been initialized.
```

You can create an object, and give it its default value if you want:

```
string str; // Not initialized.
string str2 = new string (); // Initialized to "".
string str3 = new string ("Initial Value"); // contains "Initial
value"
```

Declaring Functions

All C# functions are declared inside a class or a struct.

A function declaration contains any optional modifiers, the return type, the name of the function, any parameters, and the body of the function. Take a look at the following:

```
public int foo () {
  return 5;
}
```

To define a function that does not return a value, specify a return type of **void**:

```
public void bar () {
  // do work...
}
```

Member functions may be instance functions, or they may be class functions. Class functions are declared using the **static** keyword. **Static** functions can be called without an instance of the class (e.g., the **Main** method).

Declaring Delegates and Events

Delegates are a new C# concept. They are related to function pointers and function objects in C++ but have some new, interesting properties. You declare a delegate using the **delegate** keyword:

```
delegate int fooDelegate ();
```

You initialize a delegate by giving it a function that matches the delegate signature:

```
public int foo ();
fooDelegate f = new fooDelegate (foo);
```

You call a delegate by simply dereferencing it:

```
fooDelegate f = new fooDelegate (foo);
f (); // call the delegate.
```

Delegates have many more interesting facets; one particular use of delegates is to define events. Events are delegates declared with the **event** keyword:

```csharp
public delegate int fooDelegate ();

public interface Ifoo {
  event fooDelegate MyFoo;

  void FireFoo ();
}

public class CFoo : Ifoo
{
  public event fooDelegate MyFoo;

  void FireFoo ()
  {
    if (MyFoo != null)
      MyFoo ();
  }
}
```

Related solution:	Found on page:
Using Properties for Delegates	147

Using Branching Statements

You use branching statements to select between different execution paths in your program. Whenever there is a choice between different paths, you will use one of the branching statements.

Using the **return** Statement

The **return** statement exits a function. It is necessary for any function that does return a value:

```csharp
int func ();
{
  return 5; // necessary to get the value out of the function.
}
```

```
void func ();
{
  // do work.
  return; // optional return happens anyway.
}
```

You can also use **return** to exit a function prematurely, usually as a result of another branching statement:

```
void func ()
{
    // do something.
    return;
    // Never do this.
}
```

Using the **if/else** Statement

C# contains two different syntax elements that control branching: **if/else** and the **switch** statement.

You use **if** and **else** to control execution based on a Boolean expression. Look at the following code:

```
if (val > 5)
  func1 ();
else
  func2 ();
```

If this expression is true, the next statement is executed. If the expression is false, the next statement is skipped, and the statement after the optional **else** is executed. Often, you will want to execute more than one statement when the expression is true. C# does not add extra keywords for this. Instead, use the block statement described in the "Using Blocks { }" section earlier in this chapter to execute a block of statements:

```
if (val > 5)
{
  // do something.
  // do more.
} else {
  // do other things.
  // do more other things.
}
```

C# does not have an explicit **elseif** statement. However, the **else** clause can contain another **if** statement to get the same effect:

```
if (val < 5)
{
  // do something.
} else if (val < 20) {
  // do something else when val is between 5 and 20.
}
```

Also, notice in this example that the **else** clause is optional. Simply omit the **else** clause, and execution continues with the next statement. This has some interesting implications as to which **if** matches a given **else**, as shown in the following example:

```
if (val < 5)
  if (val > 2)
    func1 ();
  else // coupled with 'if (val > 2)'
    func2 ();
```

Here, **func1** is called if **val** is greater than 2 and less than 5. **func2** is called if **val** is less than 5 and not greater than 2. If you want the **else** to match the **if (val < 5)** clause, you need to add braces to make block statements, as shown here:

```
if (val < 5)
{
  if (val > 2)
    func1 ();
} else // coupled with 'if (val < 5)'
  func2 ();
```

> **NOTE (C++ Users):** *The Boolean expression must evaluate to true or false. You can use an integral expression in C#, as you can in C and C++.*

Using the **switch/case/break** Statement

The **switch/case** statements provide a multiway branching statement. The **switch** statement defines the variable to use as the branching element. Each **case** statement defines the beginning of a block. That block is executed only when the value control variable has a value equal to the value in the **case** statement.

```
switch (day) {
  case "Monday":
    func1();
    break;
  case "Wednesday":
    func2();
    goto case "Thursday"; // execute Thursday too.
  case "Thursday":
    func3();
    break;
  default:
    func4();
    break;
}
```

NOTE (C++ Users): *You will notice a number of differences between the C# **switch** statement and the corresponding **switch** statement in C++ or Java.*

*The C# **switch** statement can use strings. The **switch** statement cannot use any value, but any integral value or any string value is allowed. Also, each **case** block must end with some kind of a jump statement. If you omit a **break** statement, the code will not compile. Notice that you can still get the cascade effect using a **goto** statement, as shown in the example where Wednesday also executes the **case** block for Thursday.*

Using Iteration Statements

You use iteration statements to execute a block of code multiple times. Usually, you will do this to perform the same action with multiple related data items.

Using **while** and **do/while** Statements

C# contains statements that let you execute a series of statements multiple times. The **while** loop and the **do/while** loop are closely related:

```
int i=0;
while (i < 10)
{
  func1 (i);
  func2 (i);
  i++;
}
```

This example calls **func1** and **func2** for every value of **i** from 0 to 9. The **do/while** loop works almost the same:

```
int i=0;
do {
    func1 (i);
    func2 (i);
    i++;
} while (i < 10);
```

The only difference between the **while** loop and the **do/while** loop is that a **do/while** loop is always executed at least once. The **while** loop evaluates the Boolean expression before entering the block of code. The **do/while** loop evaluates the Boolean expression only after executing the block of code the first time.

Using **for** Loops

The code in the preceding section can be just as easily written using a **for** loop. A **for** statement contains three clauses: The first clause sets the initial value of the looping variable; the second clause defines the loop termination expression; and the third clause defines the expressions that modify the looping variable. The first and third clauses may contain multiple statements separated by commas. The second clause must evaluate to a single Boolean expression:

```
for (int i=0, j=0;((i < 10) & (j < 50));i++, j+=5)
{
    func (i,j);
}
```

The **for** loop executes in the following order:

- The initialization clause (first clause) is executed.

- The Boolean expression (second clause) is evaluated. While it is true, the statements in the block are executed, followed by the iteration clause (third clause).

- The expression is evaluated again. If false, the loop exits. If true, the block and the iteration clause are executed again.

Using **foreach** Loops

The **foreach** statement is a new looping construct in the C# language. It provides a shortcut to loop through a collection, as in the following example:

```
foreach (string s in args)
{
  SayHello (s);
}
```

The **foreach** statement has some very innovative features. It works with any of the collection types or any other class that supports certain interfaces defined in most collection classes.

Related solution:	Found on page:
Using Arrays	335

Using **break/continue** in Loops

You use the **break** and **continue** statements to modify the execution paths of loops. The **break** statement terminates the block being executed inside the loop and exits the loop. The **continue** statement terminates the block being executed inside the loop and starts the next iteration.

```
for (int i=50; i < 100; i++)
{
  if (IsPrime (i))
    continue; // Primes can't be perfect squares.
  if (IsPerfectSquare (i))
    break; // exit when we find a perfect square.
}
// i now has the value 64. (8 * 8).
```

When the **continue** statement gets hit, the iteration expression is evaluated, and the loop continues. As soon as the **break** statement gets executed, the loop exits, and the next statement after the **for** loop block is executed.

The **break** and **continue** statements are examples of jump statements. You should use jump statements judiciously, however, because they violate the principles of structured programming. You can always rewrite loops to avoid the jump statements:

```
for (bool found=false, int i=50; ((i < 100) && (!found); i++)
{
  if (!IsPrime (i))
    if (IsPerfectSquare (i))
      found = true;
```

```
    }
    // i now has the value 64. (8 * 8).
```

Depending on the particular loop, the version with **continue** or **break** may be more readable.

Programming with Exceptions

This section defines the keywords that are part of exceptions. Exceptions are the way in which C# handles catastrophic errors.

Using **throw/try/catch/finally** Statements

C# uses the **throw/try/catch/finally** statements to handle exceptions. Here is how each statement is used:

- **throw**—Raises an exception

- **try**—Creates a block that is tested for exceptions

- **catch**—Specifies a block that handles a particular type of exception

- **finally**—Specifies a block that will be executed whether or not exceptions have been generated

Exception syntax is quite simple. The **throw** statement creates an exception. Program execution continues with the first **catch** statement that can handle the exception. The following examples show a block of code that generates an exception and a block of code that catches an exception:

```
void func (System.IO.Stream stream)
{
    if (!stream.CanWrite ())
    {
        throw new MyException ();
    }
    // do stream things...
    stream.Write (data);
}
```

This function tests to see if the input parameter is opened for writing. If not, it signals the failure by throwing an exception.

```
System.IO.Stream myStream;
try {
  myStream = file.getStream ();
  func (myStream);
} catch (MyException e)
{
  System.Console.WriteLine ("func Failed!");
}
catch (System.Exception se)
{
  System.Console.WriteLine ("something else failed.");
  throw; // rethrow.
}
finally {
  myStream.Close (); // Always executed.
}
```

This block of code uses the function from the preceding block of code. The call to **func( )** is wrapped in a **try** block because it might throw exceptions. If **func( )** throws a **MyException**, the first **catch** block gets executed. If **func( )**, or some other function, throws an exception, the second **catch** block is executed. The code inside the **finally** block gets executed whether an exception gets thrown or not. You can use a **try** block with no **catch** statements and just a **finally** block if you have no reason to process the exceptions but simply need to execute some cleanup code in the event of exceptions.

```
try {
  myStream = file.getStream ();
  func (myStream);
}
finally {
  myStream.Close ();
}
```

Here are some quick guidelines on exception processing syntax:

- Wrap code that might throw exceptions in a **try** block.

- List **catch** clauses in order from most specific classes to most general. Otherwise, the bottom-most clause can never be executed.

- Put code that must be executed in a **finally** block after all **catch** clauses.

Related solutions:	*Found on page:*
Catching Exceptions	232
Throwing Exceptions	234

Using **checked/unchecked** Statements

The **checked** and **unchecked** statements define how to handle arithmetic overflow in integral operations. Any operation that is checked will throw an exception on overflow. Any operation that is unchecked will ignore an exception. The **checked** statement can surround a single operation or a block of code:

```
// If any of these overflow, an exception is thrown.
int a = checked (b + c);
checked {
  int a = b + c;
  int d = a * 2;
}
```

The **unchecked** statement works the same, but suppresses exceptions from being generated:

```
// No checking done here.
int a = unchecked (b + c);
unchecked {
  int a = b + c;
  int d = a * 2;
}
```

Checked and **unchecked** also control compile time checking for overflow:

```
// Does not compile:
int a = checked (2147483647 * 2);
// Max int * 2.
```

However, this will compile and will result in **a=−2**.

```
int a = unchecked (2147483647 * 2);
// Max int * 2.
```

Using Types and Reflection

This section discusses the keywords that handle type interrogation
and reflection. That is how you find out the runtime type of a variable
and query it for its capabilities.

Using **as/is** to Test Type Information

The **as** and **is** keywords are used to query and work with the runtime
type of an object. The **as** keyword attempts to convert an object to
the target type. Instead of an exception, it returns null if the conversion fails.

The **is** keyword tests to see if an object can be converted to a given
type. If the conversion would succeed, the **is** expression is true; if the
conversion would fail, the **is** expression is false. If the object being
tested is null, it always returns false:

```
void foo (System.Object o)
{
  if (o is MyClass) {
    // This conversion won't fail because the type
    // has been tested.
    MyClass myO = (MyClass) o;
    myO.func ();
  }
}
```

The **as** expression can shortcut this test somewhat:

```
void foo (System.Object o)
{
  MyClass MyO = o as MyClass;
  if (MyO != null)
    MyO.func ();
}
```

The **as** expression returns either a valid reference cast to the correct
type or null if the conversion fails.

These conversions can succeed in one of two ways. If the object is of
the correct type, it succeeds. Also, if the object is of a type that has a
conversion to the correct type, the conversion succeeds (e.g., converting an int to a long).

Using **typeof** to Get Type Information

The **typeof** operator returns a **System.Type** object that describes the type of its operand:

```
System.Type t = typeof (MyClass);
```

The operand of the **typeof** operator must be a type. The following does not compile:

```
string s;
System.Type t = typeof (s); // Doesn't compile.
```

The only way to get the runtime type of an object is to use the **GetType( )** method:

```
string s;
System.Type t = s.GetType ();
```

Learning Other Syntax

The statements in this section are a bit diverse. You can use this section as a reference to the less common areas of C#.

Using Labels and **goto** Statements

Labeled statements and **goto** statements are available in C#. You should use these statements judiciously because they break the principles of structured programming. You can always write correct programs without these statements.

```
for (int i=50; i < 100; i++)
{
  if (IsPrime (i))
    continue; // Primes can't be perfect squares.
  if (IsPerfectSquare (i))
    goto Done; // exit when we find a perfect square.
}
Done: // define a label.
// i now has the value 64. (8 * 8).
```

Using the **new** Operator

You can use the **new** operator to create a new instance of a type:

```
string s = new string ();
string s = new string ("Initial Value");
```

NOTE (C++ Users): You must use **new** to create an object. You do not use **new** to determine where storage for an object is allocated. If you are creating a reference type, **new** allocates storage on the managed heap and then initializes the object using its constructor. If you are creating a value type, **new** initializes the object using the appropriate constructor.

Managing Lifetime with **using**

The **using** statement provides syntactic support for the dispose pattern. The dispose pattern relates to garbage collection and nondeterministic finalization. The CLR will reclaim any memory resources when an object is garbage collected. Finalizers can reclaim nonmemory resources when an object is garbage collected. However, nondeterministic finalization means that these finalizers will get called at some point after you are done with the object, but you cannot be sure when.

Because of the nondeterministic nature of destruction and finalization, many C# objects implement the **IDisposable** interface. You can release nonmemory resources by calling the **Dispose()** method on any object that implements the **IDisposable** interface. However, this can be tricky when exceptions might be present in the system. The **using** statement helps make sure that the **Dispose()** method gets called even if an exception is present. You use the **using** statement like this:

```
using (MyObject o = new MyObject ())
{
  o.func ();
  o.func2 ();
}
```

The C# compiler translates that code so that it is exactly the same as:

```
MyObject o = new MyObject ();
try {
  o.Func ();
  o.Func2 ();
}
```

```
finally {
  if (o != null)
    o.Dispose ();
}
```

So, anytime you are using an object that implements the **IDisposable** interface, and you are programming with exceptions, consider using this statement to handle resource acquisition and cleanup.

Using **this/base** to Specify Class Access

The **this** keyword lets you explicitly access the current object. Anywhere inside an instance method, you can refer to the current object using **this**. You would do this for two reasons. The first is to qualify member variables when parameters have similar names:

```
public setName (string name)
{
  this.name = name;
}
```

In this function, **name** refers to the function parameter, and **this.name** refers to a member variable of the same name.

The second use is to pass the current object to a function:

```
AddValue (this);
```

You can also use the **this** keyword to call a specific constructor from another constructor:

```
public class MyClass {
  public MyClass (int val)
  {
    this.val = val;
  }

  public MyClass ()
  {
    this (0); // Calls MyClass (0) to construct the object.
  }
}
```

And you can also use the **this** keyword to declare an indexer. An indexer is a property named **this** that lets you treat an object as an array. You declare the index inside square brackets. The following example declares an int indexer that is referenced using a **string**. **value** contains the value to be set in a property:

```
public int this [string name]
{
  get { return MyDictionary.GetAt (name);}
  set { MyDictionary.SetAt (name, value);}
}
```

The **base** keyword lets you access the base class of the current object. The **base** keyword has two uses. The first is to call a method in the base class that has the same name as a method in the current class:

```
public override void DoCalculations ()
{
  base.DoCalculations ();
  // Do more work here...
}
```

The **base.DoCalculations ()** line calls the base class's implementation of the **DoCalculations ()** function.

The second use is to call a specific constructor for the base class:

```
class Derived : MyBaseClass
{
  public Derived (int val) :
    base (val) // Initialize MyBaseClass.
  {
    // Do more initialization...
  }
}
```

Related solution:	Found on page:
Creating Indexers with Visual Studio .NET	109

Using **lock** for Thread Safety

The **lock** statement creates a Monitor, also known as a critical section for multithreaded programs. Typically, you lock the current object, do some work, and unlock it:

```
public void AccessCriticalResource ()
{
```

```
lock (this)
{
  // Do work ...
} // unlock happens here.
}
```

Related solution:	*Found on page:*
Passing Data to a New Thread	290

Using **out** and **ref** to Modify Parameters

out and **ref** are modifiers for parameters passed to functions. The **ref** parameter means that the function will modify the value, and the value is passed by reference:

```
void ModifyValue (ref int val)
{
  val++;
}
```

NOTE (C++ Users): *The **ref** keyword must be present on the call to the function, as well as the function definition:*

```
int v=5;
ModifyValue (v); // Will not compile.
ModifyValue (ref v); // That's it.
// v == 6 here.
```

Notice that I initialized **v** before calling the function. **ref** parameters must be initialized before the function call. If you have a parameter that does not need to be initialized, you can use the **out** keyword, which specifies that the value will be initialized in the function:

```
void InitializeValue (out int val)
{
  val = CreateValue ();
}
```

InitializeValue can be called using a noninitialized integer. Like **ref** parameters, the **out** keyword is required on the function call, as well as the function definition:

```
int v;
InitializeValue (out v);
```

This example is simplified and would be better served with an **int** return value. In real programs, **ref** is used when more than one value must be returned.

Using **params** to Create Flexible Parameter Lists

The **params** keyword lets you define a function with a variable number of arguments; it also lets you define a variable length array to get passed into your function.

The **params** keyword is a little like the C++ **varargs** structure, but type safety is preserved.

```
public void parseArgs (params int [] list)
{
  // list must be integers...
}

public void parseObjects (params object [] list)
{
}
```

To call these functions, simply list the parameters you want:

```
parseArgs (5,8,12,27);
parseObjects (5, 2.4, "This list");
```

Because **params** does enforce type safety, the following does not compile:

```
parseArgs (5,8,"strVal");
```

Learning Unsafe Programming Syntax

C# provides mechanisms to interact with native code, even ways to write native code. This section defines the keywords that are part of native code.

Using **sizeof** to Get the Size of a Variable

The **sizeof** operator returns the size of a value type:

```
int a = sizeof (int); // returns 4.
```

The **sizeof** operator can be used only in unsafe mode.

Using **extern** to Access Native Methods

The **extern** keyword imports a native method from a DLL:

```
[DllImport("User32.dll")]
public static extern int MessageBox
  (int hWnd, string message, string caption, int type);
```

Using **unsafe/fixed** to Access Raw Memory

The **unsafe** keyword marks a block of code that executes in an unsafe context. It is usually used in context with the **fixed** statement. The **fixed** statement prevents the garbage collector from moving an object.

```
unsafe void CopyBytes (byte [] src, byte [] dest, int size)
{
  fixed byte* pSrc = src;
  fixed byte* pDest = dest;
  for (int i=0;i<size; i++)
    *pDest++ = *pSrc++;
}
```

This example marks the function **CopyBytes** as unsafe. The **pSrc** and **pDest** variables are fixed. This means that if a garbage collection operation occurs, the garbage collector will not move the arrays **src** or **dest**.

Using **stackalloc** with Unmanaged Types

stackalloc creates an array of unmanaged types:

```
{
  int* vec = stackalloc int[25];
  // do stuff with vec.
} // vec goes away here.
```

This allocates an array of 25 unmanaged integers. This code must be in an unsafe context. Also, the memory allocated by **stackalloc** will not be garbage collected. **stackallocs** can occur only inside a function. The memory is released when the block exits.

Learning Operators

Expressions and operators define how the language manipulates numeric and logical elements. An expression is a statement that contains some combination of operands and operators. Expressions are used to compare and assign variables and values.

C#, like C++, lets you overload operators. That means that when you define a class or a struct, you can define the meaning of some of the operators in the language for your object. This section is a quick reference for the operators defined in the C# language.

Using Arithmetic Operators *Overloading?*

The C# language provides the usual arithmetic operators. C# follows the heritage of C in that you can combine all the arithmetic operators with the assignment operator. For example:

```
int i = 4;
i = i + 10;
```

can be written as:

```
int i = 4;
i += 10;
```

This is more than syntactic convenience. The compiler can optimize the compound assignment constructs better. You should always try to use the compound assignment version of any arithmetic operator rather than the longer equivalent. The performance improvements are even greater when more complicated types are involved.

C# also provides two operators for incrementing and decrementing values because these are very common:

- ++ increments the value.
- -- decrements the value.

Increment has two variants known as pre-increment and post-increment. The difference is in the return value. Pre-increment returns the value after the increment; post-increment returns the value before the increment:

```
int j = 5;
int i = ++j; // i is 6, j is 6.
int k = i++; // k is 6, i is now 7.
```

Decrement works the same way:

```
int j = 5;
int i = --j; // i is 4, j is 4.
int k = i--; // k is 4, i is now 3.
```

Pre-increment generates faster, more efficient code than post-increment. When possible, you should use the pre-increment form. You can overload all of the arithmetic operators.

Related solution:	Found on page:
Defining Additive Operations	128

Using Assignment Operators

The assignment operator uses a single = sign:

```
int j;
j = 5; // Assignment.
```

C# contains a variety of assignment operators, known as compound assignment. Basically, every mathematical operator has a corresponding compound assignment. For example, the following two statements are logically the same:

```
int j = 5;
j = j + 5; // simple assignment.
j += 5; // compound assignment.
```

The **+=** means "Take the left-hand operand, add the right-hand operand, and store the result in the left-hand operand."

If you have used C, C++, or Java, this is old hat. If, however, you are new to any of these languages, try to get accustomed to the compound assignment and the increment and decrement operators. All of these allow the compiler to perform extra optimizations because the operand also stores the result.

You cannot overload the assignment operator or any of the compound assignment operators.

Using the Equality and Comparison Operators

↗ overloading?

C# contains operators that let you compare values:

- **==** tests for equality.
- **!=** tests for inequality.
- **>** tests for greater than.
- **<** tests for less than.
- **>=** tests for greater than or equal to.
- **<=** tests for less than or equal to.

All of these work in exactly the same way. They compare two values of the same type and return a Boolean value:

```
if (a == b)
{
  // do stuff
}
```

Related solution:	Found on page:
Defining Comparison Operators: ==, !=	131

Using the ?: (Ternary) Operator

The **?:** operator is called the "ternary" operator or the conditional operator. Consider the following code that returns the max of two integers:

```
int max (int a, int b)
{
  return (a > b) ? a : b;
}
```

The above is equivalent to:

```
int max (int a, int b)
{
  if (a > b)
    return a;
  else
    return b;
}
```

The conditional operator is a simplified form of the **if/else** statements that you can use in some situations. Namely, anytime you would pick a different right-hand side of an assignment based on some condition, the conditional operator will be more concise and elegant.

You cannot overload the **?:** operator.

Using the Shift Operators

The shift operators are **<<** and **>>**. The shift operators shift the bit pattern in integral values. The **<<** shifts bits to the left, and the **>>** shifts bits to the right.

NOTE (C++ Users): *C# does not follow the C++ convention of using the shift operators for I/O (input/output).*

The left shift always fills the low order bits with 0s. The right shift fills the high order bits with 0s on unsigned quantities and fills the high order bits with the sign bit for signed quantities:

```
int i = 4;
int val = i << 2; // Multiply i by 4.
int val2 = i >> 5;
```

There are also compound assignment versions for the shift operators: **<<=** and **>>=**. User-defined types can overload the shift operators.

Chapter 3

Classes I: Creating Classes

In Brief

The last chapter introduced you to all the syntax elements of the C# language. Now, it is time to begin putting those pieces together to solve real world programming problems. This chapter explains how to create C# classes and organize code into classes. C# is a strong, object-oriented language in that every piece of code must belong to a class. Classes, the building blocks for C# programs, serve as both descriptions for objects and as organizing containers for related functionality. A *class* is a scope that is introduced with the *class* keyword, and everything inside the scope of that class is said to be a *member* of the class. This chapter not only introduces you to the class concepts but also shows you how to start building classes.

Classes can contain:

- *Constants*—Nonchanging values that are defined at compile time
- *Enumerations*—Sets of named values
- *Fields*, or *data elements*—Data stored in an object
- *Functions* or *methods*—Methods that act on an object
- *Constructors* (instance and class)—Special functions that initialize an object
- *Properties*—Smart fields, or methods that act like data fields
- *Indexers*—Special functions that let you treat an object like an array
- *Operators*—Special functions that redefine how operators work on objects
- *Events*—Special functions that raise events
- *Other classes*—Classes that may be nested inside other classes to limit access

Class Design Guidelines

You create classes to solve some particular purpose. A class is a collection of data and functions that implement some particular programming feature. A class is also a description for a runtime object. The terms *object* and *class* are often used as synonyms; they are not synonymous, however, because a class is only a description of one particular object type, and an object is a runtime instance of a class. Like in Java, C# classes are all written inline in one source file. There is no facility to split the definition of a class and its implementation across different source files.

A common mistake is to create a class that tries to do too many disparate things. This kind of a design leads to a class that is both hard to use and hard to maintain. Your goal in creating and designing a class should be to make a single block of code that solves a single purpose or particular programming problem.

You should design your classes to separate their interface from the implementation of the solution. You can control the access to different parts of a class and to the class in its entirety with access modifiers. Using this feature properly makes maintaining and updating a class much easier. You can freely modify a private member function, including its signature, and know that users of your class are not affected. You can modify the internals of a more public method and know that your users will not be affected. You want to provide access to only those elements that users of your class will actually need in order to use your class effectively.

The history of object-oriented programming can help when you design your own classes. Object-oriented programming began as a means of simulating real-life systems, and for this reason it is useful to talk about classes and objects as though they are real-life things. It is also common to talk about objects in the active voice as "doing" things in which the nouns in these descriptions become classes and the verbs become methods in each of the classes. Classes become animated objects during design reviews. You will hear things like "The DBReader class reads a record from the database and returns the value of the date column." As you read through the Immediate Solutions that follow, you will see that I do the same with the classes I design for this chapter. Most object-oriented design methodologies use some form of this class discovery, and the more you work in object-oriented design and programming, the more natural this vernacular becomes.

Class Access

Access modifiers control what code can access a particular class. You want to limit the access to a class as much as possible and still have the class be useful. The more limited the access to a class is, the less points in code you need to test when you change a class. C# provides five different access modes you can choose from:

- **public**—Accessible anywhere

- **internal**—Accessible only to other classes in the same assembly

The following access modifiers are only valid for nested types. Nested types are classes declared inside other classes:

- **protected**—Accessible only to derived classes (see Chapter 9 on inheritance)

- **protected internal**—Accessible to derived classes *and* other classes in the same assembly

- **private**—Accessible only to the enclosing class

I have found **public** classes to be the most common. Generally speaking, you create a class because you need a piece of functionality in more than one place. Creating a public class that you can use in many places is the best way to accomplish that. It is far less often that you need a piece of code in only one context, which would be the time for nested classes and more restrictive access to classes. The default class created by Visual Studio .NET has an access mode of "public." If no access modifier is present, the access would be defined as "internal."

Related solution:	Found on page:
Understanding Inheritance	180

Constructors

When you create a class, you can control the state of an object when it first gets created. You do this by defining one or more constructors. A *constructor* is a special function that initializes a new object of the class type. Constructors have the same name as the class; they have no return value (not even void). Two interesting rules relate to constructor declarations:

- If you do not declare any constructors, the C# compiler adds a default constructor for you.

- If you do declare any constructors, this default constructor is not created automatically. You must create it yourself.

WARNING (C++ Users)! *Unlike C++, no copy constructor is generated by the compiler for you under any circumstances. You may declare one, however, if you want.*

Generally, the constructor sets a value to all the fields inside your object. You can initialize values in a class in two different ways:

- You can initialize any data value when you declare the field in the class. The syntax is the same as when you declare a constant.

- You can initialize the fields in the body of the constructor. To determine which method works best, you need to understand the order of initialization:

  - Any variable initializers are executed first.

  - The base class (or **System.Object**) constructor is executed.

  - The body of the constructor is executed.

C# also adds two syntax elements that are missing in C++. You can use the **this** keyword to call a different constructor.

*WARNING (C++ Users)! Unlike in C++, you cannot use initializers to set the values of fields in a class. Also, you use the **base** keyword to call a base class constructor rather than the class name to call a specific base class constructor.*

WARNING (Java Users)! You must use the initializer syntax to call a base constructor or another constructor for the current class. You may not add that call in the body of the constructor.

C# also includes a facility to initialize static member variables, called a *static constructor*. A static constructor is declared like this:

```
static DistanceCalculator ()
{
  // Initialize any static member variables
}
```

C# has many different ways to initialize the static and instance fields of your classes. Your goal should be to initialize all fields exactly once. Here are tips for when to initialize fields and how to best choose when to use which strategy:

- Initialize constants in their declaration. (You have no real choice here.)

- Initialize static values in the declaration when possible. This is possible with value types, and reference types when a constructor call is sufficient to get the object initialized.

- Create a static constructor when more program logic is required to initialize static variables.

- Initialize instance variables when they are declared if they will always be initialized with the same value.

- Create a default constructor whenever some instance variables are not initialized in their declarations.

- Create other constructors as necessary to let clients of the class initialize objects of your class properly. Your goal should be that once an object is created, it is ready to use. Users should not need to create an object, then call other initialization methods, and then use it.

Writing constructors properly is an exercise to achieve two goals:

- To initialize every member variable to some known value before using it.

- To initialize each field only once, no matter what the execution path. It also means trying not to duplicate any code in multiple constructors.

Class and Instance Methods

After an object gets created, you will want to invoke methods on the object so it can do work for you. Objects perform actions when you invoke methods on the object. You can define methods in your class to modify the state of an object or to have the object perform some work. Methods are functions defined inside a class. A method definition contains an optional access modifier, the return value type, the name, and an optional list of parameters:

```
public double getDistance (double time,
   DistanceUnits measurement)
```

This method definition defines a public method named **getDistance** that returns a double value. The **public** modifier indicates that this method can be accessed by all code. If you do not specify an access modifier, the default access of **private** is implied. You can apply any of the access modifiers described previously in the "Class Access" section to a method. You can also create internal, protected, protected internal, and private methods. **Internal** methods can be accessed by any other class in the same assembly. Any class derived from the current class can access protected methods. Protected **internal** methods can be accessed by any class that can access either protected or internal methods. **Private** methods cannot be accessed outside of the current class.

For example, consider this method:

```
static private double convert (double ft,
   DistanceUnits measurement)
```

This defines a private static method. As a private method, **convert** can be called only from inside the same class. As a static method, it is not called using an object. Instead, it is called using the class.

When a user calls the function, the return value can be set to any variable. Suppose that **obj** is a variable of type **DistanceCalculator**. Here is how you would call this function:

```
double dist = obj.getDistance (30,
   DistanceCalculator.DistanceUnits.feet);
```

The first period (.) specifies that you are accessing a member of the **obj** object, in this instance, the **getDistance ()** method. Then, all the parameters follow. Notice that the units must be scoped using the period (.) operator to indicate that **feet** is a member of **DistanceUnits**, which is a member of **DistanceCalculator.**

WARNING (VB Users)! When you call a function, all the parameters to a function must be enclosed in a single set of parentheses and separated from each other by a comma.

Fields or Member Variables

In addition to methods, most classes store some kind of data. You store that data in fields defined in the class. You declare a member variable anywhere inside a class, as in the following:

```
private readonly double accel;
```

This statement declares the member variable **accel**. The **accel** variable is private; no code outside of the class can access this member variable. The **readonly** modifier declares that this variable cannot be modified once it is initialized and must be initialized during construction. Refer to the "Constructors" section earlier in this chapter for more information on that process.

The remainder of the declaration is the type (**double**) and the variable name (**accel**).

I strongly recommend that you get in the habit of creating all your member variables as private. There is no reason not to do so. Properties can provide access to member variables and still shield the implementation of the particular variable.

Properties

Properties are a new feature in C# that are not present in either C++ or Java. They are also called "smart fields" and are elements that get treated like data members outside classes. But a property is implemented like a method or pair of methods inside the class.

A property is defined using an access modifier, the type of the property, and its name. Inside the brackets that define the property you can declare a **get** and a **set** function for the property. You can declare a property to be any type at all, without restriction. A property definition looks like this:

```
public double Acceleration
{
    get
    {
        return accel;
    }
    set
    {
        accel = value;
        if (accel > 10.0)
            accel = 10.0;
        else if (accel < -10.0)
            accel = -10.0;
    }
}
```

This defines a public property called **Acceleration**. This property supports both **get** and **set** operations. You can also create read-only or write-only properties. Read-only properties do not contain **set** methods; write-only properties do not contain **get** methods. The code inside the brackets following the keyword **get** defines what code gets executed to return the value to a caller. In the example, it simply returns the value of an internal member variable. You can execute code to support lazy evaluation or late reading from a database, or whatever scheme is necessary to evaluate the value of the property. The code inside the brackets after the **set** defines the code that executes when the user tries to set the value of a property. The keyword **value** defines the object used to set the value of the property. The **value** must be of the same type as the property. The example code sets the member variable and then tests and brackets the value of the member variable. You can execute any code inside the **set** portion of the property. The setter on a property cannot return any value. If you need to indicate some kind of error condition in a property setter, you must use an exception (see Chapter 15).

You could access this property simply like a public data member, as in the following:

```
if (obj.Acceleration > 10)
{
  // do something.
}
```

You set a property just like you would set any value, as follows:

```
obj.Acceleration = 28;
```

All the code inside the **set** portion of the property is executed.

Related solution:	Found on page:
Creating Properties with Visual Studio .NET	107

Looking Forward—Programming with Classes

Classes are a large concept in C#. Every bit of executable code in the C# language takes place inside a class. So far, this chapter has shown you some of the simple elements that make up a class. The remainder of this chapter shows many of the steps you need to take to build a simple class and add all the elements to it. You will see examples of many of the elements of a class.

Upcoming chapters expand on the knowledge you acquire here and show you ways to create more robust classes with more functionality and establish better support for your design ideas.

Immediate Solutions

The class I build with you in this chapter performs calculations based on a simple physics formula:

$$d = at^2$$

where d is the distance, a is the acceleration, and t is the time. For example, the acceleration due to gravity is 32 feet per second per second. Using the formula, then, you can see that the distance an object falls in feet in a given time is 32 times the number of seconds squared.

Creating a Simple Class

Let's build this class into a .NET assembly. (Chapters 19 and 20 cover assemblies and how to work with them in detail.)

To start a new project, perform the following steps:

1. Start Visual Studio .NET.

2. Select File|New|Project.

3. Under the Visual C# Projects tree item, select Class Library. I placed the code for this project in "C:\CSLBB\Chapter3". (See Figure 3.1.) Visual Studio .NET creates two source files for this project: a class file, named Class1.cs, and an assembly info file, named AssemblyInfo.cs.

The Class1.cs file created by Visual Studio .NET looks like this:

```
namespace Newton
{
  using System;

  /// <summary>
  ///     Summary description for Class1.
  /// </summary>
  public class Class1
  {
    public Class1()
```

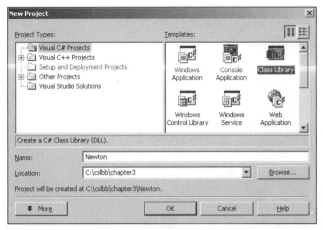

Figure 3.1 The New Project dialog box lets you select different kinds of projects. Visual Studio .NET will create the project files and initial source files.

```
    {
      //
      // TODO: Add Constructor Logic here
      //
    }
  }
}
```

You should change several defaults here. First of all, Class1.cs is very nondescriptive.

4. Rename the file to "Newton.cs". Do this by right-clicking on the file node in the Solution Explorer and changing the name.

   The default namespace is the same name as the project. To keep track of all the projects in the book, I create a nested namespace in the next step.

5. Change the **namespace Newton** in the first line of the file to **namespace CSharpLittleBlackBook.Chapter3**. (Nested namespaces are covered in Chapter 9.)

6. Change the name of **Class1** to "**DistanceCalculator**", which is much more descriptive of the kind of work this class will do.

Now you have created the first class.

3. Classes I: Creating Classes

Creating Enumerations

This class will return distances traveled in a variety of English units. An enumeration lets you specify a list of named constants for a set of values, as in the following:

```
public enum DistanceUnits
{
    inches,
    feet,
    yards,
    miles
}
```

This code creates an enumeration with four values—inches, feet, yards, and miles. This enumeration is public, meaning that any code can use this enumeration. I have not used any of the other optional information on this enumeration, so it is equivalent to the following:

```
public enum DistanceUnits : int
{
    inches = 0,
    feet = 1,
    yards = 2,
    miles = 3
}
```

The base unit specifier **int** indicates that the underlying form of this enumeration is an **int**. You may pick any integral unit other than **char**. The default is **int**.

The initializers specify the integral value used by each named constant. In this code, the default values work fine. The default is to start at 0 and increment by one. You can specify any values you want or need. This is quite common for enumerations that specify a bit pattern. As an example, consider the following enumeration for directions:

```
public enum Direction : short
{
    North = 0x01,
    East = 0x02,
    South = 0x04,
    West = 0x08
}
```

You can mix the compass points to get another direction: North|East would have the value 3; South|West would have the value 0x0C.

Use enumerations over unrelated constants when there is a logical grouping of elements—your intent will be more obvious.

Creating Constants

A constant describes a value that never changes. Constants define a symbolic notation for some known value. In fact, the compiler replaces a constant definition with the literal when compiling your code.

In this application, I want to add a constant that specifies the acceleration due to gravity. Gravity exerts a force of 32 feet per second per second. So, this is the constant declaration:

```
public const double GRAVITY = 32;
```

I have given this constant public access because I would expect any client of the class to be able to use this value. The **const** declaration declares this value as a compile time constant. Constants must be given a value when declared and are, by definition, static. If you add the **static** modifier to a constant declaration, the C# compiler flags it as an error.

WARNING (C++ Users)! *const in C# is different than const in C++.* *See the fields for unit conversion for a description of "read-only", which more closely resemble C++ const members.*

Constants do not need to be public. This class also contains methods to convert between different distance units and defines private constants to help with those conversions:

```
private const double FEET_PER_INCH = 1.0 / 12.0;
private const double FEET_PER_YARD = 3.0;
private const double FEET_PER_MILE = 5280.0;
```

Notice the definition of **FEET_PER_INCH**. You can specify operations to define the value of a constant, as long as all the operands are known at compile time. Those operands can be either literals or other constants.

Adding Methods

Visual Studio .NET has a wizard that lets you automatically add methods to your class (see Figure 3.2). I added the first method using the wizard. This method is a public method that retrieves the distance traveled at a point in time. The method parameters are a **double** that represents the time and a **DistanceUnit** that specifies the units to return.

The Visual Studio .NET wizard creates an empty method for you:

```
public double getDistance (double time,
  DistanceUnits measurement)
{
  return 0;
}
```

All you need to do is fill in the body of the function, as follows:

```
public double getDistance (double time,
  DistanceUnits measurement)
{
  double f = accel * time * time;
  return convert (f, measurement);
}
```

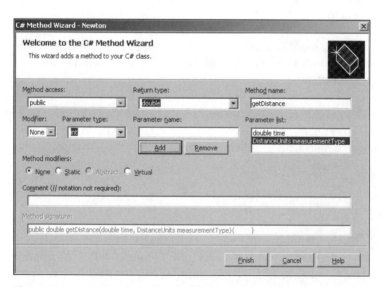

Figure 3.2   The Visual Studio .NET Method Wizard lets you create new methods by entering properties in a dialog box.

You can also simply type the method in the code, instead of using the wizard. Visual Studio .NET does format code for you automatically. Choosing Tools|Options gives you ways to change the formatting options for your code.

I want to add one more public method to this class: a method to retrieve the velocity at a given moment in time. This method is shown in the following code:

```
public double getVelocity (double time,
  DistanceUnits measurement)
{
  double f = accel * time;
  return convert (f, measurement);
}
```

Creating Static Methods

Notice that after calculating the velocity in feet per second, the methods in the preceding section call a function, called **convert**. This method is a private method to convert between different English units of measurement. It assumes the input distance is measured in feet, as in the following:

```
static private double convert (double ft,
  DistanceUnits measurement)
{
  double distance;
  switch (measurement)
  {
  case DistanceUnits.inches:
    distance = ft / FEET_PER_INCH;
    break;
  case DistanceUnits.feet:
    distance = ft;
    break;
  case DistanceUnits.yards:
    distance = ft / FEET_PER_YARD;
    break;
  case DistanceUnits.miles:
    distance = ft / FEET_PER_MILE;
    break;
  default:
    distance = 0;
    break;
```

```
    }
    return distance;
}
```

This method shows two different modifiers possible on member functions. It is private to indicate that it cannot be accessed outside of this class, and it is a static method. Static methods are part of the class but are not considered part of an *instance* of that class, differing from instance methods in a few ways:

- You cannot access any nonstatic member variables in a static method.

- You cannot use the **this** keyword in a static method. There is no object to which **this** refers.

- Static methods are slightly more efficient than instance methods. Static methods do not have an implicit parameter (**this**) and never participate in late binding. (Late binding relates to inheritance and is covered in Chapter 10.)

- Static methods cannot call instance methods directly.

I made this a static member because it does satisfy all these conditions without any undue work to access an instance of this class. Even though it accesses three different constants in this class, the constants are static members, and this is allowed. If you were to call a static method, you would need to scope it using the class name:

```
DistanceCalculator.convert (32,
    DistanceCalculator.DistanceUnits.inches);
```

As I said, this particular method is private, so you can't call it from outside the class. Static methods are often public. You can call static methods without needing to create an instance of that class. This is the mechanism used to call the **Main** method.

Adding Fields or Member Variables

You can declare a member variable anywhere inside a class, as in the following:

```
private readonly double accel;
```

This statement declares the member variable **accel**. The **accel** variable is private; no code outside of the class can access this member variable. The **readonly** modifier declares that this variable cannot be modified once it is initialized and must be initialized during construction. See the "Creating Constructors" section for more information on this process.

The remainder of the declaration is the type (**double**) and the variable name (**accel**).

Adding Properties

In this sample, I would like users to be able to query, or read, the value of the acceleration. You define a property like this:

```
public double Acceleration
{
  get
  {
    return accel;
  }
}
```

A property is defined using an access modifier, the type of the property, and its name. Inside the brackets that define the property you can declare a **get** and a **set** function for the property. You can declare a property to be any type at all, without restriction. This property is declared **public** because I want it to be used by all clients.

You could access this property simply like a public data member, as in the following:

```
if (obj.Acceleration > 10)
{
  // do something.
}
```

Suppose that I wanted to let users set the acceleration within some bounds. I could write that as follows:

```
public double Acceleration
{
  get
  {
    return accel;
  }
```

```
set
{
  accel = value;
  if (accel > 10.0)
    accel = 10.0;
  else if (accel < -10.0)
    accel = -10.0;
}
}
```

You can set a property as you would set any value, as follows:

```
obj.Acceleration = 28;
```

All the code inside the **set** portion of the property is executed.

You can define write-only properties as well. Write-only properties contain only the **set** portion of the property, not the **get** portion. These are somewhat more rare in practice.

You should use properties anytime you want to expose internal data to your clients. You can let your clients use data like syntax to access properties, and you can hide the details of the implementation from your clients. The property form adds syntax support to the common **get_varname** and **set_varname** idiom to support getting and setting a value for your class.

Creating Constructors

Visual Studio .NET created a default constructor for the class. Let's look at the two constructors for the **DistanceCalculator** class:

```
public DistanceCalculator () :
  this (GRAVITY)
{
}

public DistanceCalculator(double a)
{
  accel = a;
  //
  // TODO: Add Constructor Logic here
  //
}
```

The first constructor is the default constructor. It will be called when you declare a new **DistanceCalculator** and do not explicitly initialize it with a value. Notice how the first constructor calls the second version to explicitly initialize the acceleration to the value for gravity. The second constructor gets called when you create a new **DistanceCalculator**, specifying an initial value for the acceleration.

Or, you could have initialized the acceleration field when it was declared. You do that by simply giving the field an initial value when you define it in the class definition:

```
public class DistanceCalculator {
  private readonly double accel = GRAVITY;
  // ...
}
```

Testing Classes

C# provides a mechanism to create a **Main** routine in each class and specify which class's **Main** will be the program main. You can write **Main** routines in each class to form a unit test for the class. This serves two purposes: First, you can test your class in isolation; second, other members of your programming team can see some example code. Here is a sample main for this class:

```
public static void Main ()
{
  DistanceCalculator d = new DistanceCalculator();
  double dist = d.getDistance(10, DistanceUnits.feet);
  System.Console.WriteLine
    ("Distance after 10 sec: {0} feet", dist);
  double v = d.getVelocity (10, DistanceUnits.feet);
  System.Console.WriteLine("Velocity after 10 sec: {0} feet /
sec", v);
}
```

You can change the build options to the C# compiler to create a test executable, or to build a DLL. Unfortunately, Visual Studio .NET does not provide a way to do that easily. This limitation should not stop you. You can easily build from the command line. For this sample, you can do the following:

```
csc /target:exe
   /main:CSharpLittleBlackBook.Chapter3.DistanceCalculator
   Newton.cs
```

The previous code should be on one command line, despite its appearance in the book. **csc** is the name of the C# compiler. The **/target** option specifies to create an executable. The **/main** option specifies which class to use for the **Main** method. Notice that you need to completely specify the class, including any namespaces for this to work properly. This command creates an executable file called Newton.exe. Running Newton.exe tests this class and produces the expected output:

```
Distance after 10 sec: 3200 feet
Velocity after 10 sec: 320 feet / sec
```

Chapter 4

Structs

In Brief

C# treats structs and classes differently, in more ways than C++ does. A *class* is a reference type. This means that a variable of a class type is actually a pointer, or a reference to an object on the managed heap. A *struct* is a value type. This means that a variable of a struct type is placed inline in objects and on the stack in functions. The distinction between reference types and value types also affects the way values are copied and assigned. This chapter explains those differences and shows you how to choose between structs and classes in your designs.

C# has a number of limitations on structs:

- You should use them for small objects, typically not greater than 64 bytes.

- You cannot treat structs *polymorphically* (so they cannot inherit from any other class), nor can you use them as a base class (structs can implement interfaces, though).

- You cannot declare virtual functions in structs.

- Structs always implicitly inherit from **System.ValueType**, so you can override the functions declared in that class.

The distance calculator class from last chapter has one big deficiency—the internal units are assumed and not part of the data. This limits its use and also increases the chances of errors. What you need to correct this problem is a set of objects that carry the units along with the magnitude of any measurement being used. This is exactly the kind of usage structs are designed for.

Structures and System.ValueType

The inheritance hierarchy for structs is somewhat inconsistent, but it does help quite a bit when you are using structs. Any struct you define inherits from **System.ValueType**, which inherits from **System.Object**. So, in some sense, all structs do inherit from **System.Object**. You cannot, however, add any further inheritance hierarchies to structures. Any struct you declare is implicitly sealed.

Four virtual methods are defined in **System.ValueType**, or **System.Object**, that are potential overrides in any struct:

```
public override bool Equals (object obj)
public override int GetHashCode ()
public override string ToString ()
protected override void Finalize ()
```

It is somewhat rare that you would need to override the **Equals ()** method. **System.ValueType** provides an implementation that compares values, as opposed to the **System.Object** version that compares references. You would need to override this function if some of the values in your struct are for optimizations and do not participate in the "equality" of two different objects.

The next method is **GetHashCode ()**. You would often override **GetHashCode ()** to provide a more efficient hash function for the values in a collection. The hash-based collections call **GetHashCode ()** when storing and retrieving values in a collection.

ToString () returns a string representation of your object. You will almost always want to override **ToString ()**. The default implementation of **ToString ()** prints out the name of the struct. Writing your own method lets you print some or all of the values in the struct.

Finalize () is part of the CLR memory management strategy. You should very rarely add a **Finalize** method to a struct. The **Finalize** method is meant to release nonmemory resources when your object is no longer in use. Structs cannot hold members of reference types, so it is very rare to require a **Finalize** method. In fact, if you design a struct that does need a **Finalize** method, you should really consider converting that struct into a class.

Related solutions:	Found on page:
Designing Disposable Objects	254
Using Arrays	335

Data in Structs

C# also places limitations on the types of fields that you can create in a struct. Rather simply, structs can contain only other value types as data members. Also, when a struct is constructed, all of the fields are initialized to 0. So, you should make sure that all 0s is a valid state for your struct. If you think you can change this behavior by writing your own default constructor or initializers for your struct data, you can't— it won't compile.

Fields in a struct cannot have protected internal access. It makes no sense, because structs cannot be used as base classes.

Properties in Structs

You can add properties in structs to insulate your struct from changes in the underlying representation of the data.

Properties in a struct work exactly the same as properties in a class. So, you should make the data members private and add properties to get and set the values in the struct.

There are versioning reasons to get in the habit of doing this, even when the properties are simply pass-through functions. If you modify the code inside a property, that change would be compatible, and you need not update client assemblies. However, if you change from raw data access to a property when you find you need one later, you will need to recompile all clients of your structure.

Related solution:	Found on page:
Using Versions	401

Structs Containing Other Structs

Structs cannot contain members of a class type. They can, however, contain values of other value types. To finish off my sample, I created a struct that defines a velocity. A distance per time unit defines a velocity. Rather than create this from whole cloth, I can store a **Distance** struct and the enumeration that defines a time unit:

```
public struct Velocity : ICloneable
{
  private TimeUnits tm;
  private Distance dist;

  // ...
}
```

Be careful when you use this technique. The CLR is optimized to work with smaller structs. If your structs grow to more than 64 bits, you should start thinking about using a class instead.

Methods in Structs

A common fallacy for many programmers is that structs contain only data. Actually, you can create both instance methods and static methods in your structs. You can make you structs easier to use, creating more efficient programs by anticipating the uses of your structs and writing methods for the common uses. In fact, creating overloaded operators for structs is very common.

Related solution:	Found on page:
Defining Comparison Operators	131

You will also want to create constructors for your structs so that users can set values other than the default when they initialize a struct. Finally, structs often implement interfaces. This means that you will be writing overridden functions that are part of different interfaces.

Common Interfaces

Structs and classes behave very differently with respect to assignment. Consider these two statements:

```
DistanceCalculator c1 = new DistanceCalculator ();
DistanceCalculator c2 = c1;
```

Because **DistanceCalculator** is a class, not a struct, **c1** and **c2** both refer to the same object. Any changes to **c2** will also be seen in **c1**. The way to make two different objects that have the same value is to use the clone method, as in the following:

```
DistanceCalculator c1 = new DistanceCalculator ();
DistanceCalculator c2 = (DistanceCalculator)c1.Clone ();
```

With a struct, the two forms are equivalent, as follows:

```
Distance d1 = new Distance ();
Distance d2 = d1;
Distance d3 = (Distance) d2.Clone ();
```

The **Clone ()** method is the only method defined in the **ICloneable** interface. You should implement this interface in all your structs. You should try to make the distinction between a class and a struct as transparent as possible to the users of your objects. That does give you some flexibility if you need to change a struct into a class at some later date. One way to get this flexibility is to implement the **ICloneable** interface, which lets users copy your struct-based objects the same way that they copy class-based objects. In addition, if you want to put your structs into some of the .NET collection classes, you need to implement the **ICloneable** interface.

You can implement as many interfaces in your struct as you need. The **ICloneable** is the most common, with the **ISerializable** a close second.

Related solution:	Found on page:
Understanding Interface Implementation Rules	202

Structs or Classes? When to Use Which

Structs have more limitations than classes. However, they can be much more efficient, especially for small objects. As mentioned at the beginning of this chapter, you should consider using structs when all of the following are true:

- You do not need to derive from any particular base class. You can implement interfaces in a struct, if necessary.
- You do not need to treat this object polymorphically.
- The size of the object is small—64 bits is a good guideline.
- The object should have value semantics.

If any of these items is false, use a class instead.

Related solution:	Found on page:
Understanding Inheritance	180

Immediate Solutions

First, let's make a struct that holds a distance and a magnitude. I pre-fer keeping each class or struct in a separate file. Doing so makes for smaller compilation units, and they are easier to work with. To make a new source file in Visual Studio .NET, perform the following steps:

1. Right-click on the project node in the Solution Explorer window.

2. Select Add and New Item from the context menu.

3. Select a new C# Class template.

4. Give it the name **distance.cs** (see Figure 4.1).

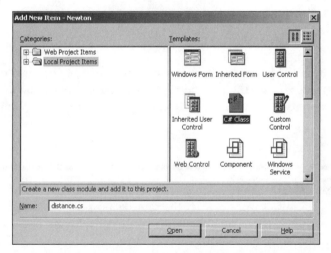

Figure 4.1   The IDE gives you commands to create a new source file and add it to the project automatically.

Adding Data

The struct that manages distance will hold two values: one represent-ing the magnitude of the distance, the second representing the units used (see Listing 4.1).

Listing 4.1 Initial struct definition.

```
namespace CSharpLittleBlackBook.Chapter4
{
  using System;
  using System.Text;

  public enum DistanceUnits
  {
    inches,
    feet,
    yards,
    miles
  }

  public struct Distance
  {
    public double mag;
    public DistanceUnits units;
  }
}
```

The definition in Listing 4.1 creates a structure that you can use to store distances and use them in the distance calculator from Chapter 3. But, it is pretty unsatisfactory from an object-oriented standpoint.

Defining Properties

Properties in a struct work exactly the same as properties in a class. So, you should make the data members private and add properties to get and set the values in the struct, as follows:

```
private double mag;
private DistanceUnits units;

public double Magnitude
{
  get { return mag; }
  set { mag = value; }
}

public DistanceUnits Unit
{
  get { return units; }
  set { units = value; }
}
```

Most data elements inside a struct should support both **get** and **set** properties.

Related solutions:	Found on page:
Creating Properties with Visual Studio .NET	107
Creating Indexers with Visual Studio .NET	109

Adding Methods

The **Distance** struct now insulates the fields from the outside world, even if only slightly. This is a perfectly usable struct. But, you can do better. Structs can contain methods that make them easier to use. To perform any of the calculations necessary using the distances, all distance values need to be converted to the same units. Using the properties, any client could perform those calculations. But, writing them once will make smaller, more efficient programs. So, you can define methods to retrieve a distance using any of the defined distance units (see Listing 4.2):

Listing 4.2   Public methods in the **Distance** struct.

```
public double AsInches ()
{
  double inches = 0;
  switch (units)
  {
  case DistanceUnits.feet:
    inches = mag * INCHES_PER_FOOT;
    break;
  case DistanceUnits.yards:
    inches = mag * INCHES_PER_FOOT * FEET_PER_YARD;
    break;
  case DistanceUnits.miles:
    inches = mag * INCHES_PER_FOOT *
      FEET_PER_YARD * YARDS_PER_MILE;
    break;
  case DistanceUnits.inches:
  default:
    inches = mag;
    break;
  }
  return inches;
}
```

4. Structs

```
public double GetAs (DistanceUnits u)
{
  switch (u)
  {
  case DistanceUnits.inches:
    return AsInches ();
  case DistanceUnits.feet:
    return AsFeet ();
  case DistanceUnits.yards:
    return AsYards ();
  case DistanceUnits.miles:
    return AsMiles ();
  default:
    return 0;
  }
}
```

You can define any number of methods in a struct. However, you cannot create virtual methods in a struct. Structs can override methods in the **System.ValueType** class.

Overriding **System.ValueType** Behavior

You should add the **ToString ()** method to the **Distance** struct, as shown in Listing 4.3. The signature must match the version in Listing 4.3: a public override method that returns a string, or the compiler will warn you that you have created a new method, not an override. Notice that I am using the **StringBuilder** class to create the output string instead of the **string** class. The **string** class creates an immutable string; every time you modify the string, you actually create a new string object. The **StringBuilder** class, on the other hand, lets you append and modify a series of characters. See Listing 4.3 for the **ToString** method for the **Distance** struct.

TIP: *Anytime you are creating a string using multiple statements, try to use the* **StringBuilder** *class instead of the* **string** *class.*

Listing 4.3   This method prints the values in a **Distance** struct. The framework will call this method to print an object to an output stream.

```
public override string ToString ()
{
```

```
StringBuilder rVal = new StringBuilder ();
rVal.Append (mag.ToString ());
switch (units)
{
case DistanceUnits.inches:
  rVal.Append (" in");
  break;
case DistanceUnits.feet:
  rVal.Append (" ft");
  break;
case DistanceUnits.yards:
  rVal.Append (" yd");
  break;
case DistanceUnits.miles:
  rVal.Append (" mi");
  break;
default:
  break;
}
return rVal.ToString ();
}
```

Implementing Common Interfaces

To implement the **ICloneable** interface, you need to add the **ICloneable** interface to the list of the interfaces your struct supports, as in the following:

```
public struct Distance : ICloneable
```

Next, you need to implement the **Clone ()** method, as illustrated in Listing 4.4. The clone method returns a new object that has the same value as the current object.

Listing 4.4 Implementing the **Clone ()** method to return a copy of the object. This method should create a new struct that is equal to the current object and return the new object.

```
public object Clone ()
{
  Distance d = new Distance (mag, units);
  return d;
}
```

Using Structs

The CLR handles structs a little differently than it does classes. First of all, assignment copies the *value* of a struct, rather than its reference. Secondly, structs are always passed to functions by value, rather than by reference. The copy of a struct inside a function is a local object that is equivalent in value, but not the same as the object outside of the function. If you want to modify a struct inside a function, you need to use the **ref** or **out** modifiers on the parameter declaration, as in the following:

```
public static void DoubleVal (ref Distance d)
{
   d.Magnitude *= 2.0;
}
```

By specifying the **ref** modifier on the function call, you ensure that changes made inside the function do carry over outside the function. You must also specify a **ref** parameter on the call to the function:

```
Distance dist = new Distance ();
Distance.DoubleVal (ref dist);
```

You can write slightly more efficient code by using the **out** modifier on parameters that are created inside a function, as follows:

```
public static void makeDistance (out Distance d)
{
   d = new Distance ();
   d.Magnitude = 32.0; // calls Magnitude property of Distance
                       // struct.
   d.Unit = DistanceUnits.inches; // Calls Unit property
                                  // of Distance struct.

}
```

The **makeDistance** function can be called on a variable that has not been initialized. Whereas, the **DoubleVal ()** function can be called only on a variable that has been initialized, or it will generate a compiler error. Take a look at the following:

```
Distance dist;
Distance.DoubleVal (ref dist); // does not compile.
Distance dist2 = new Distance ();
Distance.DoubleVal (ref dist); // works fine.
```

```
Distance dist3;
Distance.makeDistance (out dist3); // works fine.
Distance.DoubleVal (ref dist3);    // also works.
                                   // Dist3 has been initialized
                                   // by makeDistance().
```

Assigning structures does create a value copy. However, you still need to initialize a structure before you use it. Unlike in C++, declaring the variable does not initialize it; you need to use the new operator to initialize a structure.

4. Structs

Chapter 5

Properties and Indexers

In Brief

This chapter covers the topics of properties and indexers. You can use properties and indexers with either classes or structs. Properties and indexers may seem like some extra syntax with minimal usage, but they are actually very powerful constructs. Using properties, you can give the appearance of exposing data in your class, even though properties are actually implemented as methods. You have a number of advantages due to this dual expression. Previously, I said that you should always make member variables private in C#, something you can do without any penalty because of properties and indexers. By using properties and indexers instead of relaxing the access to your data members, you have several advantages. Let's consider those advantages.

A *property* is a group of accessors that lets you export a data item in your classes. The calling code sees the property as a data item, yet internally, you implement the property as a function. You can create properties that expose any type: simple data types, classes, or even interfaces. Simply, you can use any object as a property.

An *indexer* is a way to treat any object as though it were an array of some type. Users access an indexer by placing brackets, [], after the object name. You can specify any number or type of parameters to the indexer: You can use integral types, floating-point numbers, strings, dates, or any other object.

Properties and indexers are very similar in many ways (the bulk of the following discussion applies to both). Also, properties and indexers work the same way whether they are defined in a class, struct, or interface. For simplicity, I use the term *class* throughout the discussion in this chapter unless a discussion applies only to some other elements.

Clearer Syntax

C++ and Java both contain conventions for properties with **get** and **set** methods. C# properties turn those conventions into full-fledged language features. If you want your class to support **get** and **set** for some item, you can make that a property. When you look at a class that someone else has created, the design intent is very clear. You don't need to browse the entire file to find the **get** and **set** methods for each individual item. Instead, you just need to look for the properties.

Although this may appear to be a minor concern, it is also quite helpful when you start working with reflection. The metadata for a class differentiates between methods, properties, indexers, and data. In short, your code will be much cleaner when you use this new syntax, both to other programmers and to the .NET tools that work with your code.

When you use properties defined in other classes, you specify the property as though it were a variable, as follows:

```
System.IO.File foo;
Initialize (foo); // connect to a real file.
if (foo.Length > 1024) // Length is a read-only property.
{
  // File is more than 1 K.
}
```

foo.Length accesses the read-only property **Length** that is a member of the **File** class. It appears just like you are accessing a public variable in the class. Class users get to use a very natural syntax to access a piece of data held in the object.

Restricted Access

In addition to shielding data access inside methods, properties and indexers provide for more flexibility in the way you can define and restrict access to the underlying data. You can restrict access in two different ways:

- Support read or write access independently
- Limit the access to the property as a whole by adding access modifiers

Read-Only and Write-Only Properties

When you create a property or an indexer, you can specify whether it supports reading, writing, or both. This feature is far more versatile than exporting data. The underlying value need not be constant, or even a read-only data value, and you can still protect from clients changing it. In fact, you can calculate and update the value of a property anytime, without letting users modify it.

Write-only properties are much more rare. However, you can define properties that support **set** methods without supporting the corresponding **get** method. I cannot, however, come up with a good reason to let client code modify a value without letting that same code query it. It is supported by the C# language and the runtime.

Access Modifiers

You can use *access modifiers* to create properties that are public, protected, internal, protected internal, or private. Typically, you will create public properties to provide access to private data. You can also create protected properties or internal properties to expose private data to a more limited set of clients.

Parameter Validation

Because properties and indexers are implemented as functions, you can verify any parameters to these functions and protect the internal state of your object. You can ensure that property values are in a valid range or are non-null.

The only way you can indicate a failure in the functions making up a property or indexer is to throw an exception, because the return value is the value of the property. So, you need to be a bit careful about coding these functions to define exceptions that notify callers when they incorrectly use the properties you have defined.

Related solution:	Found on page:
Throwing Exceptions	234

Lazy Evaluation

Sometimes a property may be expensive to calculate. It may require database retrieval or extensive computation. In those cases, it would not be wise to do all the work to retrieve a data value if it is never used. Properties can help you avoid expensive calculations until requested. When you define the accessor for a property, you can examine if the value has already been calculated. If not, you can calculate the value and cache it for later use, as shown in the following example:

```
int MyProperty {
  get {
    if (myvar == null)
```

```
    myvar = func ();
  return myvar;
}
}
```

Polymorphism and Properties

You can also use properties to create polymorphism with data elements. You can indicate that derived classes can or must override the definition of the property. There are some restrictions on how derived classes can override properties and indexers. First off, to override a property or indexer, you need to have exactly the same parameter list. If an indexer takes three integer parameters, your overridden version must do the same. To override a property or indexer, the type of the property must match the base class. Overridden properties must support **get** and **set** exactly the same as the base class. You cannot convert a read-only property into read/write in a derived class. Nor can you convert a read/write property to read-only.

You can also create abstract properties that have no implementation. You do this in a class by specifying that the property is abstract. You can also create properties and indexers in interfaces. When you create abstract properties, you must declare which of the **get** and **set** accessors are supported by the abstract property. Abstract properties let you treat your data polymorphically in C#.

You can create polymorphic indexers by creating multiple indexers with different parameter lists. These different indexers must be distinct in either the number or type of parameters. You can also create polymorphic indexers by using the **params** keyword on the parameter list. The **params** keyword indicates that the indexer takes a variable number of parameters, which lets you create an indexer that can take many different numbers of parameters.

Related solution:	Found on page:
Understanding Inheritance	180

When to Use Properties

It is quite easy to decide when to use a property: Any time you want to expose data from a class or struct, wrap that access in a property. You get better control over the internal state of your object, and you insulate users from any possible maintenance or performance changes you make to the internal layout of your objects.

5. Properties and Indexers

When to Use Indexers

Indexers let you treat an object as though it were an array or a matrix. You should consider using indexers when you design a class that exposes a set of data that is indexed using some other value. One typical example is the list of strings in a combo box. You can write an indexer to retrieve the string by its ordinal in the combo box. Another typical example is a dictionary class or a set of named properties. You can retrieve or set a named property using a string as an index.

But, consider some of the less typical examples. You could write an indexer to retrieve an account balance using the date as the index parameter. You can also write multidimensional indexers to model matrices or cubes of data.

In short, you should consider indexers anytime your object contains a collection of data that you retrieve or set based on some kind of index.

Immediate Solutions

Creating Properties with Visual Studio .NET

Visual Studio .NET contains a wizard that automates creating properties in your C# class or struct. To create a property using the C# Property Wizard:

1. Right-click on the class in the Solution Explorer window.

2. Choose Add and Add Property from the context menu (see Figure 5.1).

3. Fill in the information on the wizard (see Figure 5.2).

4. Click Finish.

The C# Property Wizard has quite a few fields for you to fill in (some of which are optional):

- *Property Access*—You use this combo box to specify the access to this property. You may pick any of the access modifiers in the list.

- *Property Type*—You use this combo box to specify the return type of the property. You can pick any of the C# predefined types, or you can type your own value into this control.

- *Property Name*—You use this edit box to type the name of the property.

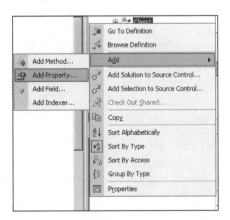

Figure 5.1   Access this menu to add a property to your class.

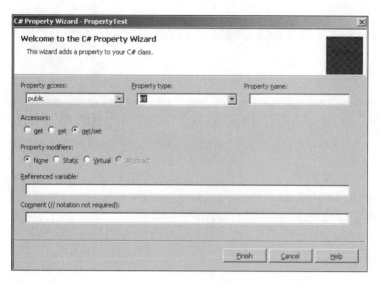

Figure 5.2   The wizard lets you define properties for your classes.

- *Accessors*—These radio buttons let you specify your property's support for **get**, **get/set**, or **set** methods.

- *Property Modifiers*—These radio buttons let you specify static, virtual, or abstract properties. The Abstract radio button will be grayed out unless the class you are editing is abstract.

- *Referenced Variable*—This field is optional. You can enter the name of a class member variable that will hold the value of this property. If you add a variable, the wizard creates a new variable in your class with protected access using the name you specify. The wizard will use this variable to write completed **get** or **set** methods in your property. The methods that the property wizard writes are simple pass-through methods to access this variable. You will need to edit the completed code to provide any additional error-checking code.

- *Comment*—This field is optional. If you type anything here, the wizard will include this comment above the property. The wizard does not place the comment inside any XML documentation tags.

I generally use the wizard when I am creating a new class. It saves me quite a bit of typing. I specify the variable, if I have not already added it. After the wizard writes its code, I change the variable access to private in the code myself. I specify the summary text as the comment and add the XML tags myself. You will often modify both the **get** and **set** accessors after the wizard has finished them. You will want to add some validation at the very least.

Creating Indexers with Visual Studio .NET

Visual Studio .NET contains a wizard you can use to create an indexer in your class. You access the C# Indexer Wizard by right-clicking on a class in the Solution Explorer window. Then, select Add and Add Indexer from the context menu. Visual Studio .NET displays the wizard shown in Figure 5.3. This wizard has many different options for you to specify the type of indexer that you want.

Here are the different fields you fill in to create an indexer:

- *Indexer Access*—This combo box lets you pick the access for your indexer.

- *Indexer Type*—This combo box lets you pick the return type for the indexer. You can select one of the C# intrinsic types, or you can type in some other class type. You can create an indexer to return any type at all.

- *Parameter Type*, and *Parameter Name*—Use these controls to add a new parameter to the indexer. You can select the type from the drop-down or write your own types in the Parameter Type box. You write a name in the Parameter Name box. Then, click Add to add a parameter. If you make a mistake, highlight the parameter in the list and click Remove.

- *Indexer Modifiers*—You can create indexers that are virtual, abstract, or neither. The Abstract radio button is grayed out unless you are editing an abstract class.

5. Properties and Indexers

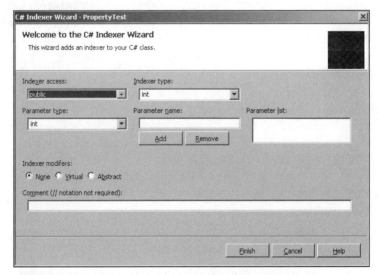

Figure 5.3   This wizard lets you define a new indexer in your class.

- *Comment*—You can add comments here that are placed in XML-style documentation comments above the indexer. This field is optional.

After you have added all the necessary information, click Finish, and Visual Studio .NET creates the indexer. Visual Studio .NET creates only read/write indexers. You can create read-only or write-only indexers, but the wizard doesn't do it for you.

Writing Properties

This is a simple property definition:

```
private decimal Percentage;
public decimal InterestRate
{
  get
  {
    return Percentage;
  }
  set
  {
    Percentage = value;
  }
}
```

This code defines a public **decimal** property named **InterestRate** that maps to the member variable **Percentage**. This property contains both a **get** and a **set**—it is a read/write property.

Writing **get** Accessors

You write the **get** accessor to read the value of the property. The example in the preceding section is as simple as a property gets—it simply returns the value. The code inside the **get** accessor can call any member function or perform any other computations necessary to return the value of the property. When you write **get** accessors, remember that code using these looks like it is just examining data. Keep the following guidelines in mind when you write a **get** accessor for any property:

- Anytime you calculate a value, cache it for later use. If client code is using a property, it will likely use it often.

- If you are returning a reference type, consider returning a copy of the internal data, not a reference to your object's internal data structure. Always return a copy if you are supporting only a **get** accessor. If you are writing a read/write property, the **get** and **set** accessors should both use copy semantics or reference semantics.

- Try to write **get** accessors that will not throw exceptions. Callers will see a simple data access and might not be prepared for exceptions. If you do throw exceptions in a **get** accessor, document them clearly.

Related solution:	Found on page:
Throwing Exceptions	234

Writing **set** Accessors

The **get** accessor handles the read portion of the property; you write a **set** accessor to set the value of a writeable property. The example shown previously in this section shows the simple pass-through version of a **set** accessor. Notice the implicit parameter to the **set** name's value. This is the parameter sent to the accessor. Every **set** accessor has one parameter **value** that is the same type as the property itself.

You will often want to perform range validation on the value of the property. When the value does not meet the range you expect, you must indicate an error using an exception. A **set** accessor cannot return a value in any other way. Take a look at the following:

```
public decimal InterestRate
{
  get
  {
    return Percentage;
  }
  set
  {
    if ((Percentage > 100) ||
        (Percentage < 0.0))
      throw new BadPercentageException ();
    Percentage = value;
  }
}
```

Be careful when you define your **set** accessor for reference types. You should be explicit about whether the value is copied, or if you keep the original reference. Either can be valid at different times. Remember the following guidelines when you write a **set** accessor:

- Validate the **value** parameter before you set any member variables.

- Indicate any invalid parameters by using exceptions.

- Decide on copy or reference semantics carefully. Make sure that your **get** and **set** accessors both use the same semantics.

Creating Static Properties

When you create a static property, you simply add the static modifier to the property definition, as is done here:

```
static public decimal InterestRate
{
  get
  {
    return Percentage;
  }
  set
  {
    if ((Percentage > 100) ||
      (Percentage < 0.0))
        throw new BadPercentageException ();
    Percentage = value;
  }
}
```

Static properties act like static data. Namely, clients access static properties using the class name, rather than a variable of that class type:

```
MyClass.InterestRate = 5.5;
```

instead of this:

```
MyClass c = new MyClass ();
c.InterestRate = 5.5;
```

When you write a static property, you need to remember some obvious restrictions on the code you can write in the **get** and **set** accessors. The restrictions are as follows:

- Static properties cannot access instance data; they can only access static data.

- Similarly, static properties cannot access instance methods.

Creating Virtual and Abstract Properties

You can now easily create virtual data accessors using the property syntax in C#. You can create three different variants of virtual properties. First, you can declare any property to be a virtual property. Take a look at the following:

```
virtual public decimal InterestRate
{
  get
  {
    return Percentage;
  }
  set
  {
    if ((Percentage > 100) ||
      (Percentage < 0.0))
      throw new BadPercentageException ();
    Percentage = value;
  }
}
```

Any derived classes can override the virtual property and give it their own definition. Derived classes declare their intention to override a virtual property, or any virtual function for that matter, using the **override** keyword as follows:

```
override public decimal InterestRate
```

You provide a complete definition for a virtual property when you define it. You have to. If you don't, the C# compiler will complain. There are times when you don't have a correct default implementation for a virtual property. In those cases, you can make the property an abstract property, as in:

```
abstract public decimal InterestRate
{
  get;
  set;
}
```

You can declare abstract properties inside an abstract class. Abstract properties do not have any implementation. You must declare which combination of **get** and **set** accessors your abstract property

5. Properties and Indexers

supports. You specify which accessors your property supports by placing the **get** or **set** keywords inside the abstract property.

Lastly, you can specify properties that must be supported by interfaces. You specify a property in an interface almost exactly the same way that you specify an abstract property:

```
public interface IArray
{
  int size
  {
    get;
    set;
  }
}
```

The only differences are those defined by interface definitions— interface members are always public. You cannot specify an access modifier on a property in an interface.

Related solutions:	Found on page:
Understanding Inheritance	180
Programming with Interfaces	198

Using Properties with Managed C++

When you create components in C#, you will often be creating components that will be accessed by other .NET languages. VB .NET supports property syntax that is exactly the same as C#. VB .NET code will see C# properties as data, just like C#.

However, managed C++ is an entirely different animal. Any property gets exposed to managed C++ as functions. The functions have the name of the property with **get_** and **set_** as prefixes for the **get** and **set** accessors, respectively. For example, the **InterestRate** property from the previous sections would create two functions:

```
decimal get_InterestRate ();
void set_InterestRate (decimal value);
```

Let's look at the MSIL generated by this property to get a deeper understanding of how this works. Figure 5.4 shows the MSIL generated for a class containing the **InterestRate** property. The C# compiler

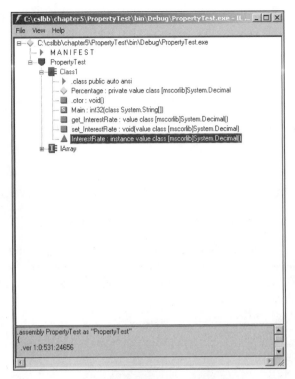

Figure 5.4 This shows the two functions and the property definition in MSIL for the **InterestRate** property.

turns the code for the property into three distinct elements in the class: two functions (**get_InterestRate**, and **set_InterestRate**) and a property definition. Managed C++ code will use the two functions directly. C# clients and VB .NET clients will use the property definition. The property definition specifies the functions that get called when client code accesses the property.

Creating Arrays with Indexers

You can use indexers to let an object be treated as an array or any number of dimensions. For example, most 2-dimensional graphic transformations use 3×3 matrices for all calculations. Suppose you made a class that represented the 3×3 matrix. It would be nice to refer to the element in the first row, second column like this:

```
Matrix m;
m[0,1] = 3.4;
```

115

You can do that by simply creating an indexer that takes two integer parameters and returns a double value, as in the following:

```
double this [int r, int c]
{
  get
  {
    return V[r,c];
  }
  set
  {
    V[r,c] = value;
  }
}
```

The **set** accessor has an implicit parameter named **value**, just like a property. Also, just like a property, you can add any amount of validation code in either the **get** or the **set** accessor, as follows:

```
double this [int r, int c]
{
  get
  {
    if (r < 0) || (r > 2)
      throw new RowRangeException ();
    if (c < 0) || (c > 2)
      throw new ColumnRangeException ();
    return V[r,c];
  }
  set
  {
    if (r < 0) || (r > 2)
      throw new RowRangeException ();
    if (c < 0) || (c > 2)
      throw new ColumnRangeException ();
    if (value > 2000) // Hey, why not?
      throw new ValueException ();
    V[r,c] = value;
  }
}
```

All of the discussions from prior sections pertaining to virtual and abstract properties apply to indexers. You can make virtual indexers in your classes, and you can create abstract indexers in abstract classes and in interfaces. There is, however, one important difference on indexers: You cannot create static indexers.

Creating Maps with Indexers

The parameters to the array boundaries do not need to be integer values. You can use any type as the parameter types to an indexer.

You can create a class that stores the temperature at a given time and day, retrieving it through an indexer. Take a look at the following:

```
Temperature this [DateTime t]
{
    get { // ... }
}
```

This indexer does not support the **set** method, for obvious reasons.

It is often common to create indexers that are *maps*—structures that store data based on some key string. A simple example would be stock quotes. You retrieve a stock's price using its symbol:

```
decimal this [string symbol]
{
    get { // ... }
}
```

As with the temperature example, this indexer does not have a setter.

Using Indexers with Other Languages

By now, you are probably thinking that indexers are really cool, and you can't wait to use them in every one of your programming tasks. But wait; there is a dark side. Indexers do not translate particularly well to other languages.

When you create an indexer in C#, you actually create two functions:

```
get_Item ()
set_Item ()
```

Yes, that's what they are called. Suddenly, this elegant syntax is lost. So, when you create indexers, be cognizant of the callers of your classes. Instead of writing this:

```
decimal price = Stocks ["MSFT"];
```

5. Properties and Indexers

Managed C++ clients will write:

```
decimal price = Stocks->get_Item ("MSFT");
```

This still works, but is much less clear and consistent. So, use indexers judiciously and only when the abstraction makes sense.

Chapter 6

Overloaded Operators

In Brief

C# provides facilities for you to define how some of the operators in the C# language behave with your new types, be they structs or classes. For those of you coming from a C++ background, you will find that you can do almost everything you could in C++, but that the mechanisms are a bit different.

Designing Overloaded Operators

The first time someone sees overloaded operators in a language, whether it is in C++ or C#, their first reaction is usually negative. The idea that you can change the meaning of a built-in operator is pretty scary.

After a few days, the scariness wears off and programmers start trying to figure out what the new meaning of every operator that can be overloaded should be. Unfortunately, this phase usually lasts a few months. Then, programmers finally start maintaining classes with very obfuscating operators. They learn that these are creating unreadable code that no one wants to examine, modify, or use.

The biggest challenge in working with overloaded operators is to create operators that make your types easier to use, but do not make your types more confusing to use. If you err, you should probably err on the side of restraint, rather than excessive operators.

Before I discuss guidelines for overloaded operators, you need to understand what overloaded operators means and how it works.

Defining Overloaded Operators

You can write a function that defines how an operator works when applied to objects of your type. For example, look back at the **Distance** struct in Chapter 4. You should be able to write the following:

```
Distance d1 = new Distance (32.0, DistanceUnits.feet);
Distance d2 = new Distance (6.0, DistanceUnits.inches);
Distance d3 = d1 + d2;
```

This is much more clear than writing something like this:

```
Distance d1 = new Distance (32.0, DistanceUnits.feet);
Distance d2 = new Distance (6.0, DistanceUnits.inches);
Distance d3 = Distance.sum (d1, d2);
```

The first form lets you use the same syntax you would use for any built-in type. You would write the function in this form:

```
struct Distance {
  // ...
  public static Distance operator + (Distance l, Distance r)
  {
    Distance rVal = new Distance ();
    // compute the answer...
    return rVal;
  }
}
```

This shows some of the typical points about defining an operator:

- The name of an overloaded operator is *operator* followed by the symbol for the particular operator you are overloading (in this case, **+**).

- C# overloaded operators are always static functions.

- At least one of the parameters or return value in an overloaded operator must be of the type containing the function (in this case, **Distance**).

Let's examine each of these points in a little more detail.

You can overload most of the operators in C#. Some of them, you can overload more than once, using different parameter lists. The .NET BCL does this in the string class: you can concatenate strings with a variety of different types. The parameters sometimes define which operator you are overloading. Consider the hyphen (-) character:

```
struct Distance {
  // ...
  // Overload subtraction:
  public static Distance operator - (Distance l, Distance r)
  {
    Distance rVal = new Distance ();
    // compute the answer...
    return rVal;
  }
  // Overload unary -.
  public static Distance operator - (Distance r)
```

```
{
  Distance rVal = r;
  rVal.Magnitude = - - r.Magnitude;
  return rVal;
}
}
```

The first function in the preceding snippet overloads binary subtraction. The second overloads the unary minus symbol. You can use it to write code like this:

```
Distance d2 = -d1;
```

C# operators are always static functions. There is no implicit **this** parameter to an operator. Because of that, you must specify both operands of a binary operator. It also means that overloaded operators cannot be abstract or virtual. If you give it a little thought, you will see that it also means that you cannot declare overloaded operators in interfaces.

At least one of the parameters in an overloaded operator must be of the type containing the function. This is just plain common sense and security. You don't want to write a class and then have someone else add operators on your class after the fact. After you finish your class, no one else can change the interface for that class. They can, however, add their own operators in their class that may use variables of your type.

Overloadable Operators

The last section showed you some of the rules for defining overloaded operators. In C#, not every operator can be overloaded. Table 6.1 shows you the unary operators you can overload, and Table 6.2 shows you the binary operators you can overload. Unary operators take only one parameter; binary operators take two parameters. In each of the tables, the parameter named l would appear on the left side of the operator, and the parameter named r would appear on the right side of the operator.

WARNING (C++ Users)! There is no distinction between the preincrement and the postincrement versions of overloaded ++ and - operators. The compiler and the runtime do the work to optimize between pre- and post-increment.

Table 6.1 This table shows the overloadable unary operators and the valid prototype for each.

Operator	Meaning	Declaration
+	unary + (positive)	**public static MyType operator + (MyType r)**
-	unary − (negation)	**public static MyType operator - (MyType r)**
!	logical not	**public static MyType operator ! (MyType r)** or **public static bool operator ! (MyType r)**
~	bitwise complement	**public static MyType operator ~ (MyType r)**
++	unary increment	**public static MyType operator ++(MyType r)**
--	unary decrement	**public static MyType operator -- (MyType r)**
true	unary definitely true	**public static bool operator true (MyType r)**
false	unary definitely false	**public static bool operator false (MyType r)**

Table 6.2 This table shows the overloadable binary operators and a valid prototype for each.

Operator	Meaning	Declaration
+	addition	**public static MyType operator + (MyType l, MyType r)**
-	subtraction	**public static MyType operator -- (MyType l, MyType r)**
*	multiplication	**public static MyType operator * (MyType l, MyType r)**
/	division	**public static MyType operator / (MyType l, MyType r)**
%	modulus (remainder)	**public static MyType operator % (MyType l, MyType r)**
&	bitwise AND	**public static MyType operator & (MyType l, MyType r)**
|	bitwise OR	**public static MyType operator l (MyType l, MyType r)**

(continued)

Table 6.2   This table shows the overloadable binary operators and a valid prototype for each *(continued).*

Operator	Meaning	Declaration
^	bitwise exclusive OR	**public static MyType operator ^ (MyType I, MyType r)**
<<	left shift	**public static MyType operator << (MyType I, int r)**
>>	right shift	**public static MyType operator >> (MyType I, int r)**
==	equality	**public static bool operator == (MyType I, MyType r)**
!=	not equal	**public static bool operator != (MyType I, MyType r)**
>	greater than	**public static bool operator > (MyType I, MyType r)**
<	less than	**public static bool operator < (MyType I, MyType r)**
>=	greater than or equal	**public static bool operator >= (MyType I, MyType r)**
<=	less than or equal	**public static bool operator <= (MyType I, MyType r)**

Those are all the overloadable operators. There is a small set of operators you cannot overload:

- **&& and ||** You cannot overload the logical AND or the logical OR operator. You actually cannot provide your own definition of these functions and still have short circuiting work correctly.

- **=** You cannot overload the assignment operator. Assignment is predefined and cannot be affected. Nor can you overload any of the compound assignment operators. Assignment means something different for reference and value types. Preventing the overloaded of these operators ensures that distinction remains.

WARNING (C++ Users)! Even though you cannot overload the assignment operator, nor any of the compound assignment operators (such as **operator +=***), the compiler generates code to call your overloaded operator + when you use a compound assignment operator. The compiler also optimizes the access to get the same benefits that the compound assignment normally gives you.*

Conversion Operators

Even if the standard operators are not enough, you can create any number of operators to convert from your type to any other type. You can create two different types of conversion operators, implicit conversions and explicit conversions, which are shown in the following examples:

```
public static implicit operator NewType (MyType r)
public static explicit operator OtherNewType (MyType r)
```

A *conversion operator* returns the new type and takes the current type as its only parameter. The distinction between the explicit and implicit conversions is in how they are called. An *explicit conversion* will be invoked only when you perform a cast:

```
MyType m = new MyType ();
OtherNewType t = (OtherNewType) m;
```

On the other hand, an *implicit conversion* will be invoked anytime the compiler needs to convert your type into another type to get your code to compile cleanly.

WARNING (C++ Users)! C# does not use conversion constructors to create temporary variables. Conversion operators are the only conversion functions examined when a different variable type is needed.

6. Overloaded Operators

Immediate Solutions

You have seen the theory behind operators and the syntax to create your own operators. Now, let's work through and create some operators for the **Distance** struct I made previously.

When you define and write overloaded operators, you need to remember one simple concept: The C# compiler wants to compile your code. Really, truly, badly, it does. If there is any way to get an expression to generate valid object code, the compiler will do it. The more operators you add, the more different paths the compiler can explore to compile your code. Often, this will result in code you did not expect to compile to generate code that does the wrong thing.

Your goal is to write code that is much less likely to be misused and compiled into code that creates runtime errors. To do this, you want to create overloaded operators in logical groups. Secondly, you will want to provide the minimum number of conversion operators to make your class easy to use. Let's look at the grouping, from the most common to the least common.

There are quite a few operators that make the **Distance** struct easier for other programmers to use.

Defining Ordering Relations: <, <=, >, >=

The ordering relations are the most common operators to overload. When you see them used, the answer should be clear:

```
Distance d1;
Distance d2;
  // Initialize d1 and d2.
if (d1 < d2) // Clear, right?
{
  // Do things ...
}
```

The actual implementation of operator **<** for the **Distance** struct is straightforward to develop:

```
public static bool operator < (Distance l, Distance r)
{
  return l.AsInches () < r.AsInches ();
}
```

If you add this code to the **Distance** struct and compile it, you will get some surprising results: It does not compile. C# requires that if you define operator **<**, you must also define operator **>**. So, you simply add the greater-than operator:

```
public static bool operator > (Distance l, Distance r)
{
  return r < l;
}
```

This is the *canonical* form of operator **>**. After you've defined operator **<**, you should define operator **>** in terms of it: You will generate less code at runtime, and you will have less code to maintain.

Often, when you support operator **<** and operator **>**, your objects also support **<=** and **>=**. These also must both be defined:

```
public static bool operator <= (Distance l, Distance r)
{
  return l.AsFeet () <= r.AsFeet ();
}
```

```
public static bool operator >= (Distance l, Distance r)
{
  return r <= l;
}
```

All ordering relations are *binary* functions: They take two objects of the same type and compare the values of their member data. Notice that the parameters are values. You cannot declare **ref** or **out** parameters for these functions.

You should overload the relational operators whenever you create a type that has a defined ordering. When you overload the relational operators, you will most likely overload all four of them.

You can create ordering relations between different types, but that is much less common and can be confusing for users of your class. What does it mean for a distance to be greater than a time, for example? Probably nothing.

Defining Additive Operations: **++, --, +, -**

The next set of operators you will commonly add are the additive operators. First, here are the increment and decrement operators for the **Distance** struct:

```
public static Distance operator ++ (Distance l)
{
  Distance rVal = l;
  rVal.mag++;
  return rVal;
}

public static Distance operator -- (Distance l)
{
  Distance rVal = l;
  rVal.mag--;
  return rVal;
}
```

C++ programmers are probably cringing at this code. Well, you shouldn't. There are several differences in these operators in C#. There is no distinction between the prefix and postfix version of **++** and **--** in C#. The CLR handles that difference in the calling code.

Notice that both of these operators return a new **Distance** object. Remember earlier that I said it was important to keep your structs small. Here is one example of why you should do so. You cannot write these operator functions as member functions and modify the value in place. You have no choice but to write these functions in the form shown in the preceding code.

You can also create an operator **+** and operator **-** for the **Distance** struct:

```
public static Distance operator + (Distance l, Distance r)
{
  Distance rVal = l;
  rVal.mag += r.GetAs(rVal.units);
  return rVal;
}

public static Distance operator - (Distance l, Distance r)
{
```

```
    Distance rVal = 1;
    rVal.mag -= r.GetAs(rVal.units);
    return rVal;
}
```

The **+** and **-** operators do not need to be declared as pairs. You can implement either independently in a class. The string class is the only class I can think of that implements operator **+** without implementing operator **-**. The string class also does a few other tricks relating to additive operators. Normally, you would expect the following code to print "commutative property holds":

```
MyClass a, b, c, d;
// Initialize a and b.
c = a + b;
d = b + a;
if (c == d)
{
    Console.WriteLine ("commutative property holds");
}
```

The commutative property does not hold for strings. Under most conditions, you should make sure that the commutative property holds for your classes and structs. Incidentally, that is also a reason to avoid having too many addition operators defined with different operands. That makes it much more difficult to ensure that the commutative property holds. I could have written a number of different addition operators for the **Distance** struct:

```
public static Distance operator + (Distance l, Distance r)
public static Distance operator + (Distance l, double r)
public static Distance operator + (double l, Distance r)
// could add long, int, short, but the double version works.
```

Notice that for those operators that take different operands, you need to essentially define them twice, for each order of the operands.

You should define the additive operators for any type that clearly supports addition. You should try to make sure that your overloads support the normal arithmetic properties: commutative and associative. In almost all cases, you should define *all* of the addition-related operators if you define any of them.

Defining Multiplicative Operations: *, /, %

You will probably want to define two different versions of the multiplicative operators on the **Distance** struct:

```
public static Distance operator * (Distance 1, double r)
{
  Distance rVal = 1;
  rVal.mag *= r;
  return rVal;
}

public static Distance operator * (double 1, Distance r)
{
  return r * 1;
}
```

First of all, notice that no version of the * operator takes two **Distances**—that would return an area, not a **Distance**. Secondly, notice that you need to create both versions of * that take a **Distance** and a **double**. You certainly want multiplication to be commutative. As with the relational operators, you can define one ordering in terms of the other for efficiency reasons. Division is not commutative, so you need only define one version of that operator:

```
public static Distance operator / (Distance 1, double r)
{
  Distance rVal = 1;
  rVal.mag /= r;
  return rVal;
}
```

The modulus operator (**operator %**) is typically defined only for integral values. It is defined for the built-in floating-point types, but I have yet to find it used in practice.

You should overload the multiplication operators for any type that models an entity that supports multiplication operators. But, be careful. The **Distance** struct shows how multiplication operators can change the type of the answer. Multiplication operators often introduce many other types into the set of overloads.

Multiplication operators also point out the need for clarity in overloaded operators. Remember that your goal is to create clearer code, not more confusing code. Suppose you define a matrix class. Would operator * invoke the dot product, or the cross product? Users of your class would not be certain. It is probably better to create other functions called **CrossProduct** and **DotProduct**, which would improve the clarity of your class.

Defining Comparison Operators: ==, !=

I would strongly recommend not overloading the == and != operators in your class types. Remember that class objects are reference types, and these operators compare the references to the objects. For any reference types, operator == returns true only if the two operands point to the same object. To test if two references are equivalent, you can use the **CompareTo ()** method in the **IComparable** interface, or the **Equals()** method, if it has been overloaded. Value types will only rarely need to overload these operators. The built-in == operator compares all the values in the struct, and if all the member variables are the same, the == operator returns true.

Well, that built-in behavior will not work for the **Distance** struct. You know that 12 inches should be equal to one foot, but the built-in operator == doesn't know that. So, you simply write your own:

```
public static bool operator == (Distance l, Distance r)
{
    return l.AsFeet () == r.AsFeet ();
}
```

Simple enough, right? But, like the relational operators, adding just this one method does not compile. You need to add an operator !=:

```
public static bool operator != (Distance l, Distance r)
{
    return !(l == r);
}
```

You should be learning the tricks by now: Whenever you see operators that must be defined in pairs, you should define one in terms of the other, as in the preceding example. When you define == and !=, you also need to overload **System.ValueType.Equals()** in the **Distance** struct:

```
public override bool Equals (object r)
{
    if (r is Distance)
    {
```

131

```
        Distance dR = (Distance) r;
        return this == dR;
    } else {
        return false;
    }
}
```

NOTE: *This function introduces a few ideas that have not been covered, so it bears a little more scrutiny. The **Equals()** method is a virtual function declared in **System.Object** (or **object**, in C#). The trick to this function is that the parameter is a **System.Object**, not a **Distance**. The first line in the function checks to see if the parameter r is a **Distance** object. If not, the function returns false. If it is, it casts the parameter to a **Distance**, then checks to see if they are equivalent.*

Related solutions:	Found on page:
Declaring Override Methods	172
Throwing Exceptions	234
Finding Types in an Assembly	386

The **Distance** struct compiles again, but this time you get one warning (note that the following code should be entered as a single line):

```
c:\cslbb\chapter6\newton\distance.cs(18,16): warning CS0661:
'CSharpLittleBlackBook.Chapter6.Distance' defines operator ==
or operator != but does not overload Object.GetHashCode()
```

You could stop here, but that would make your struct very confusing for users. Examine the following code:

```
Distance d1 = new Distance (12.0, DistanceUnits.inches);
Distance d2 = new Distance (12.0, DistanceUnits.feet);
if (d1 == d2)
{
  Console.WriteLine ("d1 == d2");
} else
{
  Console.WriteLine ("d1 != d2");
}
if (d1.GetHashCode().equals (d2.GetHashCode()))
{
  Console.WriteLine ("d1 Hash equals d2");
} else
{
  Console.WriteLine ("d1 Hash does not equal d2");
}
```

6. Overloaded Operators

If you ran the code, you would get the following output:

```
d1 != d2
d1 Hash equals d2
```

This output is wrong because all Distances return the same hash code.

Next, let's examine **GetHashCode( )**. You need to follow three guidelines for implementing **GetHashCode( )**:

- Two objects that are equal must return the same hash value.
- A hash function should generate a random distribution for all values.
- For reference types, **GetHashCode( )** should be based on an immutable member. Otherwise, HashTables may not work. For value types, you cannot modify a value once it is in a hash table. You can remove it and insert a new value but because of boxing and unboxing, the value stored cannot be modified.

All we need to do for the **Distance** function is to make sure that equivalent objects return the same hash code. The easiest way to do that is to make sure that they return the same units. I chose inches because that gives the greatest distribution of values, satisfying the second guideline. Notice that **Distance** objects that are not necessarily equal may return the same hash value, which is okay, just a little inefficient:

```
public override int GetHashCode ()
{
    return (int) AsInches ();
}
```

Related solution:	*Found on page:*
Working with Dictionaries	344

Lastly, types that support **Equals( ) operator ==**, and **operator !=** and the relational operators should also support the **IComparable** interface. The **IComparable** interface has one method: **CompareTo( )**.

To support this interface, first add it to the list of implemented interfaces on the **Distance** struct:

```
public struct Distance : IComparable
```

Then, implement the **CompareTo( )** method in the **Distance** struct:

```
public int CompareTo (object o)
{
  if (o is Distance)
  {
    Distance dR = (Distance) o;
    if (this < dR)
      return -1;
    else if (dR > this)
      return 1;
    else
      return 0;
  } else
    throw new ArgumentException ("Argument is not a
Distance value", "o");
}
```

Related solution:	Found on page:
Implementing **IComparable**	197

And you thought checking for equality was easy. Luckily, you do not often need to do that much work to get equality tests to work properly. Remember these guidelines:

- If you override **operator ==** and **operator !=**, you must overload **System.Object.Equals**.

- If you override **operator ==**, you should consider overloaded **System.Object.GetHashCode( )**. You must do this if your new **operator ==** would violate the guidelines for **GetHashCode( )**.

- You should overload **System.Object.Equals** in your reference types (classes) to let users check for different reference objects with the same values.

- Most types should override the **IComparable** interface to provide methods that test for equality and ordering relations.

Defining Conversions

Conversion operators export your data as another type; you should use them judiciously. These operators imply that your new type is somehow equivalent to another type. The **Distance** struct stores a

6. Overloaded Operators

double to represent the magnitude of the distance. It makes sense to provide a conversion operator that lets you treat a **Distance** as a **double**. Doing so will make working with the **Distance** struct and any existing math libraries much more convenient:

```
public static explicit operator double (Distance r)
{
  return r.mag;
}
```

This declaration creates an explicit conversion from a **Distance** to a **double**. You can use it in one of the Math library functions, as this example shows:

```
double d = System.Math.Ceiling ((double)dist);
```

The cast is necessary because the conversion operator is explicit. If you wanted to perform operations like this without the cast, you need to mark the conversion operator as implicit.

You should use implicit conversion operators with extreme care because they can be called without your knowledge when a parameter of a different type is expected. You should use explicit conversions with care because they imply an equivalence relationship between different types.

Managing State

You want to be able to treat some of your types as Boolean values:

```
if (var)
{
  // Do stuff
}
```

You can support this construct by defining **operator true( )** and **operator false( )** for your type:

```
public static bool operator true (Distance d)
{
  // define validity as non-zero magnitude:
  return d.mag != 0.0;
}
```

Just like many of the other operators we have defined, if you define **operator true**, you must define **operator false**:

```
public static bool operator false (Distance r)
{
   return r ? false : true;
}
```

Just like all the other operators that must be defined in pairs, you should define **operator false** in terms of **operator true**. This uses the ternary operator to reverse the return value of **operator true**.

You should overload the true and false operators for types that can be treated as Boolean values. My example for the **Distance** struct is not a particularly good use of this feature. A more typical use is a value type loaded from a database. In that case, these operators return true if the data has been loaded, false if not.

Chapter 7

Delegates and Events

In Brief

A *delegate* is a type of C# object that stores and uses a function pointer. Delegates provide many of the same programming idioms that function pointers provide, but they have more language support. This chapter explains the syntax used with delegates and shows you how to create your own delegates and define delegates in your own classes.

Declaring and Calling Delegates

Declaring a delegate is very much like declaring a function. Inside a class, you simply declare the prototype of a function, with the keyword **delegate**.

Imagine you wrote a class that copied large files between machines. Most clients would want to tell the user how the operation was proceeding. Delegates provide a very flexible way to do that:

```
public class FileTransfer
{
  // return true to keep going...
  public delegate bool ProgressCallback (int blocksWritten,
    int blocksTotal);

  public static void CopyFiles (string src,
    string dest,
    ProgressCallback progress)
  {
    int blocks = 0;
    int blocksLeft = 1000; // guess.
    While (blocksLeft > 0) {
      // copy a block...
      blocks++;
      blocksLeft--;
      if (!progress (blocks, blocksLeft))
        return;
    }
  }
}
```

This class declares a delegate named **ProgressCallback**. It expects client code to provide an implementation of that function that will be called as each block copy completes. Inside the **CopyFiles( )** method, the delegate object gets invoked using the delegate parameter name **progress**.

Creating a Delegate

To use the class in the previous section, you need to create a delegate that matches the specification declared there.

```
class Class1
{
  static bool MyProgress (int written, int total)
  {
    Console.WriteLine("Written {0} of {1} blocks", written,
    total);
    return true;
  }

  static void Main(string[] args)
  {
    FileTransfer.CopyFiles ("foo1", "foo2",
      new FileTransfer.ProgressCallback(Class1.MyProgress));
  }
}
```

Class1 declares a static method (**MyProgress**), which satisfies the function declaration for the **ProgressCallback** delegate declared in the **FileTransfer** class:

```
static bool MyProgress (int written, int total)
```

The call to **CopyFiles** creates a new delegate object for the **FileTransfer** class to call inside the **CopyFiles ()** method:

```
new FileTransfer.ProgressCallback(Class1.MyProgress));
```

Delegates are actually objects. Anytime you declare a delegate, you actually declare a nested class inside your class. Figure 7.1 shows the MSIL generated from this declaration and use of the **ProgressCallback** delegate.

The class declaration for **ProgressCallback** contains four methods that define the internal workings of delegates in C#. The first method is the constructor. The constructor for the delegate takes a pointer to a function that matches the delegate signature. The address of

7. Delegates and Events

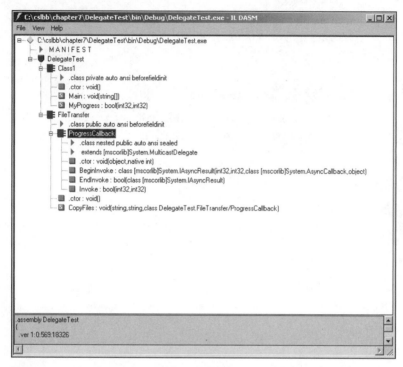

Figure 7.1   Delegate declarations actually create a class derived from **System.MulticastDelegate**.

the function is stored inside the base class object, a **System.MulticastDelegate**. The function stored in the delegate gets called by using the **Invoke** method declared in the **ProgressCallback** class. In fact, the line

```
if (!progress (blocks, blocksLeft))
```

generates the following MSIL:

```
IL_0015:  callvirt instance bool
  DelegateTest.FileTransfer/ProgressCallback::Invoke(int32,
    int32)
```

Here is the mechanism for calling and declaring delegate functions:

- Some classes declare a delegate. This actually declares a new class that is derived from **System.MulticastDelegate**.

- Another piece of code constructs an instance of the delegate object using a function that matches the calling signature found in the delegate object.

- The delegate method gets called through its **Invoke()** member. The delegate object calls the actual function using the address stored when the delegate object was created.

The example in this section uses a static method as the invoke member on the delegate. That is not a requirement; you can use instance methods just as easily. The delegate object stores all the necessary information to call both static methods and instance methods correctly.

Multicast Delegates

Delegates can be chained together to create multicast delegates or composite delegates. A *multicast* delegate object can store the address of more than one function. All delegate objects support multicasting. Delegates overload the addition and subtraction operators to add and remove functions from a delegate object. These overloaded functions simply call the multicast delegate's **Combine ()** and **Remove ()** methods. This snippet uses the addition operator to combine two delegates:

```
FileTransfer.ProgressCallback c = new
  FileTransfer.ProgressCallback(MyProgress);
c += new FileTransfer.ProgressCallback(Progress2);
```

This snippet uses the **Combine** method to produce exactly the same result:

```
FileTransfer.ProgressCallback callback1 = new
  FileTransfer.ProgressCallback(MyProgress);
FileTransfer.ProgressCallback c2 = new
  FileTransfer.ProgressCallback(Progress2);
FileTransfer.ProgressCallback c =
  (FileTransfer.ProgressCallback)
  FileTransfer.ProgressCallback.Combine (callback1, c2);
```

After both bits of code, **c** has both **MyProgress** and **Progress2** in its invocation list. The code inside the **CopyFiles()** function

```
if (!progress (blocks, blocksLeft))
```

calls both methods.

But wait, this delegate defines a Boolean return value. Which one actually gets returned to the **CopyFiles()** function? Well, like so many similar constructs, the last one wins. The return value from **Progress2( )** gets used to determine whether or not the copy operation continues.

A similar set of problems occurs with exceptions. If one of the functions in an invocation list throws an exception, none of the other remaining events in the invocation list will be called. Also, you can't always find out which method threw the exception.

So, be careful with multicast delegates. They are a powerful feature, but you need to follow some guidelines:

- Declare delegates with a void return when they are intended for multicasting.

- Be very careful when throwing exceptions in functions used as delegates. That requires extra processing by the class that calls the delegates.

Handling Events

All events in C# programs are processed using multicast delegates. An *event declaration* is a delegate declaration with a special form. All event handlers have a void return type, and take two parameters: a sender object and an object derived from **System.EventArgs**.

Anyone familiar with Windows programming of any sort should be familiar with writing event handlers—they permeate every facet of Windows code. Creating your own event handler is quite simple. You write a function that handles an event, such as this function that handles the **Click** event in a form:

```
private void OnClick(object sender, System.EventArgs e)
{
  System.Windows.Forms.MessageBox.Show (
    "Ouch, I've been clicked!");
}
```

After that, simply use the addition operator to add this event handler to the chain of event handlers already in place for the **Click** event. The following code shows the standard event wiring code in a class called **Form1** (**InitializeComponent** is a function written and maintained by Visual Studio .NET to initialize the form):

```
private void InitializeComponent()
{
  //
```

```
// Form1
//
this.AutoScaleBaseSize = new System.Drawing.Size(5, 13);
this.ClientSize = new System.Drawing.Size(292, 273);
this.Name = "Form1";
this.Text = "Form1";
this.Click += new System.EventHandler(this.OnClick);
}
```

That's all you need to do to handle events. It's quite a simple model, isn't it?

Creating New Events

Handling events is one thing, but what if you are writing a server object and you want to publish events for others to consume? That is almost as easy. Suppose you wrote a class to handle a weather station. One of the features you would want to support would be the ability to notify other objects when the weather changes. The first task is to create a class to hold the event arguments:

```
public class TempChangedEventArgs : EventArgs
{
  private readonly double temp;

  public TempChangedEventArgs (double t)
  {
    temp = t;
  }

  public double newTemp
  {
    get
    {
      return temp;
    }
  }
}
```

Next, you need to write a set of data structures that let users of your class add event handlers to the invocation list:

```
public class WeatherStation
{
  public delegate void TempChangeEventHandler (object sender,
    TempChangedEventArgs a);
```

7. Delegates and Events

```
public event TempChangeEventHandler OnTempChanged:

// etc.
```

These two declarations create a delegate signature for the tempera-
ture-changed event and an event variable. The event variable stores
the delegate that creates and manages the invocation list.

Next, you need to write the code that fires the event. Assume that
UpdateTemp () gets called when the temperature changes:

```
public void UpdateTemp (double newTemp)
{
  if (OnTempChanged != null)
  {
    TempChangedEventArgs e =
        new TempChangedEventArgs(newTemp);
    OnTempChanged (this, e);
  }
}
```

If the **OnTempChanged** variable is not null, this code creates a new
TempChangedEventArgs object and fires the event by invoking the
OnTempChanged( ) delegate.

Finally, a client needs to attach a function to the delegate instance:

```
private static void gotNewTemp (object sender,
TempChangedEventArgs e)
{
  Console.WriteLine("New Temp is {0}", e.newTemp);
}

WeatherStation w = new WeatherStation ();
w.OnTempChanged += new WeatherStation.TempChangeEventHandler
  (gotNewTemp);

// Elsewhere:
w.UpdateTemp (75.5); // generate the event.
```

The client simply adds the new event handler by using the **+=**
operator.

So, you see that you can easily create your own events, as well as
using the standard events defined in Windows or anywhere in the
class library.

Immediate Solutions

Armed with a knowledge of how delegates work in .NET and C#, let's look at some common real-world scenarios where C# delegates are used.

Using Callbacks

You will find yourself using delegates as callback functions far more often than you will use them in any other situation.

Receiving Callbacks

The regular expressions namespace in the .NET Framework library has a great example for using delegates. Regular expressions are used to replace text in a string. They are a powerful means of expressing search strings. The regular expressions library has methods that automatically edit a string and replace any matches with a new string. For example, the following bit of code replaces *This* at the beginning of the string with *That*:

```
const string inputStr =
  "This is a simple test of this RegEx System.";
Regex reg = new Regex ("^[Tt]his");
string outputStr = reg.Replace(inputStr, "That");
```

For those of you that have not used regular expressions before, the expression "**^[Tt]his**" means this:

- **^** matches the beginning of a line or the beginning of the input string.

- **[Tt]** matches either *T* or *t*.

- **his** matches the character sequence *his*.

So, together "**^[Tt]his**" matches *This* or *this* at the beginning of a line or the beginning of an input string. But, this chapter is not about regular expressions, so let's get back to delegates. The preceding example will unconditionally replace every occurrence of the string. But, what if you want your user to approve or edit changes? The **Regex** class provides an overloaded version of **Replace** that does just that.

The code in Listing 7.1 accomplishes the exact same task but gives the user the chance to approve or reject changes:

Listing 7.1   Using a delegate to control pattern replacement.

```
static string Matcher (Match m)
{
  Console.WriteLine ("Replace {0} with \"That\"? ", m.Value);
  string val = Console.ReadLine ();
  if (0 == val.ToLower ().IndexOf("y"))
    return "That";
  else
    return m.Value;
}


// Elsewhere in the code:
const string inputStr =
  "This is a simple test of this RegEx System.";
Regex reg = new Regex ("^[Tt]his");
string outputStr = reg.Replace(inputStr,
  new MatchEvaluator (Matcher));
```

First, you need to create a function that matches the signature used by the regular expression matcher delegate. Then, you invoke a different version of the **Replace()** method on the **Regex** object (see the highlighted code in the preceding example). Anytime the **Regex** object finds a string that matches the input string, your delegate gets called. Your delegate returns the string that should replace the existing string.

Receiving Callbacks with Instance Methods

The example in the preceding section uses a hard-coded string as the replacement string. To improve on this, Listing 7.2 defines a class to handle the replacement.

Listing 7.2   Using a member function as a delegate.

```
public class TextMatcher
{
  private string Replacement;

  // Constructor: Set the replacement string.
  public TextMatcher (string r)
  {
    Replacement = r;
  }

  // Delegate Member function:
```

```
public string Matcher (Match m)
{
  Console.WriteLine ("Replace {0} with {1}", m.Value,
    Replacement);
  string val = Console.ReadLine ();
  if (0 == val.ToLower ().IndexOf("y"))
    return Replacement;
  else
    return m.Value;
  }
}

// Usage:
const string inputStr =
  "This is a simple test of this RegEx System.";
Regex reg = new Regex ("^[Tt]his");
TextMatcher Matcher = new TextMatcher ("That");
string outputStr = reg.Replace(inputStr,
  new MatchEvaluator (Matcher.Matcher));
```
                        Text Matcher

This example shows you how easy it is to use an instance method. But, this example breaks some of the rules of encapsulation. It would be better if the code using the delegate did not have to create it. The answer is to create the delegate inside the **TextMatcher** class. The following section makes that addition.

Using Properties for Delegates

Making the delegate a member of the **TextMatcher** class is easy. Simply add a member variable of type **MatchEvaluator** and create the delegate object in the **TextMatcher** constructor. But, that is wasteful. Nothing is ever free, and delegates cost processing time and memory. (Delegates are managed objects, so they make the garbage collector do more work as well.) Remember properties? They are the right solution to this problem. Using properties, you can create a read-only property to return the delegate. Now, the code that uses the **TextMatcher** class just asks to use the delegate (see Listing 7.3).

7. Delegates and Events

Listing 7.3 The **TextMatcher** class encapsulates the delegate in a property. Now, the property gets created only when requested.

```
public class TextMatcher
{
  private string Replacement;
  private MatchEvaluator matchEval = null;

  public TextMatcher (string r)
```

```
          {
            Replacement = r;
          }

    public MatchEvaluator MatchEval
          {
            get
            {
              if (matchEval == null)
                matchEval = new MatchEvaluator(Matcher);
              return matchEval;
            }
          }

          private string Matcher (Match m)
          {
            Console.WriteLine ("Replace {0} with {1}", m.Value,
              Replacement);
            string val = Console.ReadLine ();
            if (0 == val.ToLower ().IndexOf("y"))
              return Replacement;
            else
              return m.Value;
          }
        }

// Usage:
Regex reg = new Regex ("^[Tt]his");
TextMatcher Matcher = new TextMatcher ("That");
string outputStr = reg.Replace(inputStr, Matcher.MatchEval);
```

The changes are highlighted in Listing 7.3. First, you need to add a delegate variable to hold the delegate created from the member function. Secondly, you need to add the property to retrieve the delegate when requested. The **get** accessor uses a lazy evaluation idiom: If the delegate has not been created, it is created in the accessor.

Related solution:	Found on page:
Creating Properties with Visual Studio .NET	107

You should use this idiom whenever you make a class that creates a delegate for use by other classes. It creates the delegate only when necessary and insulates the delegate function from client code.

Defining Callbacks

By now, you know everything you need to know about using delegates. There will be times when you undoubtedly will need to create delegates. There are some nuances here that are important as you handle callbacks from client code.

To demonstrate defining your own callbacks, I am going to use a simple application that echoes input from the user to the console.

Issuing Callbacks

You define a callback function simply by declaring a delegate. Delegate declarations do not need to be declared in classes; they can be declared anywhere. Here is the delegate definition for the keyboard echo callback:

```
public delegate void OnGetLine (string s);
```

Backing up just a bit, Listing 7.4 shows the first listener that echoes keyboard input out to the console.

Listing 7.4   First listener class.

```
public class listener1
{
  private static OnGetLine myDelegate;

  // Static constructor.
  // Initialize the delegate to null.
  static listener1 ()
  {
    myDelegate = null;
  }

  public static OnGetLine Listener1Delegate
  {
    get
    {
      if (myDelegate == null)
        myDelegate = new OnGetLine (ShowLine);
      return myDelegate;
    }
  }

  private static void ShowLine (string s)
  {
```

```
      Console.WriteLine ("\tGot text in Listener1: {0}", s);
  }
}
```

Most of this should be review from earlier in this chapter. I have added one new twist—this class has a **static** constructor. The **static** constructor initializes the delegate reference to null.

Listing 7.5 shows the code that creates and calls the delegate.

Listing 7.5   Using the delegate to publish keyboard input.

```
public class KeyboardProcessor
{
  private OnGetLine theFunc = null;

  public OnGetLine OnGetLineCallback
  {
    get
    {
      return theFunc;
    }
    set
    {
      theFunc = value;
    }
  }

  public void Run ()
  {
    string s;
    do {
      s = Console.ReadLine ();
      if (s.Length == 0)
        break;
      if (theFunc != null)
        theFunc (s);
    } while (true);
  }

  static void Main(string[] args)
  {
    KeyboardProcessor k = new KeyboardProcessor();
    k.OnGetLineCallback += listener1.Listener1Delegate;
    k.Run ();
  }
}
```

Listing 7.5 shows the class that processes the input and notifies any listeners using its delegate. It is a long listing, so let's break it down a bit. First, this class declares a private member variable to hold the delegate (**theFunc**). Next, this delegate is exported using a property named **OnGetLineCallback**, which is a read/write property, so users can set it as well as read it.

The **Run()** method handles the work of reading input and passing the string off to any delegates that have registered. This function just keeps reading input until it gets an empty string. If there are any registered callbacks, they get notified.

Finally, the **Main()** method tests these two classes. **Main** creates a new **KeyboardProcessor** object and adds a **Listener1** delegate to the list of listeners. Then, it calls the **Run** method to process the input.

Handling Multicast Callbacks

You need to do some extra work if you want to support multicast delegates robustly. The delegate object invokes all the functions in its invocation list to support multicast delegates, which causes two related headaches. The first is that you only get the return code from the last delegate called. All other return codes are discarded.

The second problem is more of a concern. If any of the delegates throw an exception, none of the other delegates get called. After that happens, you have very few options. You do not even know for sure which delegates have been called and which have not. Like so many other problems, you can fix this, but you need to do more work yourself (see Listing 7.6).

Listing 7.6   This version calls all delegates, even if an exception is thrown in the first delegate function.

```
public void Run ()
{
  // Read input.
  // If there is any listeners, publish:
  string s;
  do {
    s = Console.ReadLine ();
    if (s.Length == 0)
      break;
    if (theFunc != null)
    {
      System.Delegate [] funcs = theFunc.GetInvocationList();
```

```
        foreach (OnGetLine f in funcs)
      {
        try
        {
          f (s);
        }
        catch (Exception e)
        {
          Console.WriteLine ("Caught Exception: {0}", e.Message);
        }
      }
    }
  } while (true);
}
```

The highlighted portions of Listing 7.6 show the most important changes. Simply put, these changes mean that you call each individual delegate yourself, rather than invoking the main delegate and letting it call all the methods in its invocation list in turn. The **GetInvocationList( )** method returns an array of delegates that contains every delegate object that has been added to the list. You use the **foreach** loop to cycle through each delegate in the list and invoke it.

The **foreach** loop syntax does two important jobs. First, it is a simpler syntax for a loop using an array. Second, it performs the cast operations to return the correct object type. If, somehow, the wrong type of delegate got in the array, the cast operation fails, and the statements in the **foreach** loop are not executed.

The inside of the **foreach** loop contains a **try-catch** block to handle exceptions. The **try** block executes the invoke method on the delegate. If it throws an exception, a message gets logged to the console. Then, the loop continues with the next delegate.

The key point here is that you can invoke the members of a delegate individually to get better control. You can use the same trick to receive the return code from all the delegates, rather than getting just the return code from the last delegate invoked.

Related solution:	Found on page:
Catching Exceptions	232

Handling Events

You will start using events as soon as you start writing Windows programs. Visual Studio .NET provides wizards to wire up event handlers for you. To add an event handler to the form, follow these steps:

1. Open the form class in design mode.

2. Click on the lightning bolt icon in the Properties window (see Figure 7.2).

3. Find the event you want. Events are grouped by category. You can click the + sign to expand groups of related events.

4. Type the name of the function you want to use in the box to the right of the event name.

5. Press Enter. Now, you can edit the event handler function when you open the form class in code view mode. You can also double-click on the event definition to edit the event handler function.

You can also add common event handlers by clicking in the Form window in design mode. Doing this adds the default event handler for the class. In the case of a form, it adds an **OnLoad** event handler. For buttons, it adds an **OnClick** handler. Other controls add other events.

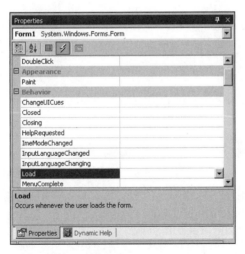

Figure 7.2   This window lets you examine and edit the events your form can receive.

7. Delegates and Events

Publishing Events

You will be creating events far less often than you will be using pre-defined event handlers. Here are the steps to follow to create and publish your own events.

Defining Custom Event Types

First, you need to create your own class type to hold the event arguments. Your class type must be derived from **System.EventArgs**.

This class defines a simple event argument type for a counter:

```
public class CounterEventArgs : EventArgs
{
  private readonly int counterVal;

  public CounterEventArgs (int val)
  {
    counterVal = val;
  }

  public int Counter
  {
    get
    {
      return counterVal;
    }
  }
}
```

Next, you need to define a delegate type to receive events of your new type:

```
public delegate void CounterEventHandler (object sender,
  CounterEventArgs args);
```

Remember that all event handlers take the same two parameter types: an object that represents the sender of the event and the event arguments type you defined in the preceding code.

Registering Events

Next, you need to add a member variable and a property to let users register event handlers. You declare the event just like the delegate, except that you add the **event** keyword:

```
private event CounterEventHandler myCounterEvent;
```

Next, you need to write a property to add and remove event handlers from the event:

```
public event CounterEventHandler OnCounterEvent
{
  add
  {
    myCounterEvent += value;
  }
  remove
  {
    myCounterEvent -= value;
  }
}
```

Writing events as properties supports different accessor syntax: instead of the **get/set** idiom, events use an **add/remove** idiom.

Publishing Events

The last step is to add the code to publish the event. This is the same as calling any other delegate:

```
if (myCounterEvent != null)
{
  CounterEventArgs args = new CounterEventArgs (counter);
  myCounterEvent (this, args);
}
```

When you receive notification that you should publish the event, simply check the event property against null and invoke the event handler.

If you need to be concerned about exception safety, you can walk the event handler list using the exact same idiom I showed you in Listing 7.6 to work with any other delegate.

Chapter 8

Namespaces

In Brief

This chapter is about *namespaces*. You use namespaces to partition code based on who supplied it and what it does. The purpose behind namespaces is to avoid naming collisions. If two (or more) vendors create components with the same name and the same function name, you need a way to specify which component and function you mean. The syntax for namespaces is simple—just two keywords control the creation and use of namespaces. There are, however, a few subtleties involved with namespaces that you need to be aware of when you use them. You can perform some interesting naming tricks when you start using namespaces and methods. This chapter shows you how and when to use the syntax supporting namespaces effectively.

Declaring Namespaces

Visual Studio .NET will always place your code inside a namespace. This is a good habit. Strictly speaking, you only need to use namespaces when you are delivering a component that will be used in other applications. You do not need to place code in namespaces when the code is part of the application.

Simple Namespaces

You declare a namespace with the **namespace** keyword:

```
namespace CSharpLittleBlackBook {
  // Code block here.
} // End of namespace
```

All the code inside the braces is part of the **CSharpLittleBlackBook** namespace. Pretty simple, huh?

Nested Namespaces

You see nested namespaces all throughout the .NET Base Class libraries: **System.Windows.Forms**, **System.IO**, **System.Drawing. Imaging**. You can declare a nested namespace in either of two ways. The first way: If your source file contains some elements inside the nested namespace along with some elements that belong in the outer namespace, you can declare the nested namespace inside the outer namespace:

```
namespace CSharpLittleBlackBook {
  class outerNamespaceClass {
    // code here...
  }

  namespace Chapter8 {
    class C8class {
      // code here...
    }
  } // End of namespace CSharpLittleBlackBook.Chapter8
} // End of namespace CSharpLittleBlackBook
```

The second way: If all the code inside a source file is part of the nested namespace, you can declare the nested namespace in one statement:

```
namespace CSharpLittleBlackBook.Chapter8 {
  class C8class {
    // code here...
  }
} // End of namespace CSharpLittleBlackBook.Chapter8
```

Both forms are equivalent. Which method you choose depends on the source in a given file.

Repeated Namespace Declarations

Namespaces are organized around functional areas of code. Namespaces may very well encompass several source files. Namespaces can even encompass multiple assemblies. You can repeat the same namespace, or the same nested namespaces, in as many source files as you need, even in different assemblies.

This freedom has one simple ramification: No access privileges are associated with namespaces. Because you can't prevent any new code from being added to an existing namespace, there would be no security if access privileges were associated with a namespace.

Namespace Guidelines

Every component and tool developer creates components in namespaces. Microsoft has recommended a hierarchy for namespace names to help avoid collisions. The outermost namespace should be the company name. The second outermost namespace should be the technology name. Inner namespaces beyond that are up to you.

This hierarchy results in code for this book having the namespaces:

```
Coriolis.CSharpLittleBlackBook.ChapterX
```

Where *X* is the chapter number. The C# compiler, however, cannot enforce these guidelines for you. If you remember to follow them, you will avoid naming collisions with other vendors.

Using Namespaces

Using a namespace is just as simple. At the top of your source file, simply add a **using** statement:

```
using System;
```

This declaration *promotes* all the types in the **System** namespace into the global namespace. Now, instead of typing **System.Console**, you can simply type **Console**.

The **using** declaration promotes only types, not namespaces. Even though the preceding declaration promotes the **System** namespace, it does not make it any simpler to use any of the namespaces inside **System**. For example, you still need to use the following:

```
System.Windows.Forms.MessageBox.Show ("Your Message Here");
```

You can't use this:

```
Windows.Forms.MessageBox.Show ("Your Message Here");
```

because it won't compile.

Now, I'll go into a bit more detail about promoting namespaces. Promoting a namespace simply means that the compiler resolves names by adding all types in the requested namespace to the list of searched types. Consider this example again:

```
using System;
// later:
Console.WriteLine ("Output goes here");
```

When the compiler sees the class name **Console**, it looks for a class called **Console** in the global namespace. There is no global class named **Console**, so this fails. Next, the compiler searches any namespace that has been promoted into the global namespace—in this case, the **System** namespace. The compiler finds a **System.Console** class, so it assumes that is what you mean.

Using Nested Namespaces

To simplify nested namespaces, you must explicitly use the nested namespace:

```
using System.Windows.Forms;
```

This promotes all the types in the **System.Windows.Forms** namespace into the global namespace. It does not have any effect on types in the **System** or **System.Windows** namespaces.

Immediate Solutions

The syntax for using or declaring namespaces is really simple. In practice, however, some of the subtleties can grab the unsuspecting programmer. The rest of the chapter is devoted to working with those subtleties.

Using a Namespace

To use a namespace, you need only specify the namespace in your source file with the **using** statement:

```
using System.Windows.Forms;
```

The **using** statement must appear in a source file before any other definitions. It may appear inside a namespace declaration, but it cannot follow any other code.

Matching Namespaces with Assemblies

To promote a namespace in your source file, you simply add a **using** directive in your source code:

```
using System.Windows.Forms;
```

That promotes the types from the **System.Windows.Forms** namespace into the global namespace. But your code still may not compile correctly.

If you have added a less common namespace, you need to reference the assembly containing that namespace when you build the project, which you can accomplish using Visual Studio .NET by following these steps:

1. Right-click the References folder in the Solution Explorer window.

2. Select Add Reference.

The dialog box shown in Figure 8.1 appears. The .NET tab lists all the shared assemblies delivered as part of Visual Studio .NET. Your list may be different than what is shown here depending on the installation options you have chosen. The COM tab lists any COM objects that can be used by .NET components. The Projects tab lists any assemblies created by other projects in the same solution.

3. Select the assembly you need and click Select. This adds the new assembly to your project.

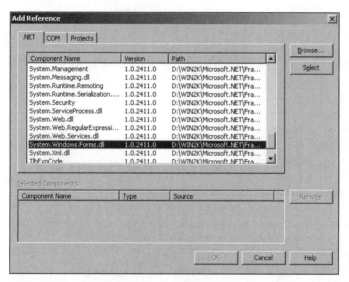

Figure 8.1   The Add Reference dialog box is where you tell the C# compiler where to find the classes you are including in your project.

Promoting Nested Namespaces

If you are using a large number of nested namespaces, you may find that you do not remember which class came from which namespace. You want to import namespaces so that you do not need to scope every variable, enumerated type, and function call. Yet, you want to organize these included types so that you can easily remember where they came from.

You can easily accomplish this by promoting a nested namespace and by giving it a new name. For example, consider the **System. Windows.Forms** namespace:

```
using Forms = System.Windows.Forms;
```

Now, you can reference the **System.Windows.Forms** namespace using the short name **Forms**:

```
Forms.MessageBox.Show ("This is a message");
```

I would recommend using this technique only on large projects where the number of namespaces you are including gets unmanageable.

Now, we come to one of those features I feel that I need to demonstrate for completeness, but I fear it is too easily misused to be practical. Actually, it is a variation on the previous example. There is no reason why the name you give a promoted namespace should have any relation to its original name. You can do the following:

```
using Charlie = System.Windows.Forms;
```

There is only one reason to do something like this. Suppose you have two different **Forms** namespaces in your application. You need a way to distinguish them:

```
using WindowsForms = System.Windows.Forms;
using MyForms = Coriolis.CSharpLittleBlackBook.Forms;
// Use the standard forms package:
WindowsForms.MessageBox.Show ("My Message");
// use my forms:
MyForms.MessageBox.Display ("Another message");
```

Remember this little feature when you are trying to integrate two different packages that have similar components in the namespaces. Without some kind of alias, you get an "ambiguous reference" compiler error.

Creating an Alias for a Class

You can use the same syntax to create an alias for a single class in a namespace. Following the same example, suppose you only needed to use the **MessageBox** class from the **System.Windows.Forms** namespace. You could promote just that class into the global namespace:

```
using MessageBox = System.Windows.Forms.MessageBox;
```

However, if you are thinking that you want to preserve some of the namespace, you might try this:

```
// Try to import just one class.
// This does not work.
using Forms.MessageBox = System.Windows.Forms.MessageBox;
```

Well, it doesn't work. You can only place a single name on the left side of this form of a **using** statement.

Organizing Functionality Using Namespaces

You are going to place your code in namespaces to keep the global namespace from getting cluttered and to help your users avoid the kinds of renaming problems I mentioned earlier. Your main goal is simply to pick namespaces that are organized around your company name and technology libraries. Follow these guidelines:

- The top level namespace should always be the company name.
- The second level namespace should be the technology name.
- The third level namespace should be the feature set, or library.

This gives you a lot of leeway. Remember that you can place code as well as other namespaces in the outer namespaces. You can place any code that is shared by all your company's technologies in the top level namespace. As an example, consider the mythical graphics library in the following section. This library is missing quite a few components, but you get the idea.

Creating a Top Level Namespace

The top level namespace is called **MyCo**, which contains the types that would be used in many of the lower level namespaces:

- **Point2D** models a point in 2D space.
- **Point3D** models a point in 3D space.
- **Velocity** models velocity.
- **Acceleration** models acceleration.

All of these classes will be used in many of the other subordinate namespaces.

Building Second and Third Level Namespaces

This graphics library would contain two different second level namespaces: a **Math** library and a **Modeling** library.

The **MyCo.Math** namespace would contain the following:

- **Matrix3×3** models a 3×3 matrix.
- **Matrix4×4** models a 4×4 matrix.

The **MyCo.Math** namespace would also contain a third level namespace: **MyCo.Math.Geometry**. The **MyCo.Math.Geometry** namespace would contain the classes and static functions necessary to support all the geometric transformations required for the graphics library.

The **Modeling** namespace would consist entirely of third level namespaces:

- **MyCo.Modeling.Lighting**—Has all the classes necessary to provide lighting models in the 3D graphics library
- **MyCo.Modeling.Images**—Has all the classes necessary to provide image support in a graphics library
- **MyCo.Modeling.Models**—Has all the classes needed to support building 3D objects and 3D worlds

The organization of namespaces and organization of assemblies need not, and in fact probably should not, match. Namespaces are used to organize your code around the perception of its use. You should try to get namespaces that can be viewed as a package of code that is meant to deliver a single feature. Organize your assemblies around how you deliver code as components. One component could very easily have elements that span multiple namespaces. Also, parts of the same namespace can be delivered in different components.

Related solution:	Found on page:
Loading and Assembly	384

Chapter 9

Class Design and Inheritance

In Brief

The chapters preceding this one have concentrated on creating classes and structs in isolation. Now let's look at how to design classes so that they work well with other classes. You want to view each class as a separate entity with one major responsibility. Doing so will help you create designs that are more stable in the face of multiple new feature requests. The rest of this section explains the techniques you can use to limit the scope of future changes in your software.

Maximize Cohesion

Cohesion refers to the singular nature of a class's responsibilities. You want to strive for classes that have one singular responsibility: achieving maximum cohesion. One test I use when I design classes is to see if I can describe a class's function in one sentence. Try this with some of the classes in the .NET Base Class Library (BCL) and you can see how it works: "A string stores a series of characters." "A form is a window that supports controls and drawing." Classes with poor cohesion are much more difficult to adequately describe in a single sentence. You will find that any single sentence leaves you missing functionality you need to describe to fully explain the class.

Minimize Coupling

Coupling describes how closely different classes must work together. You should strive to minimize coupling. Classes are coupled when you need to use both of them in order to use either of them. You will want to minimize coupling because tightly coupled classes create designs that are much harder to extend and modify. You will find that if you want to modify just one class, you end up needing to modify many different classes.

You won't find many examples of poorly coupled classes in the .NET BCL, but you will find some examples of tightly coupled classes. Inheritance creates a very tightly coupled relationship between the base class and its derived classes. So, unnecessary inheritance will create designs that are very hard to extend or change over time.

Information Hiding

Information hiding means limiting the scope of information to the code that needs it. Rather simply, you want to provide the minimum amount of access to code in order to achieve the functionality you want.

You have seen examples of information hiding already. Marking all member variables as private is one form of information hiding. Creating private methods is another. C# also has two different techniques for hiding classes and structs, as described in the following sections.

Nested Classes

Sometimes you may need to create a class that is only useful to one other class. When that happens, you can create a nested class by declaring the class inside another class. Nested classes provide a way to limit access based on the relationship with the outer class. You can declare nested classes using any of the access modifiers. This means that you can independently determine whether or not to nest a class and how accessible the class is.

Internal Classes

You can create classes inside a package and limit its access to only those classes that are in the same assembly. Any class, or struct, can be declared with internal access. Doing so limits access to classes declared in the same assembly.

Polymorphism and Inheritance

Finally, we come to one of the major topics of object-oriented programming: polymorphism. *Polymorphism* means "many forms." It means that you can treat an object as any of its base classes. Once again, you have seen examples of this already. All of the classes and structures that you have seen in this book have been derived from **System.Object**. As such, any of those objects can be treated as a **System.Object**.

Polymorphism is supported through inheritance and also through interfaces. You will be using these features in two different ways. First, you will be creating classes that are derived from other classes in the .NET BCL. Second, you will be creating classes that you intend to be base classes. You will also be creating and implementing interfaces, but that is the subject of the next chapter.

When you create classes, you will know if they are intended to be used as base classes or not, and you will know which behavior you expect derived classes to modify or extend. The C# language provides a rich syntax for you to specify exactly what you mean.

Virtual Methods

A *virtual method* is a method that can be overridden in a derived class. When you create a base class, you will want to mark each method that derived classes might re-implement with the **virtual** keyword.

The *abstract virtual method*, or pure virtual method, is a special case of virtual method. If there is no default implementation of a virtual method, you can mark the method as *abstract*. When you mark a method as abstract, you cannot provide an implementation for the method, and all derived classes must provide an implementation of those abstract methods, unless you intend for them to be abstract classes.

Override Methods

C# adds a new **override** keyword to explicitly note that you are overriding a virtual function in a base class. If you do not add the **override** keyword when you override a virtual base class method, your code will generate warnings. The compiler will not treat your overridden method as an override; instead, it will treat it as a new method, which hides the base class method. Those are two very different things, so pay attention to those warnings.

Override methods are still considered virtual methods. Further derived classes can declare a new overridden version of a method that has been overridden in its base class.

Abstract Classes

You will create abstract classes when you want to create a class that can be used only as a base class. Abstract classes can contain abstract methods.

Any class that contains abstract virtual methods must be marked as an abstract class. In fact, you will generally create abstract classes when you realize that there is no logical implementation for a virtual method in the base class.

Sealed Classes

A *sealed* class is the opposite of an abstract class: A sealed class cannot be used as a base class. No other class is allowed to derive from a sealed class. You will create sealed classes when you create a class that has no functionality you would expect another class to modify or extend.

Sealed classes can generate slightly faster code because the compiler knows that a sealed class has no virtual functions. Internally, the compiler generates code that calls virtual or overridden methods using a function pointer, a process known as *late binding*. A few extra machine instructions are needed to make a virtual function call, as opposed to a nonvirtual function call. The compiler can make use of the knowledge that no other class overrides any overridden methods defined in a sealed class to generate slightly faster code.

Protected Methods

Creating base classes adds one more nuance to your class design. Sometimes, you need to provide a method or a property to your derived classes only, not to just any user of your class. You can declare any class element as protected, which grants access to any derived class.

You should think very carefully about protected elements. Any programmer can derive a class from your class. Protected interfaces can turn into a maintenance nightmare as more and more classes are developed that derive from your base class. You should strive to create the minimum methods and properties necessary to support your derived classes when you create protected methods and properties in your base class.

Summing Up

You will spend much of your design time working out the relationships between the class you are designing and the classes with which it will interact. Your new class will interact with other classes in many ways: inheritance relationships, containment, internal assembly classes. You will want to examine these relationships carefully. The more independent your class is, the more likely it can be reused.

Immediate Solutions

The "In Brief" section explained many of the concepts that you will use to get your class to work well with other classes. This section shows you how to code those different elements in C#. Using the syntax optimally will help you express your design intent most clearly.

Deriving from a Base Class

You explicitly derive from a base class by declaring the base class in the declaration of your new class:

```
public class MyForm : System.Windows.Forms.Form
```

You simply place a colon followed by the name of the base class after your new class's name.

NOTE (C++ Users): All inheritance in C# is public inheritance; no private or protected inheritance exists. Also, only single inheritance is supported in C#. Objects may implement multiple interfaces, but they cannot derive from multiple base classes.

MyForm now can be treated as a **Form**. This means that any public method or property that is part of the **Form** class definition is now part of the **MyForm** class definition. This is most powerful for objects that use the **MyForm** class. In the same sense, any method that expects a **Form** as a parameter can take a **MyForm** object as a parameter. The **MyForm** object is not converted into a **Form** object when you treat it like a **Form**; it simply lets the **Form** portion of itself handle that **Form** behavior. This is one example of polymorphism.

Declaring Override Methods

You override an existing virtual method using the override keyword. For example, through a long inheritance list, **System.Windows.Form** eventually inherits from System.Object. The entire hierarchy goes like this: Form → ContainerControl → ScrollableControl → Control → Component → MarshallByRefObject → Object. Most classes override **ToString()** to provide a better description of the object. You declare the override method like this:

```
public override string ToString (){
  return "This is my Form.";
}
```

The **override** keyword tells the compiler that you intend for this method to be called anytime code calls the **ToString( )** method declared in the object class. Namely, you are re-implementing the same method to provide specific behavior in your type.

If you omit the **override** keyword, the C# compiler warns you about it:

```
c:\cslbb\chapter9\inheritance\form1.cs(32,17): warning CS0114:
  'Inheritance.Form1.ToString()' hides inherited member
  'System.Windows.Forms.Form.ToString()'. To make the current
  member override that implementation, add the override keyword.
  Otherwise add the new keyword.
```

This syntax is one of the great new features in C#. You must declare your intention whenever you declare a method that collides with a method declared in some base class. Look at the earlier list of base classes. It is amazingly easy to accidentally declare a method with the same signature as one of the methods declared in seven different base classes. Because the compiler warns you about it and lets you declare your intention, you can write code that is more likely to be correct. If you really are overriding a method, you must say so.

Declaring New Methods

The warning message in the preceding section mentions the **new** keyword for hiding a method. Let's suppose I wanted to hide the **ToString( )** method in the **MyForm** class. I would do that this way:

```
public new string ToString (){
  return "This is my Form.";
}
```

Now, the **ToString( )** method declared in **MyForm** has no relation to the **ToString( )** method declared in **System.Object**. In fact, it is a new method entirely. Hiding a method does not affect locations where the base class version should be used. For example, the following code calls the version of **ToString( )** declared in **MyForm**:

```
MyForm m = new MyForm ();
m.ToString ();
```

However, the following code will call the version of **ToString( )** visible in **System.Windows.Form**:

```
MyForm m = new MyForm ();
PrintObject (m);

public void PrintObject (object f)
{
  Console.WriteLine (f.ToString ());
}
```

You hid the version of **ToString( )** when the compile-time type of the object is a **MyForm**, but when the compiler thinks the object is one of the base classes, the original version becomes visible.

The exact same hiding behavior happens if you try to override a function in your base class that is not marked as virtual. All you can do is hide it with your own version.

The **new** keyword and the name hiding features are part of the language to address a specific scenario, and you should avoid using them indiscriminately. In most cases, when you get any warning about hiding the name of a base class method, property, or data item, you should change the name. You then avoid the earlier case where two identical lines of code call two different functions. The practical application of hiding involves versioning. Suppose that you have created a class. Months pass. Then, you update your class and recompile with a new version of the BCL. Suddenly you get warnings about redefining methods in your base classes that you never got before. Guess what? Version 2 of the BCL added a method with a name you were already using. You have two choices: Change the name of your method and all the calls to your old method so that no conflict exists, or add the new keyword. If the method generating the warning is called several hundred times in multiple assemblies, it is an easy choice. Hiding the base class method makes prudent sense here. You know that none of your code uses the method in the base class because it did not exist before. Any code in version 2 of the BCL should use the BCL method. In this case, having similar lines of code call two unrelated methods is the right behavior.

The moral is to use name hiding, and use the **new** modifier only when necessary because there's been an update to some base class outside your control.

Creating Base Classes

Creating a class designed to be a base class requires some different disciplines than just creating any old class. First of all, you need to consider what, if any, protected methods and properties are needed. Second, you need to think about which methods and properties of your new base class are candidates for modification in derived classes. More succinctly, you need to think about what parts of this class are polymorphic.

Creating Protected Interfaces

The **protected** interface represents those methods that your class exposes to any derived class. Declaring a method as protected is simple: All you do is mark the method, property, or data item as protected:

```
class myBase {
  protected void DoSomething () {
    // Do stuff...
  }
}
```

Just like any other method, property, or data element, you declare the method with a specific access modifier. You can declare anything inside a class protected: instance methods, static methods, instance or static properties, indexers, instance or static data, even nested classes and enumerations. If you can put it inside a class, you can declare it as protected.

A variant of protected members is protected internal members. Any members of derived classes and any code in the same assembly can access protected internal members.

Creating the protected portion of the class is simple syntax, but you need to spend time determining what should be part of the protected portions of your class. Looking at the **System.Windows.Forms.Form** class sheds some light on guidelines for creating the protected portion of the class. I am not going to cover every protected member and property because there are quite a few. Some of the properties are **DefaultSize**, which indicates the default size of the form; and **ResizeRedraw**, which indicates whether this form needs to redraw itself when it is resized. You can see where derived forms would need to modify these properties to create correct behavior in their

9. Class Design and Inheritance

implementations. However, these are not general-purpose properties that any code should be allowed to change. In fact, allowing any code to modify the **ResizeRedraw** property could introduce bugs in an application.

The protected methods are similar in nature. Good examples are **WndProc()** and **DefWndProc()**, which are used to process messages, and **CreateHandle()**, which creates the underlying window object for the form. Once again, these methods can be too easily misused if called by just any code. In fact, if methods like these were necessary to use a form, the interface would be unnecessarily complicated; it would indicate that the interface was too low level. On the other hand, classes that are creating a new form might very well need to modify the Windows message loop to provide the correct high-level behavior to client code. These make good candidates for protected methods.

The rule of thumb should be that protected members should be limited to those members that a derived class might need to access in order to override virtual methods or create new behavior. This limits the scope of the protected interfaces to those methods necessary for derived classes to modify the behavior of the base class.

Declaring Virtual Methods

You declare virtual methods to indicate those methods that you expect derived classes to modify. When you declare a virtual method, you add the **virtual** keyword to the function declaration.

Imagine a set of controls that model indicators. You might create temperature gauges, dials, bar lights, or warning lights. One way to use the indicators interchangeably would be to derive them all from a common base class: **Indicator**. One obvious virtual method would be a method to draw the indicator. You would write it using the **virtual** keyword:

```
class Indicator : System.Windows.Forms.UserControl
{
  public virtual void Draw ()
  {
    Font drawFont = new Font("Arial", 16);
    SolidBrush drawBrush = new SolidBrush(Color.Black);
    using (Graphics gc = CreateGraphics ())
    {
      gc.DrawString ("Base Indicator Control", drawFont,
        drawBrush, 0,0);
```

```
      }
    }
  }
```

The **Draw()** method is marked virtual, indicating that any derived class can supply a new version of the **Draw** method that displays a better representation of the indicator.

Declaring Virtual Properties

Remember that properties are actually methods, even though they appear to be public fields to users of your class. Because properties are methods, you can mark them as virtual as well. Consider the **Indicator** class again. You would want a property to represent the current value of the indicator. You can certainly imagine that a derived class might want to modify the implementation of this property. So, you should make it virtual:

```
class Indicator : System.Windows.Forms.UserControl
{
  private double TheValue;

  public virtual double Value
  {
    get {
      return TheValue;
    }
    set {
      TheValue = value;
    }
  }
}
```

Any derived class can override this property by creating their own. Suppose a **Dial** class can only handle values between 0 and 1,000:

```
public class Dial : Indicator
{
  public override double Value
  {
    set {
      double val = Math.Min (value, 1000);
      val = Math.Max (val, 0);
      base.Value = val;
    }
  }
}
```

Notice a few points with virtual properties. First of all, if you override a virtual property, you cannot add accessors not defined in the base class. Here, I have overridden only the **set** portion of the **Value** property. Value is still a read/write property; the read portion is still implemented in the base class.

Next, notice how the base class **set** accessor is called in the derived class **set** accessor. The code **base.Value = val** invokes the base class **set** method and stores the value.

Virtual properties are a very powerful construct. You can create data elements in the interface that are implemented differently in each particular derived class.

Creating Abstract Classes

Carefully look at the **Indicator** class in the previous section. Do you think that you would ever create an instance of an **Indicator**, or do you think you would always create objects that are specific derivations of an **Indicator** (such as **Dials**, **TemperatureGauges**, and so on)? Almost certainly, you would never create an **Indicator**, rather only derived classes. C#, like most object-oriented languages, lets you specify that a class is meant to be used strictly as a base class, never as an object that gets instantiated. To declare an abstract class in C#, you specify the **abstract** keyword on the class definition:

```
public abstract class Indicator: System.Windows.Forms.UserControl
{
  // snip.
}
```

WARNING (Java Users)! C# abstract classes do not need to have any abstract methods. Although that is fairly typical, it is not mandated by the syntax.

After making this one simple change, the following code won't compile:

```
Indicator ind = new Indicator ();
```

You get the following error from the C# compiler:

```
c:\cslbb\chapter9\indicators\indicatorstest.cs(22,18):
   error CS0144: Cannot create an instance of the abstract class
   or interface 'Indicators.Indicator'
```

This is good. It prevents any users from creating an instance of an object that is an abstraction of common elements across many specific types. Abstract base classes are marked in the MSIL with an **abstract** keyword.

Declaring Abstract Methods

As I said previously, abstract classes very commonly contain abstract methods. Look again at the implementation of the **Draw()** method in the **Indicator** class in the "Declaring Virtual Methods" section. It is a very unsatisfying implementation. You would expect every derived class to provide a better version of this method. In fact, this method does not even display the value in the particular indicator it models. Clearly, it just isn't that useful. So, you should make the **Draw** method an abstract method. That forces derived classes to create their own implementation of **Draw()**, and you do not need to write an implementation that does not satisfy anyone's expectations anyway. Declaring a method abstract is simple. Just replace the **virtual** keyword with the **abstract** keyword and remove the entire implementation:

```
public abstract void Draw ();
```

Now, all classes that are derived from **Indicator** and not marked as abstract must override the **Draw()** method. Understand that you can create a new abstract class, derived from **Indicator**, that does not implement **Draw()**. As long as the new class is abstract, that's fine. When you want to create nonabstract classes, you must add the **Draw()** method.

Creating Sealed Classes

Sealed classes can be thought of as the opposite of abstract classes: Sealed classes cannot be used as base classes. The string class in the .NET BCL is sealed. All you need to do to create a sealed class is add the **sealed** keyword to the declaration of the class:

```
public sealed class Dial : Indicator
{
  // code...
}
```

Think long and hard about sealed classes. Are you absolutely sure no one would ever want to create a new variant of your class with some new implementation of virtual functions? The preceding example is very likely a bad example. I'm sure you can imagine more than one form of **Dial** that you might want to display. Making a sealed **Dial** prevents you from inheriting any of the existing implementation from **Dial**.

If you look at the string class in the .NET BCL, however, you can't come up with behaviors that you would want to extend with a derived class. The string class designers did not anticipate deriving from that class. They did not declare any virtual methods, so they did not anticipate anyone deriving from the string class. When you cannot come up with any functions that you anticipate being virtual, you should consider making a sealed class.

Understanding Inheritance

Creating a derived class means that you inherit both the public interface and the implementation of the base class. This creates a very strong coupling between derived classes and the base class: Any change in the base class is automatically reflected in all the derived classes. On the other hand, it maximizes reuse: Your derived class has all the features of the base class with a minimum of work on your part.

You should look at inheritance as the most heavy-duty tool in your object-oriented toolbox. You can accomplish quite a bit of work in very little code using inheritance, but it makes designs very stringent. You can often accomplish many of the same goals using delegates or interfaces. Both of those language features let you treat objects polymorphically, with fewer restrictions on your class designs.

Related solutions:	Found on page:
Using Delegates	137
Defining Interfaces	199

One goal of an inheritance hierarchy is to limit the locations in the code where you need to know the specific kind of an object, but rather design the code so that you can always call virtual methods in the base class to achieve the goals you need. Figure 9.1 shows the

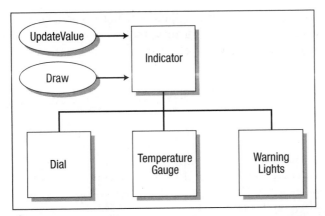

Figure 9.1 A simplified view of the interfaces in the **Indicator** class and its derived classes. The key to a good hierarchy is making sure that the methods you need are all found in the base class.

pertinent methods that drive an indicator. Notice that none of the methods needed to use an indicator are defined in a derived class. Once created, all interaction uses the base class methods. One indicator is easily interchanged with any other type. Ideally, the only time you use the derived class's methods is when you are creating and initializing the object.

Creating Nested Classes

When I opened this chapter, I said that cohesion was the property such that each class is assigned one single clear responsibility. Sometimes, this is not as easy as it sounds. When you are designing a system, you often create classes that have multiple responsibilities. Usually, these classes will be made up of other classes that you reuse in other areas. Sometimes though, you find that a class performs multiple responsibilities that are not shared by other classes. You still want to delegate each individual responsibility to some other class, though. The easiest way to do this is to create a nested class: The inner class handles one responsibility on behalf of the outer class. You create a nested class just like any other class; you simply declare it inside the outer class.

Let's examine the **Indicator** class again. If you look at it carefully, it really has two responsibilities: It stores a value between two endpoints, and it displays the current value using some visual display.

You can separate those two responsibilities using a nested class. The main responsibility is the visual display; that responsibility also exhibits the polymorphic behavior. So, it is easier to separate the responsibility of storing the value between two endpoints:

```
public abstract class Indicator: System.Windows.Forms.UserControl
{
  protected class IndicatorValue
  {
     readonly double Max = System.Double.MaxValue;
     readonly double Min = System.Double.MinValue;

     double TheValue = 0;

     IndicatorValue (double max, double min)
     {
       Max = max;
       Min = min;
     }

     public double Value
     {
       get {
         return TheValue;
       }      set {
         double val = Math.Max (value, Min);
         val = Math.Min (val, Max);
         TheValue = value;
       }
     }
  } // End of IndicatorValue class.
  // Rest of Indicator class...
}
```

Now, the value-storing responsibilities are separated in a nested class: **IndicatorValue**. This class is declared protected, so derived classes can use the **IndicatorValue** class definition. Using nested classes, you have successfully separated these two responsibilities into two different objects. Each is clearer, easier to understand, and easier to maintain. Users that create a new Indicator can use any of the methods in the **IndicatorValue** class to support the storage and retrieval of the values. The responsibilities of the storage and display of the values are separated.

Creating Internal Classes

Every class up to this point has been declared with public access. Public classes are the most common, but they are not the only classes you will create. Occasionally, you may need to create a class that will be used only as part of a given assembly. You can create a class with internal access. This limits the access to only other members of that assembly. Internal classes are usually helper classes that provide algorithms or services that are not needed outside of a given assembly. To declare an internal class, simply use the **internal** access keyword:

```
internal class Helper {
  // helper implementation.
}
```

Internal classes have quite a few limitations. All the limitations revolve around one simple rule: You can create any code that attempts to give greater access to an element, like a class. Some examples make this a bit clearer. You could not create a public property of **Helper** type that tries to give public access to **Helper**, which is defined as internal. Similarly, you could not use **Helper** as a base class to a public class. You could not even put **Helper** objects anywhere in the protected interface. So, internal classes are quite well hidden from the outside world.

Understanding Initialization Order

C# provides many ways to initialize the members of an object. When you combine those different methods with base classes and inheritance, remembering when different values are initialized can be difficult. Knowing when something gets initialized is important for two reasons. First, you cannot use a value that has not been initialized. Second, your programs will have poor performance if you are initializing values more than once.

So, here is a simple example that shows all the possibilities for member initialization. The example shows the order in which the members are initialized:

```
public class B
{
```

```
      private static int s1 - 0;
      private static int s2;
      private static int s3;

      private int m1 - 0;
      private int m2;

      static B ()           ← Static ctor!
      {
        s2 - 1;
      }

      public B ()  :
        this (1)
      {
      }

      public B ( int i)
      {
        m2 - i;
      }
  }

  public class D : B
  {
      private static int d1 - 0;
      private static int d2;
      private int dm1 - 0;     ←—
      private int dm2;

      static D ()
      {
        d2 - 1;
      }

      public D () :
        base ()
      {
        dm2 - 0;
      }

      public D(int i) :
        base (i)
      {
        dm2 - i;
      }
  }
```

This is easiest to understand if we break it down into parts and discuss how initialization is always generated by default and how you can modify it.

Static member variables are initialized first. The first time a class is loaded, the static variables are initialized. In class **B**, **s1** is initialized first, followed by **s2**, although not for the reasons you might think. The **s1** variable has an initializer as part of its declaration. It gets initialized first. The **s2** variable is initialized in an explicit **static** constructor. Static variables are initialized in the following order when the class is first loaded:

1. Any static variables declared with initializers. This step initializes **s1**.

2. Any static variables uninitialized (including the body of the static constructor) are initialized to default values. This step initializes **s3**.

3. Any static variables initialized in a static constructor. This step initializes **s2**.

Now look at the initialization of member variables when a **B** object is created. The **m1** variable is initialized first, because it has an initializer declared as part of the variable declaration. The **m2** variable is initialized second, in the **explicit** constructor. So, the rules for member initialization are pretty simple:

- Any member variables with explicit initializers are initialized. This applies to **m1** in the preceding example code.

- The body of the invoked constructor gets executed. This initializes **m2** in the preceding example code.

Inheritance hierarchies modify these rules only slightly. Let's look at what happens when class **D** is first loaded. When **D** is first loaded, it follows the rules outlined in this section for static variable initialization. This will initialize **d1** and **d2**. In this example code, the **static** constructor for **B** does not need to execute. The **static** initializations for **D** do not examine any static data in **B**, so there is no need for the runtime to load **B**. In many situations, the **static** initializers for a derived class will make use of some static data in the base class and will load the class. In those cases, the **static** initializers for **B** are invoked before they are needed.

Now, let's look at the order for the instance variables in **D** and **B** when an instance of **D** is created. The variables are initialized in this order:

- **dm1**
- **m1**
- **m2**
- **dm2**

This is noticeably different from the initialization order for C++. Here are the rules that cause this behavior:

- Any member variables with initializers specified in the variable declaration are initialized. This applies to **dm1**.

- The base class constructor is executed. I have placed an explicit call to the **base( )** constructor in the default constructor for **D**. The same code is generated whether or not that call is present. This step initializes **m1** and **m2** based on the rules outlined in this section. (Note that the **System.Object** constructor is invoked between the initialization of **m1** and **m2**.)

- The class constructor body is executed. This step initializes **dm2**.

You should try to initialize variables in their declarations if possible. If not, make sure that you initialize all variables in the body of the constructors. Whenever possible, avoid specifying initial values for member variables in both the field declaration and the constructor, which causes your fields to be initialized twice.

Interfaces

In Brief

The last chapter explained class inheritance so that you can effectively use inheritance hierarchies and polymorphism in your designs. C# limits object inheritance to single inheritance. However, any class or struct can implement multiple different interfaces.

An *interface* is simply a set of methods that are defined together to create a single cohesive function. The easiest way to explain interfaces is usually by describing the differences between interfaces and base classes. Imagine a base class that contains nothing but public abstract methods—that is more or less equivalent to an interface.

Implementing Interfaces

Interfaces are easiest to understand if you start with implementing an interface. One of the most common interfaces is the **ICloneable** interface. The **ISerializable** interface contains a method to write the object's state to a stream.

The **ISerializable** interface contains one method, **GetObjectData( )**, which writes the data to a **SerializationInfo** structure. You can implement this interface anytime you create a class that supports persistent storage. To declare that your class implements an interface, simply add it to the inheritance list on your class declaration.

```
class MyClass : MyBase, ICloneable {
  public object Clone()
  {
    MyClass copy = new MyClass (this);
    return copy;
  }
  // Other methods...
}
```

Using Interface Methods

There are two different idioms for using interfaces. In most cases, you can simply use the public methods, because interface methods are part of the class's public interface.

```
MyClass c = (MyClass)oldC.Clone ();
```

Also, you can cast any object to an interface type and use the interface methods. C# contains some syntax to make those idioms safe, whether or not the interface is supported. Suppose that you make a collection, and you want to support copying the entire container, including all the objects in the collections. You can write a copy function like this:

```
class Bag : ICloneable
{
  Bag (Bag other)
  {
    foreach (ICloneable obj in other.storage)
    {
      object newObj = obj.Clone ();
      storage.Add (newObj);
    }
  }
}
```

This code is not exception safe. If the container does not contain objects that support the **ICloneable** interface, explicit cast that is part of the **foreach** statement throws an **InvalidCastException**. To make the code exception safe, you would need to wrap the **foreach** loop in a **try** block.

Defining Interfaces

An interface definition looks similar to an abstract base class definition. The only difference is that an interface can contain only public abstract methods. Namely, interfaces cannot contain data, or concrete methods. Here is a simple interface definition:

```
interface ITest
{
  void TestMethod ();
  int TestClass();
}
```

By convention, all interface names begin with a capital *I*. This definition declares an interface named **ITest**, with two methods, **TestMethod( )** and **TestClass( )**.

Interfaces can contain items other than methods. An interface can contain methods, properties, indexers, and events. You must specify whether properties support **get** or **set** accessors when you declare a property in an interface, just like when you specify abstract properties in a class definition.

Defining Derived Interfaces

Interfaces can derive from other interfaces. You can create a new enhanced interface by deriving from the old interface:

```
interface ITest2 : ITest
{
  void TestMethod2 (object o);
}
```

Experienced COM programmers have seen this construct many times. The **ITest2** interface now declares every method in the **ITest** interface, plus the new **TestMethod2( )** function.

Related solution:	Found on page:
Understanding Inheritance	180

Implementing Multiple Interfaces

Creating a class that implements multiple interfaces is very common. You simply add the other interfaces to the list of supported interfaces:

```
class MyClass : ICloneable, IComparable, ISerializable {
  // Implementation...
}
```

Now, instances of **MyClass** can be used anywhere an object supporting **ICloneable**, an **IComparable**, or an **ISerializable** is expected.

When Interfaces Collide

The preceding example points to one possible problem when you implement multiple interfaces: Sometimes, the same method signature appears in more than one interface. C# provides a way to specify which method corresponds to which interface. Consider these two interface definitions:

```
interface IFoo {
  void DoStuff ();
}
```

```
interface IBar {
  void DoStuff ();
}
```

If you create a class that implements both the **IFoo** and the **IBar** interfaces, you introduce an ambiguity:

```
class MyClass : IFoo, IBar
{
  public void DoStuff () // IFoo.DoStuff, or IBar.DoStuff?
  {
  }
}
```

So, does the **DoStuff()** method declared in **MyClass** satisfy the requirements for **IFoo**, or **IBar**? The answer is pretty simple—both. Anytime you call the **DoStuff()** methods for **IFoo** or **IBar**, you get the same method.

That might not be the behavior you want. If **IFoo.DoStuff()** and **IBar.DoStuff()** accomplish different tasks, you may very well want different functions to implement their behavior. You specify which function goes with which interface by using explicit interface implementations. This code shows two different **DoStuff()** methods implementing the two different interfaces separately:

```
class MyClass : IFoo, IBar
{
  void IFoo.DoStuff ()
  {
  }
  void IBar.DoStuff ()
  {
  }
}
```

Now, you have two different methods for each interface's version of **DoStuff()**. But, your world isn't quite perfect yet. Look at the following code:

```
MyClass c = new MyClass ();
c.DoStuff (); // Call IFoo.DoStuff (), or IBar.DoStuff ()?
```

The compiler doesn't know which version of **DoStuff()** to call. You get an error message telling you that **MyClass** does not contain a public method called **DoStuff( )**. To fix this, you make one more version of **DoStuff( )**, this time without either interface qualifier:

```
class MyClass : IFoo, IBar
{
  void IFoo.DoStuff ()
  {
  }
  void IBar.DoStuff ()
  {
  }
  public void DoStuff ()
  {
    ((IFoo)this).DoStuff (); // More foo like than bar like.
  }
}
```

Now, invoking **DoStuff** on a **MyClass** object calls the **DoStuff( )** method without any qualifiers. The default version uses the **IFoo** implementation of **DoStuff( )**. If **MyClass** is cast to an **IFoo**, the **IFoo.DoStuff( )** method gets invoked; if **MyClass** is cast to an **IBar**, the **IBar.DoStuff( )** method gets called.

Hiding Interfaces

This section shows another interesting compiler trick with interfaces. You can use explicit interface declarations to hide interface implementations in a class. Suppose that you are implementing an interface to satisfy a library requirement. You may not want those methods to show up in your class's public interface. You can use the explicit interface implementation to hide interface methods in your public interface. Suppose that you needed to work with a library, and you needed to support the **IThirdPartyInterface**. However, the **IThirdPartyInterface** method **Do3rdPartyWork( )** was not part of your public interface design:

```
class MyClass : IThirdPartyInterface
{
  void IThirdPartyInterface.Do3rdPartyWork ()
  {
    // Do the work.
  }
}
```

Here, you are qualifying the interface method name not to avoid an ambiguity, but rather to keep the interface methods out of the public interface.

Choosing Interfaces or Inheritance

Interfaces provide a way to use polymorphism in your designs without creating the same tight coupling that is part of an inheritance hierarchy. When you inherit a class definition, you inherit the definition and the implementation of every function in the class. This can be quite constraining. Interfaces let you describe the capabilities of a class by grabbing small pieces of common functionality from many different interfaces.

Remember from the last chapter that single inheritance is the only object inheritance supported in .NET. Describing the capabilities of an object using interfaces gives you more freedom in selecting the best base class for a set of objects. A class or struct can implement any number of interfaces. However, a class or struct can have only one base class.

You should prefer interfaces to base classes in many cases. You should use base classes only when you will be using the base class as a generic type of object, and subclasses will be specific instances of the base class. Use interfaces when you want to describe common functionality that many different object types can use.

Immediate Solutions

This section focuses on common scenarios where you will program using interfaces. To do this, I create a simple class that represents complex numbers. Complex numbers are of the form $x + y * i$, where i is the square root of -1. They are used in many scientific applications.

A complex number class will contain a double representing the real part of the number and a double representing the imaginary part of the number. The complex class in Listing 10.1 shows only a portion of the possible mathematical operations for complex numbers, but it is sufficient for this example.

Listing 10.1   Complex number class without any interfaces.

```
public class Complex
{
   private double realPart = 0.0;
   private double imagPart = 0.0;

   public Complex ()
   {
   }

   public Complex (double r) :
     this (r, 0)
   {
   }

   public Complex (double r, double i)
   {
     realPart = r;
     imagPart = i;
   }

   public Complex (Complex l)
   {
     realPart = l.realPart;
     imagPart = l.imagPart;
   }

   public double Imaginary
   {
     get {
       return imagPart;
```

```
    }
    set {
      imagPart = value;
    }
  }

  public double Real
  {
    get {
      return realPart;
    }
    set {
      realPart = value;
    }
  }

  // A few mathematical functions:
  static public Complex operator + (Complex l, Complex r)
  {
    Complex result = new Complex (l);
    result.realPart += r.realPart;
    result.imagPart += r.imagPart;
    return result;
  }

  static public Complex operator * (Complex l, Complex r)
  {
    Complex result = new Complex ();
    result.Real = l.Real*r.Real-l.Imaginary*r.Imaginary;
    result.Imaginary = l.Real*r.Imaginary + l.Imaginary*r.Real;
    return result;
  }

  static public bool operator == (Complex l, Complex r)
  {
    return ((l.Real == r.Real) &&
      (l.Imaginary == r.Imaginary));
  }

  static public bool operator != (Complex l, Complex r)
  {
    return ! (l == r);
  }

  static public bool operator > (Complex l, Complex r)
  {
    double normL = l.imagPart * l.imagPart +
      l.realPart * l.realPart;
```

```
      double normR = r.imagPart * r.imagPart +
        r.realPart * r.realPart;
      return normL > normR;
    }

    static public bool operator < (Complex 1, Complex r)
    {
      return r > 1;
    }

    public override bool Equals (object o)
    {
      if (!(o is Complex))
        return false;
      Complex c = (Complex) o;
      return ((c.Real == Real) && (c.Imaginary == Imaginary));
    }

    public override int GetHashCode ()
    {
      return (int)(Real + Imaginary);
    }
  }
```

This example shows only a few of the possible mathematical operations that are part of complex numbers. The class supports addition and multiplication. You can also test complex values for equality, and use the greater-than (**>**) and less-than (**<**) operators for ordering functions.

The next section shows you how to make this class much easier to use with the .NET Framework by implementing some of the most common .NET BCL interfaces.

Using Typical Interfaces

You will use two interfaces with many of your objects: **ICloneable** and **IComparable**.

Implementing **ICloneable**

The complex class in the previous code example has a copy constructor:

```
public Complex (Complex 1)
{
```

```
    realPart = 1.realPart;
    imagPart = 1.imagPart;
}
```

When you create a class or struct that has a copy constructor, you should implement the **ICloneable** interface. Implementing the **ICloneable** interface lets any code make a copy of a complex number object, without knowing its type:

```
public class Complex : ICloneable
{
  public Complex (Complex 1)
  {
    realPart = 1.realPart;
    imagPart = 1.imagPart;
  }

  public object Clone ()
  {
    return new Complex (this);
  }
  // other details omitted.
}
```

Now, using the **ICloneable** interface, you have expressed the same concept as the copy constructor using a standard .NET interface.

Implementing **IComparable**

The complex class contains operators for testing equality and greater-than and less-than. These three operators together constitute the **IComparable** interface. The **IComparable** interface contains one method, **CompareTo**, that compares two similar objects:

```
public class Complex : ICloneable, IComparable
{
  public int CompareTo (object o)
  {
    if (!(o is Complex))
      throw new ArgumentException
        ("Object is not a complex number");
    Complex c = (Complex)o;
    double norm = imagPart * imagPart + realPart * realPart;
    double norm0 = c.imagPart * c.imagPart +
      c.realPart * c.realPart;
    if (norm > norm0)
      return 1;
```

```
        else if (norm0 > norm)
          return -1;
        else
          return 0;
    }
    // Other details omitted.
}
```

Some classes will support more than one sort order. If you write a class that supports multiple sort orders, the **IComparer** interface lets users pick which sort order to use.

The new version of **Complex** does not do anything different than the original, but it can be incorporated more easily with the .NET BCL libraries. The lesson here is that by declaring the appropriate interfaces to your classes, you create a class that you can use in other different situations. As you are about to see, you can write routines that depend on interface declarations rather than class types. You can reuse these routines in more situations.

Programming with Interfaces˙

Programming with interfaces is a simple matter of casting an object to an interface and using that interface. These operations are often done in conjunction with the .NET collection classes. The collection classes store references to **System.Object**. You need to cast the objects in the collections to the kind of objects you expect. Using interfaces will let you write routines that work with more different objects.

This routine returns the largest value in a collection. It uses the **IComparable** interface to determine which value is the largest. It also uses the **IEnumerable** interface to iterate over the collection. In the same way that **IComparable** makes this routine useful with other different classes or structs, using **IEnumerable** means that this routine will work with any of the collection classes.

```
public static IComparable theMax (IComparable seed,
    IEnumerable coll)
{
    foreach (IComparable c in coll)
    {
        if (c.CompareTo(seed) > 0)
        {
```

```
      seed = c;
    }
  }
  return seed;
}

// Usage:
Complex [] cArray = new Complex[100];
// Fill the array with real values...
Complex max = new Complex(0,0);
max = (Complex) Complex.theMax (max, cArray);
```

The lesson here is to use interfaces as parameters whenever possible, instead of using object types that support the interfaces. By doing so, you will get code that is far more reusable.

Related solution:	Found on page:
Enumerating Collections	340

Defining Interfaces

Interfaces are declared with the **interface** keyword. You simply define the methods that your interface supports. Interface methods are implicitly public, so you do not add that keyword. Suppose you wanted to write methods to check the valid state of objects, a common object-oriented validation technique. The easiest way to integrate that into your designs is to declare a validation interface:

```
interface IValid {
  bool IsValid ();
}
```

This interface declares the **IValid** interface, with one method, **IsValid()**. Client code can call the **IsValid()** method to ensure that an object is in a valid state.

Defining Properties in Interfaces

Looking at the **IValid** interface definition in the preceding section, the **IsValid()** method feels more like it should be a property of an object, rather than a method. Interfaces do support properties, so let's change the interface to expose **IsValid** as a property:

199

```
interface IValid {
  bool IsValid {
    get;
  }
}
```

You can simply place any property in an interface definition. You must declare which accessors the property supports. Any class that implements the **IValid** interface must declare the matching property, with the same set of accessors.

Defining Indexers in Interfaces

You can declare indexers in an interface, just like you can declare properties. However, that is not often recommended. Remember that you should design interfaces to be combined with other interfaces and a base class. You can declare only one indexer in your class that returns a given data type. Adding indexers to your class will limit the ability of class designers to use your interface without interfering with their class designs. Adding indexers to your interface designs will increase the likelihood of causing name collisions when classes implement your interface.

I recommend that you limit your use of indexers in interfaces to those times when an interface is meant to model array or matrix access:

```
interface IMatrix {
  double this [int row, int col] {
    get;
    set;
  }
}
```

The **IMatrix** interface declares an indexer to return the value at a given location in the matrix structure.

Hiding Interface Implementations

Implementing multiple interfaces will add more methods and properties to the public interface of your class. When you do not wish to expose the interface methods as part of the class interface, you can hide them using an explicit interface declaration.

Consider the **Complex** class again. You can intuitively use the over-loaded operators to compare **Complex** objects; you can also use the copy constructor to create a copy of an existing **Complex** object. The **Clone()** and **CompareTo()** methods are more cumbersome because they involve casts. You want to encourage clients of the **Complex** class to use the more efficient methods. Yet, you want to support the standard interfaces. You can accomplish this by hiding the implementation of these interfaces.

To hide any interface method, you make two changes to the function declaration. First, remove the public access modifier. Second, add the interface name as part of the function declaration:

```
object ICloneable.Clone () {
  return new Complex (this);
}
```

```
int IComparable.CompareTo (object o) {
  if (!(o is Complex))
    throw new ArgumentException
      ("Object is not a complex number");

  Complex c = (Complex)o;
  double norm = imagPart * imagPart + realPart * realPart;
  double norm0 = c.imagPart * c.imagPart +
    c.realPart * c.realPart;
  if (norm > norm0)
    return 1;
  else if (norm0 > norm)
    return -1;
  else
    return 0;
}
```

Now, the **Complex** class still supports the standard operations provided by the **ICloneable** and **IComparable** interfaces. In addition, users are encouraged to use the complex number member functions when working with complex numbers. The interface methods are used only when client code is written to specific interfaces rather than objects.

Declaring Events in Interfaces

You can create interfaces that fire events. The following code produces an alarm interface that fires an **AlarmEvent** to notify clients
of some condition:

```
public delegate void AlarmEvent(IAlarm sender);
public interface IAlarm {
   event AlarmEvent IssueAlarm;
}
```

Any class that implements the **IAlarm** interface can notify clients of
bad conditions through the **IssueAlarm** event.

Related solution:	Found on page:
Defining Custom Event Types	154

Understanding Interface Implementation Rules

Interfaces are meant to be single pieces of functionality. As such, you
can implement all or nothing in an interface. If you create an abstract
class that implements an interface, that class must declare all the
methods of the interface. You can declare any (or all) of the methods
abstract, but you must declare all the functions of the interface in the
class declaration.

Simply put, any class or struct that declares support for a particular
interface must explicitly declare each function in that interface. The
declaration may be concrete or abstract, but it must be there.

Designing Interfaces

Interfaces are meant to be used to create small, discrete elements of
functionality that can be implemented by any number of classes. You
should strive to create interfaces that are as small as possible. The

smaller an interface is, the more likely it can be reused by many different classes and structs. Interfaces should always represent one single piece of functionality.

You will also find a large number of interfaces throughout the .NET BCL. This chapter has shown you two of the most common. You should spend time becoming familiar with the interfaces defined in the .NET BCL so that you can provide your class's functionality in the most widely understood idioms. That means supporting the interfaces that make sense for your class.

Chapter 11

Programming with Attributes

In Brief

Attributes are the way in which C# performs declarative programming. *Attributes* are annotations placed on some element of code, be it an assembly, a class, a method, or a data member. These annotations are actually instances of a class and can inject code to modify the annotated item or to help explain it. In this chapter, you will learn some of the more common C# attributes and how to use them. You will also learn how to create your own attribute classes. Finally, you will see how to work query attributes at runtime.

Using Attributes

Many attributes are defined in the .NET BCL. You can use these attributes to provide conditional compilation and automate common programming tasks. I cover some of the most common attributes to show you how attributes are used to control common programming actions.

Conditional Attributes

The conditional attribute lets you create code that gets executed only when a particular preprocessor symbol has been defined.

You mark a method for conditional compilation using the **Conditional** attribute. The following example shows code that is marked for debug builds only:

```
[Conditional ("DEBUG")]
public void CheckValid ()
{
    System.Windows.Forms.MessageBox.Show ("Validating Object");
}
```

The **CheckValid( )** method gets marked for debug builds. If you examine the MSIL, you will find that the **CheckValid( )** method is compiled in all builds, whether or not the **DEBUG** symbol is defined. However, any calls to the **CheckValid( )** method are added to the objects only when the **DEBUG** symbol is defined. The attribute communicates with the compiler to determine whether a given call should be included in a particular build. For an example of MSIL code, see Listing 11.1.

Listing 11.1 MSIL code for a conditional method.

```
.method private hidebysig instance void CheckValid()
  cil managed
{
  .custom instance void
  [mscorlib]System.Diagnostics.ConditionalAttribute::.ctor
  (string) = ( 01 00 05 44 45 42 55 47 00 00 )
  // ...DEBUG..
  // Code size       12 (0xc)
  .maxstack  8
  IL_0000:  ldstr       "Doing the Validate Thing"
  IL_0005:  call        valuetype
[System.Windows.Forms]System.Windows.Forms.DialogResult
  [System.Windows.Forms]System.Windows.Forms.MessageBox::Show
  (string)
  IL_000a:  pop
  IL_000b:  ret
} // end of method Form1::CheckValid
```

The routine creates an instance of the **System.Diagnostics. ConditionalAttribute** class, using the string "**DEBUG**".

The compiler checks the string in the attribute and sees if that string is defined when compiling any code that calls the **CheckValid( )** method. If the **DEBUG** symbol is defined, the call to the code is included in the build. If not, the call is removed from the build.

This strategy is more efficient, and more likely to be correct than using the preprocessor to include or exclude code. The compiler can remove control logic along with a call to the removed method. For example, look at the following code:

```
c.DoStuff ();
if (value > 1000)
  c.CheckValid ();
c.DoMore Stuff ();
```

The C# compiler removes the **if** statement logic, as well as the call to **CheckValid( )** if the **DEBUG** symbol isn't defined.

Web Service Attributes

The .NET BCL contains a number of attributes that make creating Web services with C# much easier. When you create C# Web services, you will use three attributes that make the job easier. The first is the **WebMethod** attribute. Marking a method with the **WebMethod** attribute exposes it as a method that can be called across the Web. This attribute tells the ASP.NET components that this method is capable of receiving and processing XML SOAP messages.

The **XmlRoot** and **XmlAttribute** attributes play important roles in serializing data structures via Web services. You mark any class that you intend to return as part of a Web service message with the **XmlRoot** attribute. ASP.NET uses this attribute to generate a schema and corresponding code to serialize objects of that type as XML data structures. You add the **XmlAttribute** to each data member or property that should be serialized as part of a Web method.

Interoperability Attributes

A large number of attributes also help with COM interoperability. The simplest is the **DllImport** attribute. You can mark a definition of an external method with the **DllImport** attribute to tell the C# compiler where to locate a particular external native method. The **DllImport** method contains properties for the DLL name, the function name, or ordinal, the return type, and the parameter lists.

Many other attributes are concerned with interoperability between C# code and native COM objects. You can use these to create COM objects in C# or to import COM objects into C# programs.

Obsolete Code Attribute

The **Obsolete** attribute tells the compiler that a method should no longer be used:

```
[Obsolete ("This is going away")]
void BadMethod ()
{
}
```

The **Obsolete** attribute contains an error message, and indicates whether calling the method should be an error or a warning.

Creating Attributes

All attributes work in essentially the same way. Attributes inject class variables into your code stream. Some code that is interested in the presence of particular attributes queries for the presence of these variables and takes appropriate action. Let's consider the **Obsolete** attribute. The compiler reads each assembly you reference when it compiles your code. It searches for the **Obsolete** attribute on all the methods you reference. If it finds the **Obsolete** attribute, it notes that information and generates the warning or error message whenever it finds a call to that method.

The lesson: Attributes are created to be read by some other software. That software learns more about the code and can do more based on the presence of attributes. You can create your own attributes to mark your own code and later take action based on the presence or absence of specific attributes.

Creating Attribute Classes

Creating a new attribute is as simple as creating any other class. Attributes have four conventions you must follow:

- Your new attribute class must derive from **System.Attribute**.

- You have to attach the **AttributeUsage** attribute to your new attribute class. This tells the runtime where your attribute can be used. It can specify that your attribute be placed on an assembly, a class, a method, or any combination of them.

- You create a constructor that takes any mandatory parameters to your attribute.

- You create properties to define any optional parameters on your attribute.

That's all there is to it. The following sections explain these steps in more detail.

Attribute Usage

You apply the **AttributeUsage** attribute to your attributes so that the C# compiler knows where your new attribute can be used. (I tried several times to write that sentence with fewer instances of the word *attribute*, but it never worked.) The usage is simple:

```
[AttributeUsage (AttributeTargets.Class |
   AttributeTargets.Method)]
public class BeenTestedAttribute {
  // etc.
}
```

This defines that the **BeenTestedAttribute** class can be placed on either a class or any class method.

Mandatory Parameters

Sometimes, your attribute must have specific parameters associated with it to be meaningful. For instance, the .NET BCL **Obsolete** attribute needs a message to print when you try to call the obsolete method. The way you enforce mandatory parameters on attributes is to make them parameters to constructors, and do not create a default constructor for your attribute class. Then, anyone using your attribute class must specify those parameters in the creation of the attribute. The following constructor specifies that you must state whether the tests passed or failed when you create it:

```
[AttributeUsage (AttributeTargets.Class |
  AttributeTargets.Method)]
public class BeenTestedAttribute {
  public enum TestResult {
    passed,
    failed
  }

  BeenTestedAttribute (TestResult f)
  {
  }
  // etc.
}
```

Before you can create the **BeenTestedAttribute**, you would need to specify the result of the tests:

```
[BeenTested (TestResult.passed)]
```

Named Parameters

There may be occasions in which you have information that you want to add to the attribute only some of the time. These optional parameters are specified internally as properties. You create read/write properties in your attribute class. Users then add a **name=value** string to the attribute designation to set the named property. These named properties must have reasonable defaults, or you should replace them with mandatory parameters. These named parameters are defined as properties when you create the attribute:

```
[AttributeUsage (AttributeTargets.Class |
  AttributeTargets.Method)]
public class BeenTestedAttribute {
```

```
public enum TestResult {
  passed,
  failed
}

public TestResult Results {
  get {
    return m_Result;
  }
  set {
    m_Result = value;
  }
}
// etc.
}
```

To use this attribute, you can specify the result as a named parameter:

```
[BeenTested (Results = passed)]
```

Attributes in Assemblies

Attributes get compiled into the MSIL for an assembly just the same as any other code. To retrieve the attributes from an assembly, class, or method, you use the reflection and metadata APIs. These methods will return a collection of attributes that you can examine and iterate. Usually, when you define custom attributes you will also write some tool using these APIs to process the attribute information.

You can use attributes to create information for internal use, for external documentation, or for any other purpose. All you need to do is to write the code that can read and process attributes as well as writing the attributes.

Immediate Solutions

This section shows you the most common cases when you will use attributes in your C# programs. Some of these are common engineering situations, and some are specific scenarios that the C# design team felt were common enough programming tasks to automate.

Controlling Conditional Compilation

By far the most common programming attribute you will use is to mark code for conditional compilation. If you have come from a C or C++ background, you have been doing this for years using the preprocessor. Although you could still do the same thing in C#, the C# language provides a better mechanism using the **Conditional** attribute. When you conditionally compiled code in C++ using the preprocessor, you had to use macros to define the actual function calls. That way, you were not calling nonexistent functions when the preprocessor symbol was false. Also, you had to make sure that libraries were compiled with the same preprocessor symbols that were in use when the client code was compiled, lest there be linking errors when you find that the library was created with different preprocessor symbols defined than the executable was compiled with. Subtle bugs could also show up when statements were removed from code because a certain preprocessor symbol was not defined.

The C# **Conditional** attribute makes all those problems go away. When you mark methods with the **Conditional** attribute, that one attribute controls both the compilation of the member and all calls generated to it. Marking a member for conditional compilation is simple—simply mark it with the **Conditional** attribute:

```
[Conditional ("DEBUG")]
void CheckState ()
{
  // Check the state of the object.
}
```

All the examples I have shown for the **Conditional** attribute have used the **DEBUG** symbol, simply because this is the most common.

You can write conditional code based on the presence of any preprocessor symbol. In fact, you can write code that relies on two different
symbols and is executed if either symbol is true:

```
[Conditional ("DEBUG"), Conditional ("TRACE")]
void PrintValues ()
{
  // Print all the values in the object.
}
```

Before you get too carried away thinking that this is the greatest thing
in the world, there are some restrictions:

- You cannot apply the **Conditional** attribute to a constructor or
  destructor.

- You cannot apply the **Conditional** attribute to an overloaded
  operator, property, or indexer.

- You can apply the **Conditional** attribute only to methods that
  return void types.

- You cannot apply the **Conditional** attribute to override methods.
  However, you can apply it to virtual methods, and that implicitly
  marks all overrides with the same conditional attribute.

- You cannot mark interface implementation methods with the
  Conditional attribute.

Remember that the **Conditional** attribute affects the compilation of
calls to the method and you will understand these restrictions. The
behavior and the correctness of code would change based on preprocessor symbols without these restrictions.

Related solution:	Found on page:
Writing Invariant Functions	409

Marking Obsolete Code

The next attribute you are very likely to use is the **Obsolete** attribute.
The obsolete attribute contains one mandatory parameter and one
optional parameter.

To mark a method as obsolete, you add the **Obsolete** attribute and
add a message that points users to the proper replacement method:

```
[Obsolete ("Use the DoNewStuff () method instead.")]
public void DoStuff ()
{
  // ...
}
```

If a user calls the existing **DoStuff( )** method, he gets the following warning:

```
c:\cslbb\chapter11\dbattributes\form1.cs(79,6): warning CS0618:
  'Class1.DoStuff()' is obsolete: 'Use the DoNewStuff () method
  instead.'
```

After a period of time to let users adjust to this impending change, you can set the second parameter to the **Obsolete** attribute, changing the warning into an error. This parameter defaults to false, emitting a warning:

```
[Obsolete ("Use the DoNewStuff () method instead.", true)]
public void DoStuff ()
{
  // ...
}
```

Now, when a user calls the **DoStuff( )** method, he gets an error instead of a warning:

```
c:\cslbb\chapter11\dbattributes\form1.cs(79,6): error CS0619:
  'Class1.DoStuff()' is obsolete: 'Use the DoNewStuff () method
  instead'
```

As you find that a method becomes obsolete, you can use this attribute to notify users of an impending change. Make sure that your warning message points to the possible workaround to address the functionality that method had been using.

Serializing Web Methods

The .NET design team spent quite a bit of time adding functionality so that it would be as easy as possible to create Web services using the .NET Framework, and C# in particular. Briefly, Web services are binary objects that expose functionality across the Internet. They receive requests as SOAP messages using the HTTP protocol. They return values by sending XML using HTTP.

In fact, the .NET Framework team thought that Web services would be so common, they created a wizard that makes creating Web services easy. Using the wizard and the attributes it uses lets you concentrate on the functionality of your Web service, not on the technological aspects of HTTP, XML, and SOAP.

Using the C# Web Service Wizard

To create a C# Web service, simply select File|New|Project in Visual Studio .NET. Then, select ASP.NET Web Service from the list of C# Project Templates (see Figure 11.1).

After you create the Web service, you need to add methods to the **Service1** class to create the interface you want to export via the Web. To illustrate the attributes involved in creating a Web service, I created a dummy Web service that returns the high and low temperature for the past week.

Declaring Serializable Classes

Often, you will create Web methods that return structures more complicated than simple data types. The temperature Web service will return a structure that contains the high and low temperature as a point for each day. The easiest way to do this is to create a class that holds these datapoints. Listing 11.2 shows a simple class to create this kind of class.

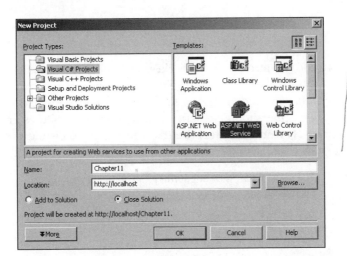

Figure 11.1   The Visual Studio .NET AppWizard provides a template for creating ASP.NET C# Web services.

Listing 11.2   A class that holds the high and low temperature for a single day.

```
public class TemperatureData
{
  private double low = 32.0;
  private double high = 212.0;

  public TemperatureData()
  {
  }

  public double LowTemp {
    get{
      return low;
    }
    set {
      low = value;
    }
  }

  public double HighTemp {
    get {
      return high;
    }
    set {
      high = value;
    }
  }
}
```

You need to add two attributes to this class so that it can be serialized across the Web. You need to add the **XmlRoot** attribute to the class declaration, and you need to add the **XmlAttribute** attribute to each data or property that should be serialized. Those two attributes are defined in the **System.Xml.Serialization** namespace. Listing 11.3 shows the new class, with the changes highlighted.

Listing 11.3   The same class, now supporting XML serialization for Web services.

```
[XmlRoot ("HighLow", Namespace="WeatherService")]
public class TemperatureData
{
  private double low = 32.0;
  private double high = 212.0;

  public TemperatureData()
```

```
    {
    }

  [XmlAttribute ("Low")]
  public double LowTemp {
    get{
      return low;
    }
    set {
      low = value;
    }
  }

  [XmlAttribute ("High")]
  public double HighTemp {
    get {
      return high;
    }
    set {
      high = value;
    }
  }
}
```

ASP.NET reads these attributes and interprets them to build the serialization methods for this class whenever it should be returned via a Web service method.

Declaring Web Methods

To return one of these objects using a Web method, you need to write a Web method that returns the new class. Again, attributes make this easy. Suppose that you had the following method:

```
public TemperatureData GetTodaysTemp () {
  TemperatureData t = new TemperatureData();
  t.HighTemp=98;
  t.LowTemp=55;
  return t;
}
```

To make this method callable across the Web, you simply add the **WebMethod** attribute:

```
[WebMethod]
public TemperatureData GetTodaysTemp () {
  TemperatureData t = new TemperatureData();
```

```
t.HighTemp=98;
t.LowTemp=55;
return t;
}
```

Now, ASP.NET knows that this method should be callable via the Web using the SOAP protocol.

The great thing about these attributes is that you just write a class, add a few keywords, and you get much more functionality. You do not need to spend any design or coding time understanding or manipulating the low-level details associated with Web services. You simply add the proper attributes, and the ASP.NET components do the rest. Later sections show you how you can do the same with your attributes.

Testing Web Services

Visual Studio .NET also includes capabilities to make testing your ASP.NET Web services easy. ASP.NET adds some extra pages along with your Web service so that you can invoke your ASP.NET Web service from Internet Explorer. You can then see the response back from your Web service in another window. Figure 11.2 shows the response from this prototype temperature Web service.

The point of all this: ASP.NET uses attributes so that you don't have to concentrate on the underlying technical aspects of creating your

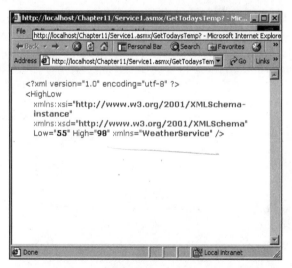

Figure 11.2   Displaying Web service responses in Internet Explorer.

own Web services. Instead, you can concentrate on your own problems and solutions and let the ASP.NET runtime create the proper code to fit the solution into the Web services framework.

Related solution:	Found on page:
Creating Web Services	371

Creating Your Own Attributes

The earlier sections of this chapter showed you how the .NET Framework uses some common attributes to make programming easier. You can apply the same strategies when you design systems so that your users can get the same benefits.

Let's suppose that you are creating a system that has a capability for users to add modules to the system. You define an interface for user-created modules to support. To keep it simple, here is the interface for a user-defined module:

```
public interface IModule {
  string GetCapabilities ();
}
```

Okay, it's not that useful, but this chapter is about attributes. The problem you need to solve is how to find classes that support the **IModule** interface and how to create those objects. The best way to solve this problem is to use attributes. If you tell users to mark any class that supports the **IModule** interface with a particular attribute, you can find those classes. Further, if you instruct clients to create a static method that creates the object that supports **IModule** and mark that method with an attribute, you can find the creation method and use it. So, here is an example of a class that supports the **IModule** interface, complete with the attributes on it:

```
[Module]
public class MyModule : IModule {
  [ModuleLoader]
  public static IModule CreateMyModule () {
    return new MyModule();
  }

  public string GetCapabilities () {
```

```
    return "I don't do much";
  }
}
```

This class supports the **IModule** interface. The class is marked with the **Module** attribute, to mark it as a user-created module, and the static method **CreateMyModule()** is marked with the **ModuleLoader** attribute to note that it is the static method that creates the object supporting the **IModule** interface.

To get this to work, you need to create two attribute classes. Here are the definitions for the **Module** and **ModuleLoader** classes:

```
[AttributeUsage (AttributeTargets.Class)]
public class ModuleAttribute : System.Attribute {
  public ModuleAttribute () {
  }
}

[AttributeUsage (AttributeTargets.Method)]
public class ModuleLoaderAttribute : System.Attribute {
  public ModuleLoaderAttribute () {
  }
}
```

These are both simple attributes. The **AttributeUsage** attribute defines that they can be placed on a class and a method, respectively. To create more complicated attributes, you define constructors that take positional parameters and properties to support named parameters.

Finding Attributes Using Reflection

Once you have defined the attributes, you need to use the reflection APIs to find and use the attributes. Listing 11.4 shows the code to find attributes in a module.

Listing 11.4   Finding attributed code.

```
System.Reflection.MemberInfo info;
info = typeof (MyModule);
object [] atts;
atts = info.GetCustomAttributes(typeof (ModuleAttribute),false);
if (atts.GetLength (0) != 0) {
  ModuleAttribute a = (ModuleAttribute)atts[0];
```

Same expr, different cast!

```
Type t = typeof (MyModule);
foreach (System.Reflection.MethodInfo method
  in t.GetMethods()) {
  foreach (Attribute t in
    method.GetCustomAttributes (true)) {
    object result = t.InvokeMember(method.Name,
      System.Reflection.BindingFlags.Public |
      System.Reflection.BindingFlags.InvokeMethod |
      System.Reflection.BindingFlags.Static,
      null,null,null);
    IModule i = (IModule)result;

    System.Windows.Forms.MessageBox.Show
      (i.GetCapabilities());
  }
 }
}
```

11. Programming with Attributes

The first section of the code

```
System.Reflection.MemberInfo info;
info = typeof (MyModule);
object [] atts;
atts = info.GetCustomAttributes(typeof (ModuleAttribute),false);
if (atts.GetLength (0) != 0) {
  ModuleAttribute a = (ModuleAttribute)atts[0];
```

loads a module and determines if the module has a class with the **Module** attribute attached to it. After that has been found, the next section

```
foreach (Attribute t in method.GetCustomAttributes (true)) {
  object result = t.InvokeMember(method.Name,
    System.Reflection.BindingFlags.Public |
    System.Reflection.BindingFlags.InvokeMethod |
    System.Reflection.BindingFlags.Static,
    null,null,null);
```

finds if any of the members are tagged with the **ModuleLoader** attribute. If so, that method is invoked, and the return value is the object that supports the **IModule** interface.

Related solutions:	Found on page:
Lodging an Assembly	384
Finding Methods	389

Much of this code is new and different. Chapter 18, on metadata and reflection, goes into this type of programming in more detail. The important point is that when you create attributes, you are tagging code so that you can find it later using the reflection APIs—making it easier for your users to write code that satisfies the requirements of your interface, without concentrating on that fact. Rather, they can concentrate on the programming tasks at hand and use your attributes to mark code that you need to use.

Chapter 12

Programming with Exceptions

In Brief

C# uses exceptions to handle serious runtime errors in a program. The .NET Base Class Libraries (BCL) use exceptions to report serious errors. You cannot write production quality C# programs without understanding exceptions and writing code that handles exceptions properly.

Exceptions Defined

Exceptions are a more efficient way of handling runtime errors in large programs. They also provide a more object-oriented strategy for error handling. Before the introduction of exceptions, each routine needed to return some kind of a success or failure code. These error codes were usually integer values. Organizations building large systems went to some interesting lengths to ensure that these integer error codes were unique throughout the entire system; the error codes were essentially global constants.

In addition, using these integer error codes meant that constructs like the following were commonplace:

```
int rVal = DoFirstThing ();
if (rVal > 0)
  return rVal;
rVal = DoSecondThing ();
if (rVal > 0)
  return rVal;
rVal = DoThirdThing ();
if (rVal > 0)
  return rVal;
```

Or worse, if this same code had to acquire resources:

```
HANDLE h = GetHandle (); // Must be freed to avoid resource leak.
int rVal = DoFirstThing ();
if (rVal == 0) {
  rVal = DoSecondThing ();
  if (rVal == 0) {
    rVal = DoThirdThing ();
  }
}
```

```
rVal = FreeHandle (h);
return rVal;
```

That's with only three functions, and no other control logic such as loops or branching statements as part of the function's main logic. Put any of those functions returning error codes inside a loop, and suddenly you can end up with code that is more than 50 percent related to recovering after errors. If these three routines usually return success, many programmers will reach the point where they write this:

```
HANDLE h = GetHandle ();
DoFirstThing ();
DoSecondThing ();
DoThirdThing ();
return FreeHandle (h);
```

This is just plain wrong. However, it is the kind of error that will most likely be caught only in the field or in a code review. The temptation to write this kind of erroneous code gets pretty great though. The alternative: checking each method's return code, which starts to obfuscate a routine's real meaning. Exceptions give you the best of both worlds. You can write code that expresses your algorithms clearly, and you can wrap that code in **try/catch** or **try/finally** blocks to handle errors:

```
HANDLE h = null;
try {
  h = GetHandle ();
  DoFirstThing ();
  DoSecondThing ();
  DoThirdThing ();
} finally {
 if (h != null)
    FreeHandle (h);
}
```

This code performs the exact same correct functionality that the second example did. It acquires the resource, calls three functions, and releases the handle. Any errors—in this case, exceptions—are propagated to the caller. And, the resource is freed at the end of the routine. In fact, if this block of code is several function calls away from the point where the error can be addressed, the exception will automatically propagate to the point where the exception can be handled.

There is another case for exceptions as an error mechanism. Some of the functions you write in C# have defined return types. Constructors do not have any return value; many operators have particular return types defined. If these functions encounter any error conditions, the only way to propagate that information is to use exceptions.

In short, exceptions provide a mechanism to separate error handling and recovery from general program logic.

Raising Exceptions

You raise an exception using the C# **throw** statement, which takes one argument: an exception object that gets "thrown." You can throw any type that is derived from **System.Exception**, which is the root of all exception types. You want to throw exceptions that are rich in content so that you give users the best opportunity to fix or recover from the error conditions. The .NET BCL contains many different exception classes for just this purpose. In general, you will want to use the type of exception to explain the particular error that happened. You will want to include properties in the exception object that help to diagnose and fix the error condition. For example, the following statement throws a **System.ArgumentException** because you could not cast an object to the proper type:

```
if (!(o is Complex))
    throw new ArgumentException ("o is not a complex number");
```

Throwing an **ArgumentException** object indicates that the argument (**o**) was not of the proper type. The message inside the **ArgumentException** tells the user the reason for the exception.

Handling Exceptions

If you throw an exception, someone somewhere must catch it. You catch exceptions by placing code that might generate exceptions inside a **try** block. Following the **try** block, you can cascade different **catch** clauses to handle different possible exception types. The **catch** clauses are processed in order, so you need to be careful regarding their order. For example, the following code puts some calls inside a **try** block and catches two different exceptions that might show up:

```
try {
    DoSomething ();
    DoMoreStuff ();
```

```
} catch (ArgumentException e1) {
  // cleanup for an argument exception.
} catch (Exception e) {
  // cleanup for other problems.
}
```

If you were to reverse the order of these two **catch** clauses the clause that catches the **Exception** type will be called even when the type of the exception is an **ArgumentException**.

finally Clauses

Sometimes you need to perform some code at the end of the routine whether the function executes normally or has an exception pass through it. You can perform any mandatory cleanup steps using a **finally** clause. The same example from the beginning of this chapter shows you how the **finally** clause provides a way to execute cleanup code:

```
HANDLE h = null;
try {
  h = GetHandle ();
  DoFirstThing ();
  DoSecondThing ();
  DoThirdThing ();
} finally {
 if (h != null)
    FreeHandle (h);
}
```

The code inside the **finally** clause is executed if all four other functions work properly. The **finally** clause also gets executed when one of the other functions throws an exception of any type.

Exceptions and Program Control Flow

Exceptions can seriously complicate the control flow in your program. The error-generating code can be many function calls away from the code that actually handles the error. This is one of the advantages of programming with exceptions. If you are writing functions that cannot fix the particular errors, simply let them pass through your function. Also, you can be safely assured that any generated exceptions do get propagated to a function upstream from the current execution point that can address the exception.

That description begs the question: What happens if no **catch** clauses are in place anywhere upstream from the current execution point? Exceptions must be handled. If an exception gets generated that does not have any appropriate handler, the runtime terminates your program. You should really avoid this situation. At the very least, in your main function, or somewhere near the top level of your program, you should put in a **catch** clause that gives the user the chance to save his work before the program terminates.

The Exception Safety Guarantees

The discussion thus far hopefully got you interested in exceptions as a better method of handling errors. However, there is another side to this discussion. You need to follow some important guidelines in order to make your programs robust in the face of exceptions. If you write well-formed programs, you will find that you are well on your way to writing exception-safe code. Two exception safety guarantees—the weak exception safety guarantee and the strong exception safety guarantee—are a result of many years of trial, experimentation, and discussion among the C++ community. These same guarantees apply equally well to the C# language. However, you need a few different techniques necessary to implement these guarantees.

The Weak Exception Safety Guarantee

The weak exception guarantee states that the following properties are true after a function executes, whether or not that function exits normally or as a result of an exception:

- When exceptions are thrown through the function, no resources are leaked.

- Any exceptions generated as part of the function execution get propagated to the caller.

- The object is in a stable and usable state.

Let's go through each of these statements so that you fully understand what you must do to satisfy this guarantee.

Plugging Resource Leaks

The use of the .NET runtime garbage collector by C# removes much of the burden for this promise. However, objects must be cleaned up when they are no longer needed. Most of these object types will implement the **IDisposable** interface. Simply call the **Dispose( )** method to clean up after these objects.

Related solution:	Found on page:
Implementing the **IDisposable** Interface	254

Propagating Exceptions

You can accomplish this portion of the weak exception guarantee in three ways:

- *Simply do nothing.* Any exceptions generated during the course of the function processing will automatically propagate through the function up to the caller.

- *Perform any necessary cleanup and rethrow the exception.* In C#, you rethrow an exception by using an empty **throw** statement.

- *Throw some other exception and set the **InnerException** property to the original exception.* This is a new C# idiom that lets you process exceptions in your classes and still propagate the original exception. This option is the best—it gives the callers the most information about the problem and gives them the best option of fixing it.

The best option here is to pass on the original exception, if that is sufficient for any users of your class. If not, create a new, more descriptive exception and use the **InnerException** property to preserve the original exception.

Keeping Objects Usable and Stable

This one takes a bit more work and forces you to understand that any function call can possibly generate exceptions. After each statement or function call, you need to make sure that the state of the object is usable. In many classes, this is always true and can be considered a class invariant. You need to be careful anytime you create a class where one field somehow relates to another field. For example, look back at the complex number class from Chapter 10. In that form, the only fields are the real part and the imaginary part of the complex number. Any other values are calculated only when needed and are never stored.

Suppose that you later discovered that too much processing time was spent calculating the norm of a complex number for ordering comparisons. So, you decide to store the norm as part of the object. This changes the **Real** property as follows:

```
public double Real {
  get {
```

```
      return realPart;
   }
   set {
     realPart = value;
     norm = realPart * realPart + imagPart * imagPart;
   }
}
```

This code no longer satisfies the weak exception safety guarantee. It is possible that either of the multiplications or the addition can throw an **OverflowException**. In that case, the **norm** field no longer reflects that actual state of the object. That puts the object in an unstable state. Some operations will be incorrect because the object is in an inconsistent state.

The Strong Exception Safety Guarantee

The weak exception guarantee states that an object is usable when exceptions happen. The strong exception safety guarantee goes one step further—it satisfies everything in the weak exception guarantee, and the following statements are also true:

- If the function exits normally, all of its side effects have occurred.

- If the function exits throwing an exception, the internal program state—namely the state of the object and all reference parameters—is unchanged.

Here is where the comment I made earlier about exception safety and good programming practice comes into play. The strong exception guarantee is much easier to implement if the function performs only one side effect. You can then safely perform all changes to a temporary object, which then can be copied to the actual object by using operations that cannot throw exceptions. A simple change of order fixes the exception problem from the previous section:

```
public double Real {
   get {
     return realPart;
   }
   set {
     norm = value * value + imagPart * imagPart;
     realPart = value;
   }
}
```

The statement that sets **norm** might throw an overflow exception when the new value is computed. If that happens, the value of **norm** does not change. The statement that sets the new **realPart** of the object cannot throw an exception; it is a simple assignment. Now, if any exceptions occur in the accessor function of this property, the state of the object is unchanged.

Immediate Solutions

Exceptions are light on syntax and heavy on semantics. Only three keywords or statements have any relationship to exceptions. But because exceptions can pass through any function you write, you must always be aware of exceptions whenever you write C# code. The remainder of this chapter shows you how to work with exceptions in your programs. This is a bit different than many of the other chapters' "Immediate Solutions" sections. The most important part of working with exceptions is understanding when to do which operations so that you write exception-safe code. You need to always be cognizant of how exceptions can alter the path of execution in any given function. Armed with that knowledge, you can write code that will function properly whether or not exceptions are present in the runtime environment.

Catching Exceptions

You need to follow two steps in writing code that catches exceptions. First, place the code blocks that might generate exceptions in a **try** block:

```
try { // any of these might throw exceptions.
  DoStuff ();
  DoMoreStuff ();
  YetEvenMoreStuff ();
}
```

Next, you need to add at least one **catch** clause to process any exceptions that might get thrown. If you want to catch everything in one clause, use a single **catch** clause with the **System.Exception** class:

```
try { // any of these might throw exceptions.
  DoStuff ();
  DoMoreStuff ();
  YetEvenMoreStuff ();
} catch (System.Exception e) {
  // Fix all problems here...
  System.Console.WriteLine ("Stuff did not happen");
}
```

This single **catch** clause will catch every exception that can be thrown. Sometimes that is sufficient, but more often, you will want to use multiple **catch** clauses to handle different types of exceptions. That way, you can respond differently to different types of error conditions. To create multiple **catch** clauses, simply chain them one after the other:

```
try { // any of these might throw exceptions.
  DoStuff ();
  DoMoreStuff ();
  YetEvenMoreStuff ();
} catch (System.IO.DirectoryNotFoundException e1) {
  // Create the directory and try again...
} catch (System.IO.FileNotFoundException e2) {
  // Create the file and try again.
} catch (System.Exception e) {
  // Something else bad happened...
  System.Console.WriteLine ("Stuff did not happen");
}
```

Here, I have added two new **catch** clauses to catch different file-related exceptions. If an exception is thrown, the **catch** clauses are examined in order to see if any of them can catch this particular exception. When you use multiple **catch** clauses, you need to be sure to place them so that a base class does not catch exceptions that you want handled by the derived classes. In this case, I have placed two file system–specific exceptions before the more generic **System.Exception** class. Should one of the methods throw the *directory not found* exception or the *file not found* exception, you can use a more specific error-handling technique for the remaining exceptions that were thrown.

Let's examine the MSIL that gets generated by the **catch** clauses:

```
.method private hidebysig static void  Main(string[] args)
  cil managed
{
  .entrypoint
  // Code size       37 (0x25)
  .maxstack  1
  .locals ([0] class
[mscorlib]System.IO.DirectoryNotFoundException
    V_0,
  [1] class [mscorlib]System.IO.FileNotFoundException V_1,
  [2] class [mscorlib]System.Exception e)
```

```
.try
{
IL_0000:  call    void Exceptions.Class1::DoStuff()
IL_0005:  call    void Exceptions.Class1::DoMoreStuff()
IL_000a:  call    void Exceptions.Class1::YetEvenMoreStuff()
IL_000f:  leave.s    IL_0024
} // end .try
catch [mscorlib]System.IO.DirectoryNotFoundException
{
  IL_0011:  stloc.0
  IL_0012:  leave.s    IL_0024
} // end handler
catch [mscorlib]System.IO.FileNotFoundException
{
  IL_0014:  stloc.1
  IL_0015:  leave.s    IL_0024
} // end handler
catch [mscorlib]System.Exception
{
  IL_0017:  stloc.2
  IL_0018:  ldstr     "Stuff did not happen"
  IL_001d:  call      void
                [mscorlib]System.Console::WriteLine(string)
  IL_0022:  leave.s    IL_0024
} // end handler
IL_0024:  ret
} // end of method Class1::Main
```

The main point here is that each **catch** clause creates a new handler for the particular exception class being processed. The handlers get examined in order when an exception occurs.

Throwing Exceptions

Throwing an exception is as simple as using the **throw** statement. You create a new exception type and throw it. For example:

```
if (System.IO.Directory.Exists ("c:\\test") == false)
  throw new System.IO.DirectoryNotFoundException(@"The test
    directory does not exist");
```

This statement simply creates a new **System.IO.DirectoryNot FoundException**. The exception is thrown to the caller. No other work happens here.

Constructing Exceptions

There are four different constructors to the **System.Exception** class. Each of these is usually mirrored in all the derived classes:

```
public Exception ();
```

This is the default constructor for the **System.Exception** class. I would not recommend using this constructor because it gives very little information to the callers that would help diagnose or fix the problem.

```
public Exception (string msg);
```

This constructor gives a textual message to the caller indicating the reason for the failure. As you will see a bit later, this textual information will usually be displayed for the end user. The textual message should give the user any information necessary to fix or diagnose the problem.

```
public Exception (SerializationInfo info, StreamingContext cxt);
```

This constructor creates a new exception that can be serialized, usually with an XML stream. You will want to use this type of constructor when you create an exception in a Web service or Web application and the exception needs to be processed on another machine.

```
public Exception (string msg, Exception innerException);
```

This constructor creates a new exception that has been translated from some other exception type. You will use this form when you create your own exceptions to report errors generated by system calls inside your library. This way, you can return your own exception type, yet preserve the original cause of the exception.

Notice that each exception has an inner exception property. In some circumstances, you can create code that generates a chain of exceptions, with each library creating a new exception type and setting the inner exception to the type of exception it caught. In most cases, there will not be more than one inner exception at any given time.

Using Exception Properties

The **System.Exception** class has a number of properties that callers can query to determine more information about the exception. Most of these properties are read-only: the inner exception, the message text, a stack trace, and a target site. You can set the inner exception and message text by using the appropriate constructors outlined in the preceding section. The stack trace and target site are set by the runtime when the exception is created. You can query these to help find the location in the program where the exception was created. You can use these properties to help ascertain and fix the cause of exceptions:

- The **TargetSite** property is a string that gives the name of the routine that generated the original exception. This would be set to **void DoStuff( )**, or one of the other functions later in the example code in the "Catching Exceptions" section.

- The **Source** property is a string that gets set to the application or assembly name that generated the original error.

- The stack trace is a string that contains each method between the exception generation point and the catch point. Each method is listed in one single line.

That gives you the properties you can set on the **System.Exception** class. Each derived class has additional properties that you can set and retrieve. Consult the documentation for each exception-derived class for more information.

Designing Exception Classes

You will design your own exception classes when you write libraries that need to respond to error conditions using exceptions. The .NET team has created a different class to use as the base class when you create your own exception types—**System.ApplicationException**, which is derived from **System.Exception** and adds no new functionality. Using **System.ApplicationException** is a convention so that users can differentiate between third-party library exceptions and .NET BCL exceptions.

The **ApplicationException** class has exactly the same set of constructors that the **System.Exception** class contains. You will want to define all four constructors in your new exception class.

Other than that, you will most likely not add any extra functionality to your own exception classes. Exceptions do not perform real work; they simply carry information from the point where an exception occurs to the point where exceptions are caught. Different exception types provide the mechanism to differentiate between different exception causes. So, you will define different exception classes to handle different error types.

Understand that the only reason to define new exception types is to differentiate between error causes. So, do not define one exception type for your entire library—it won't help differentiate the cause of errors. You can consider creating one abstract base class for your library's errors and define different derived classes for specific errors that can be generated by your library. This lets users find errors generated by your library and differentiate between errors that your library can generate.

Related solution:	Found on page:
Deriving from a Base Class	172

Using **finally** Clauses

Sometimes you need to perform some cleanup in a function, whether it finishes normally or generates an exception. For example, consider this function that needs to update a large bitmap:

```
private void copySet ()
{
  this.Cursor = Cursors.WaitCursor;
  UpdateBitmap ();
  this.Cursor = Cursors.Default;
}
```

If the **UpdateBitmap( )** function throws an exception, the assignment that replaces the default cursor never happens. This particular function does not need to catch and process exceptions, but it does have bad side effects when an exception passes through it. You can fix this problem by using a **finally** clause:

```
private void copySet ()
{
  try {
    this.Cursor = Cursors.WaitCursor;
    UpdateBitmap ();
  } finally {
```

```
        this.Cursor = Cursors.Default;
    }
}
```

This second version of the function is exception safe. The **finally** clause gets executed if the **UpdateBitmap( )** function exits normally or if that function throws an exception. In either case, the cursor gets restored to its default value.

You can also place a **finally** clause at the end of any number of **catch** clauses to place all the method's cleanup code in one place. Consider this updated version of the original example:

```
Cursor = System.Windows.Forms.Cursors.WaitCursor;
try { // any of these might throw exceptions.
    DoStuff ();
    DoMoreStuff ();
    YetEvenMoreStuff ();
} catch (System.IO.DirectoryNotFoundException e1) {
    // Create the directory and try again...
} catch (System.IO.FileNotFoundException e2) {
    // Create the file and try again.
} catch (System.Exception e) {
    // Something else bad happened...
    System.Console.WriteLine ("Stuff did not happen");
} finally {
    Cursor = System.Windows.Forms.Cursors.Default;
}
```

Adding the highlighted code lets you specify any cleanup in one place, rather than repeat it in each of the **catch** clauses, and once outside the **catch** clauses for the normal case where exceptions are not generated.

Use **finally** clauses in every function that must perform some explicit cleanup operations. By doing so, your methods never leak resources or leave the system in an unpredictable state.

Passing Exception Information to Callers

Having designed exceptions and figured out where you need to throw exceptions in your code, now you need to work out what information callers need to diagnose and correct any problems. You can do this in two ways. You will want to have a reasonably detailed message in the exception so that users and client code will know what went wrong. Also, most exceptions start out somewhere in the .NET BCL. So, you will want to use the inner exception property to pass on both the original and specific exception.

Let's consider a different example from a previous chapter. I wrote a simple complex number class to demonstrate interfaces in Chapter 10. That version used double values to store the real and imaginary parts. Let's suppose that for performance reasons, you wanted to work with complex numbers based on integers. So, the real and imaginary numbers would be integers instead of doubles. Let's consider this function:

```
static public Complex operator * (Complex l, Complex r) {
  Complex result = new Complex ();
  result.Real = l.Real*r.Real-l.Imaginary*r.Imaginary;
  result.Imaginary = l.Real*r.Imaginary + l.Imaginary*r.Real;
  return result;
}
```

Either of the two multiplications could overflow. As this function is coded right now, it is sufficient: Any exceptions do propagate to the caller. However, this is not particularly useful. The multiplication will generate an overflow exception, but the caller will have no idea why. To fix this, you need to create your own exception class and use both the inner exception and message properties in **System.Exception**. First, you need to create a new exception class to handle any exceptions from complex arithmetic:

```
public class ComplexOverflowException : ApplicationException {
  public ComplexOverflowException () :
    base () {
  }
  public ComplexOverflowException (string msg) :
    base (msg) {
  }
  public ComplexOverflowException (SerializationInfo info,
    StreamingContext cxt) :
    base (info, cxt) {
  }
  public ComplexOverflowException (string msg,
    Exception inner) :
    base (msg, inner) {
  }
}
```

This is simply a re-implementation of the original **System.Exception** methods, published through the new, more specific exception class.

Once you have created this new exception class, you need to modify the original multiplication routine to package any existing exceptions in the new exception class to indicate exactly where the overflow occurred:

```
static public Complex operator * (Complex l, Complex r) {
  Complex result = new Complex ();
  try {
    result.Real = l.Real*r.Real-l.Imaginary*r.Imaginary;
  } catch (System.OverflowException o) {
    ComplexOverflowException e = new
      ComplexOverflowException ("Overflow calculating real.",
      o);
    throw e;
  }
  try {
    result.Imaginary = l.Real*r.Imaginary + l.Imaginary*r.Real;
  } catch (System.OverflowException o) {
    ComplexOverflowException e = new
    ComplexOverflowException
      ("Overflow calculating imaginary.", o);
    throw e;
  }
  return result;
}
```

Callers now get a bit more specific information. They know which term in the result generated the overflow. The original exception is preserved in the inner exception property.

Using Checked and Unchecked Code

You can control whether overflow operations generate exceptions or are silently ignored. First of all, you can control whether an entire source file generates or ignores overflow exceptions by using the **/checked** compiler option:

- **/checked+** turns on all overflow checking.
- **/checked-** turns off all overflow checking.

You can also set this option by using the Visual Studio .NET IDE. Right-click on the solution in the Solution Explorer window and select Properties, which lets you edit the compiler options for the project. Turn on the setting for Check For Arithmetic Overflow/Underflow (see Figure 12.1). The default for this option is off (False).

You can also control checked and unchecked blocks of code individually by using the **checked** and **unchecked** keywords in your source code. Suppose that you had the rest of the application compiled with the **/checked+** keywords, and you wanted the complex type multiplication to ignore overflows. You can wrap the code in an **unchecked** block to make it proceed without overflow checking:

```
static public Complex operator * (Complex l, Complex r) {
  Complex result = new Complex ();
  unchecked {
    result.Real = l.Real*r.Real-l.Imaginary*r.Imaginary;
    result.Imaginary = l.Real*r.Imaginary + l.Imaginary*r.Real;
  }
  return result;
}
```

12. Programming with Exceptions

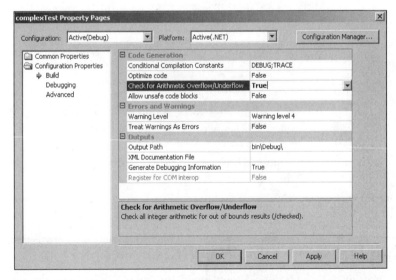

Figure 12.1 You can control whether or not integer arithmetic operations generate exceptions with the **/checked** compiler switch. The Visual Studio .NET IDE lets you set this option using this dialog box.

Of course, you can do the opposite as well. If the entire application was created as an unchecked application, and you needed overflow checking on the complex number multiplication, you simply use the **checked** keyword instead:

```
static public Complex operator * (Complex l, Complex r) {
  Complex result = new Complex ();
  checked {
    try {
      result.Real = l.Real*r.Real-l.Imaginary*r.Imaginary;
    } catch (System.OverflowException o) {
      ComplexOverflowException e = new
        ComplexOverflowException
        ("Overflow calculating real part.", o);
      throw e;
    }
    try {
      result.Imaginary = l.Real*r.Imaginary +
        l.Imaginary*r.Real;
    } catch (System.OverflowException o) {
      ComplexOverflowException e = new
      ComplexOverflowException
        ("Overflow calculating imaginary part.", o);
      throw e;
    }
  }
  return result;
}
```

In short, you can use the checked compiler option, along with the **checked** and **unchecked** keywords to tailor the performance of your application. When you know that overflow is not an issue, you can turn off the extra checking in the runtime. You can turn it on again when you need the extra checks.

Implementing the Weak Guarantee

Earlier in this chapter, I mentioned the weak exception guarantee. The weak exception guarantee is easier in C# than it is in C++. Most of the time, if you do not do anything, your code will successfully implement the weak exception guarantee. The only time you need to be concerned is when you use nonmemory resources that need to be cleaned up when your function exits. You can do this two ways in C#. You can use a **finally** clause, as I showed you previously. The other method involves the **using** statement.

Many times, you will be using a resource that implements the **IDisposable** interface, and you need to clean up after that resource. Any object that implements **IDisposable** expects you to call **Dispose()** when you are done using the object:

```
Foo f = new Foo ();
DoThingsWithFoo (f);
f.Dispose ();
```

Clearly, if **DoThingsWithFoo()** throws an exception, the **Dispose()** method doesn't get called. You could use the **try/finally** block I showed earlier, but C# gives you an easier and clearer way to describe the same functionality. A **using** block wraps code that works with a resource that implements **IDisposable**. These two blocks are identical:

```
Foo f = null;
try {
  f = new Foo ();
  DoThingsWithFoo (f);
} finally {
  if (f != null)
    f.Dispose ();
}
```

This is the same construct with the **using** keyword:

```
using (Foo f = new Foo ()) {
  DoThingsWithFoo (f);
}
```

I think you will agree that the second is a bit more concise and clear. Use a **using** clause whenever you have resources that require a call to **Dispose**. Use the **finally** clause when you need to use some other method to restore the system state.

Related solution:	Found on page:
Designing Disposable Objects	254

Implementing the Strong Guarantee

The strong guarantee is more about how you structure code that modifies the state of an object or of one of its parameters. When you have that kind of function, you need to make a few decisions and decide how to structure your code.

First, try to implement the strong guarantee. You need to do all your work on temporary objects, and then using only operations that cannot throw exceptions, set the state of the actual objects. You may find this prohibitively expensive in terms of time and memory. When that is the case, you need to fall back on the weak exception guarantee.

Consider this routine in the complex number class. It scales a complex number by some factor:

```
public void Scale (double val) {
  checked {
    realPart *= val;
    imagPart *= val;
  }
}
```

This simple function does not satisfy the strong exception guarantee. If the second statement overflows, some of the side effects have happened, but not all of them. Namely, the **realPart** of the complex number has been updated, but not the imaginary part. To fix this, you need to create one temporary variable and use it to store the result until you can be sure that no exceptions will occur:

```
public void Scale (double val) {
  checked {
    double tempImaginary = val * imagPart;
    realPart *= val;            What about this?
    imagPart = tempImaginary;
  }
}
```

Notice that I need to create only one temporary variable here. If either of the multiplications overflows, the internal state of the object has not changed. Only after any statements that might cause an exception have executed does the internal state of the object get modified.

Chapter 13

Memory Management and Object Lifetimes

In Brief

In one sense, memory management in C# programs is very easy: Let the garbage collector (GC) do it. But, there can be quite a bit more to it. The GC does handle memory resources automatically, but you need to manage any nonmemory resources properly. Also, the GC contains a set of APIs that let you manage memory resources when you need to modify the default behavior. This system lets you use the built-in memory management algorithms to your best advantage, and yet get more control of the operating environment when you need to.

Reference-Based Systems

The .NET Common Language Runtime (CLR), and therefore C#, is a reference-based system. This is a big difference for anyone accustomed to programming in value-based languages such as C++. Anytime you assign class objects in C#, you are assigning a reference, not creating new copies of the object. This is also true when you pass class objects to methods as parameters. You need to understand this simple principle: By default, there is one actual copy of an object, and several labels (variables) that refer to it. If you put objects in collections, store them as member variables, or pass them as parameters to methods, it is still just one object and several labels. The runtime system keeps track of whether these objects are still accessible or if your application has no way to reach them anymore.

The key point to any reference-based system is that your variables are simply labels that refer to the actual object, not the object itself. Having more variables simply means more labels that refer to the same object. In any reference-based system, the system must manage the actual object. You do not know how many labels still refer to a given object; therefore, you cannot know when to destroy that object.

Garbage Collection in .NET

The .NET GC is responsible for freeing memory in your application. The GC manages the heap for you and your application. It does this by periodically walking the list of allocated objects and removing those that are no longer needed. The GC performs two jobs when it manages this heap. The first is obviously managing the memory resources.

The second is to call any necessary cleanup methods on any object that requires extra cleanup. This extra cleanup is referred to as *finalization*.

Figure 13.1 shows a slice of memory before and after a garbage collection operation. The shaded objects show objects that are still in use. The .NET GC uses a *Mark and Compact* garbage collection algorithm. This means that it does not actually try to find objects that can no longer be referenced. Instead, it starts with the main application object and determines which objects can still be referenced. All of these objects are marked as *in use*. In Figure 13.1, Obj A, Obj C, Obj E, and Obj F are still in use. Next, the GC examines all the objects that are no longer in use. Any unused object that requires finalization is placed in a *Ready for Finalization* queue. This catches Obj B. The actual object is not moved, but rather a reference to it is placed in this queue. These objects are marked as "in use." Next, the GC compacts the heap. This moves all objects to overwrite those regions of memory that are no longer needed. In Figure 13.1, this moves Obj E and Obj F down over the memory that had held Obj D. The GC calls the finalization methods on any objects in the Finalization queue as its last step. You cannot control the order in which the Finalization thread finalizes objects in its queue. You will have to write your **finalize** methods so that they can be called in any order.

Notice from this simple scenario that any object that requires finalization survives the first garbage collection after it can no longer be

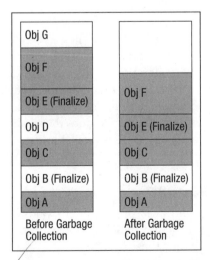

Figure 13.1   A slice of memory before and after a garbage collection.

13. Memory Management and Object Lifetimes

referenced by your program. Any object that requires finalization takes up resources longer than necessary. You should try to avoid designing objects that require finalization.

This scenario is not precisely accurate, but it gives you an idea of how the GC works. In reality, the GC spawns threads to walk the heap finding objects and calling finalization methods. Your program stops executing only for the step that involves compacting the heap.

The GC actually uses two different heaps: a small object heap and a large object heap. The GC uses the large object heap for objects of greater than 20K. This helps performance by limiting the amount of copying as objects are moved in the compaction portion of a GC operation. The large object heap will need garbage collection less frequently than the small object heap.

The GC has one more algorithm optimization for large programs: *generations*. Every object has a generation associated with it. A newly created object gets its generation set to 0. The GC increments the generation number of every object that survives a garbage collection. In practice, the longer-lived an object is, the more likely it is to still be referenced by the program. Your global data structures are probably allocated early in the life of your program, and they live for the entire life of the program. Local variables get created every time execution enters a routine, and they are no longer referenced as soon as the routine exits. Other data structures, such as dialogs and forms, might live for several function calls, but not as long as the global data structures.

The GC first examines all the objects that still have their generation number set to 0. This first pass is almost always sufficient to get enough memory. If not, the first-generation (generation number set to 1) objects are examined. If this still does not free enough memory, which is highly unlikely, the second-generation (generation number set to 2) objects are examined. The end result is that the GC does the smallest amount of work to try to get memory resources available for your program.

Nondeterministic Destruction

This section is primarily for C++ and COM programmers. Both C++ and COM use a deterministic destruction strategy. However, every reader will benefit from understanding these issues.

The question, When does an object get finalized? The answer is simple, yet not very helpful: sometime after the object cannot be referenced by your program. The point of that vague statement is that you cannot know exactly when the object actually gets finalized. In practice, this is not a major issue. It never matters exactly when memory resources are freed, as long as they are. You need only be concerned with when nonmemory resources get freed. C# provides a different idiom to handle freeing nonmemory resources.

Handling Nonmemory Resources

To specify cleanup of an object's nonmemory resources, you implement two functions. First, you implement the **IDisposable** interface. Second, you create a **finalize** method.

C# replaces the **Finalizer** syntax with destructors. You must implement the **finalize** method using the C++ destructor syntax: **~ClassName( )**. Both functions are exactly the same. In fact, the C# compiler converts destructor methods into **finalize** methods. I use these two terms interchangeably throughout the rest of the chapter.

The Dispose Idiom

Any class that uses nonmemory resources should implement the **IDisposable** interface. You free these resources by calling that class's **Dispose( )** method. Most objects are no longer stable or usable after calling **Dispose( )**. You should get in the habit of setting a reference to null after calling **Dispose( )**. You might get very unpredictable results using an object that you have disposed.

Remember that you should call **Dispose( )** even if your methods exit with exceptions. You can do this by using either **finally** clauses or the **using** statement.

Related solution:	Found on page:
Using Typical Interfaces	196

Destructors

What happens if you forget to call **Dispose( )**? If you are designing a class, how do you make sure your objects clean up after themselves?

The only way to guarantee that nonmemory resources are freed when a class object gets destroyed is to write a destructor. The destructor should perform the same operations that your **Dispose( )** method performs. As I said previously, finalization can seriously affect system performance. The .NET BCL provides a way to minimize this problem. You will create both a **Dispose( )** method and a destructor. Inside the **Dispose( )** method, you can call **GC.SupressFinalize( )** to notify the GC that the object does not need to have its **finalize** method called.

You need to know about some restrictions when you write destructors. First of all, there is no guarantee as to the relative order of destructor calls. You cannot guarantee that member variables are still valid in a destructor. If that type has its own **finalize**, it may already have been called. This means that if your only reason for implementing a destructor is to call **finalize** on a member variable—don't do it; the runtime will call that object's **finalize** method automatically. It may even be called before your **finalize** method, so this can actually cause errors.

Second, the thread that calls the destructors is unspecified. You should not try to access thread storage inside a destructor; it almost certainly will not be the same thread.

Finally, the runtime ignores any exceptions thrown by destructors. Any errors thrown by destructors are silently caught and ignored.

Boxing and Unboxing

The collection classes are designed to work with reference types, not value types. If you put value types in a collection, they will be *boxed* when they are inserted into a collection and *unboxed* when they are accessed from the collection. Simply put, the value type is placed inside a reference type, and it is taken out of the reference type when needed to match the interface of the collection.

Boxing allocates a new object and copies the value of the value type into the box. Unboxing copies the value out of the box into a new value type. Anytime you work with value types in collections, or anywhere else that objects are expected, you will be boxing and unboxing objects. You will always be working with copies of the values in those instances.

Related solution:	Found on page:
Enumerating Collections	340

Weak References

Weak references provide a way for you to recover objects before they have been garbage collected. A *weak reference* points to an object that can be garbage collected. If you don't access the weak reference before a garbage collection occurs, the GC removes it from memory. But, if you try to access the target of the weak reference before a garbage collection happens, the weak reference returns the object. For very large objects, you can get the advantage of reusing an object instead of reallocating a new object. And, the object can be reclaimed if the system needs the extra memory.

Controlling Garbage Collection

The GC is a class in the .NET BCL: **System.GC**. You can use several methods to customize the behavior of the GC for your application. The two methods you will often use are **GC.SuppressFinalization()**, which tells the GC that an object doesn't need to be finalized, and **GC.Collect()**, which forces a garbage collection at a time that is convenient for your application. In most applications, you will be better off just letting the GC do its work.

The other GC methods let you wait for the finalizer thread to finish, query the generation of an object, and perform other advanced operations. I show you how to use those in the next section, but I would recommend against using them without a careful study of your program's runtime characteristics. The GC has already been optimized for most normal situations. You will often cause more harm than good by modifying that behavior.

Immediate Solutions

The GC does its work behind the scenes. It was designed to handle most normal programming situations. The techniques I describe in this chapter are necessary when your classes have some special characteristics that do not fit the mold the GC expects.

Letting the GC Work

This solution does not have any code—this is the point. The GC has been designed so that you do not need to concern yourself with memory management. You should be thinking about how to solve your programming problems, not how to manage memory resources. So, keep this point in mind throughout the rest of this chapter. The remaining immediate solutions are predicated on some special cases that I outline in each section. Most of the time, these special cases don't apply. So, most of the time, simply let the GC do its thing.

Using Disposable Objects

Many objects in the .NET BCL implement the **IDisposable** interface. In practice, determining which objects implement **IDisposable** is pretty easy: They all manage some resource besides memory. For example, classes that work with files, IO streams, Graphics Device Interface (GDI) objects, and threading primitives all implement **IDisposable**.

Related solution:	*Found on page:*
Using Typical Interfaces	196

Anytime you use a disposable object, you should call the **Dispose( )** method when you are done using it. You need to structure your code so that you call the **Dispose( )** method even when exceptions are thrown through your method. I have written a small program that

splits files into smaller parts so that I could copy them between machines when my home network was down. I run the splitter to turn
one large file into many smaller ones. On the other machine, I run a
combiner to put the small files back together into a large file again.
Examine the following method, which performs the splitting. It can
throw exceptions in many different places. Notice that the **Dispose( )**
method calls on the streams are placed in **finally** clauses to ensure
that they are closed no matter that happens:

```
public void Split (int blockSize) {
  FileStream inStream = null;
  FileStream outStream = null;
  try {
    inStream = File.OpenRead (inputFile);
    byte [] block = new byte [blockSize];
    int fileNum = 0;
    while (0 != inStream.Read (block,0,blockSize)) {
      string oName = outputFileBaseName;
      oName += "."+fileNum.ToString ("d5");
      outStream = File.OpenWrite (oName);
      outStream.Write (block, 0,blockSize);
      ++fileNum;
      ((IDisposable)outStream).Dispose ();
      outStream = null;
    }
  } finally {
    if (inStream != null)
      ((IDisposable)inStream).Dispose ();
    if (outStream != null)
      ((IDisposable)outStream).Dispose ();
  }
}
```

You can make this routine somewhat simpler by making use of the
using clause. The preceding method adds a **try** and a **finally** block,
but it does not catch any of the exceptions to fix or report any errors.
When you find that you are adding **try** blocks only to call **Dispose( )**,
you can write the method more clearly making use of the **using**
statement:

```
public void Split (int blockSize) {
  FileStream outStream = null;
  using (FileStream inStream = File.OpenRead (inputFile)) {
    byte [] block = new byte [blockSize];
    int fileNum = 0;
```

```
    while (0 != inStream.Read (block,0,blockSize)) {
      string oName = outputFileBaseName;
      oName += "."+fileNum.ToString ("d5");
      using (outStream = File.OpenWrite (oName)) {
        outStream.Write (block, 0,blockSize);
        ++fileNum;
      }
    }
  }
}
```

Most objects that implement the **IDisposable** interface will implement finalizers. So, you won't introduce errors in your programs by
forgetting to call **Dispose()**. However, you will cause performance
problems by forgetting to use **Dispose()**. This is one of the advantages of the C# language: The system will help you write correct programs. You will need to use the tools effectively to write fast programs
in C#.

Related solution:	Found on page:
Implementing the Weak Guarantee	242

Designing Disposable Objects

There are two cases when you will want to implement the **IDisposable**
interface for your classes:

- When you add **IDisposable** objects as member variables to your
  class
- When your class contains unmanaged objects as member data

Implementing the **IDisposable** Interface

When you add a member field that implements the **IDisposable** interface, you should implement the **IDisposable** interface in your class.
This is the only time when you would implement the **IDisposable**
interface without providing a finalizer in your class. Your **Dispose()**
method will call **Dispose()** on all the disposable objects that are
members of your class. You do not need a finalizer because it happens too late. When your object starts being finalized, the member
data objects are already in the finalization queue. You can just let the
finalization process work. In practice, this means that you will rarely

need to implement finalizers in your classes. You will normally do this only when your class contains some unmanaged data.

Let's demonstrate by making a couple modifications to the file split-ter application. First, move the input file stream to a member vari-able, and open the stream in the constructor:

```
public Splitter(string inFile, string outFile) {
  outputFileBaseName = outFile;
  inStream = File.OpenRead (inFile);
}
```

Now, you need to have the **Splitter** class implement the **IDisposable** interface:

```
public class Splitter : IDisposable {
```

Last, you need to implement the **Dispose( )** method:

```
void IDisposable.Dispose () {
  ((IDisposable)inStream).Dispose ();
  inStream = null; // Reference destroyed. Good Practice.
}
```

All this **Dispose( )** method does is forward the **Dispose( )** call to the **inStream** member variable. After that, I set the **inStream** member variable to null. You should make this a habit whenever you dispose of an object. Using an object that has been disposed is a bad practice, and it almost always results in unpredictable behavior.

Creating Finalizers

As I said previously, creating finalizers is rare. You will only want to create a finalizer if your class uses unmanaged resources as member data. In fact, I could not come up with a good real-world example that required a finalizer. Any unmanaged type I could think of using—file handles, threads, database connections, sockets, or HTTP connec-tions—all had managed objects in the .NET BCL. I didn't want to cre-ate an example that shows a solution that is inefficient and extra work. So, I show you how to create a finalizer using an imaginary class. You can easily modify this example should you find yourself creating a managed object that uses an unmanaged resource.

Let's assume this simple class:

```
class MyClass {
  private HANDLE unmanagedResource = null;
```

```
MyClass () {
  // Call function to acquire the resource.
  UnmanagedResource = AcquireResource ();
}

// Other functions use the resource.
}
```

Clearly, the unmanaged resource will not be freed. You can easily fix this by implementing the **IDisposable** interface:

```
class MyClass : IDisposable{
  private HANDLE unmanagedResource = null;
  MyClass () {
    // Call function to acquire the resource.
    unmanagedResource = AcquireResource ();
  }
  IDisposable.Dispose () {
    if (unmanagedResource != null)
      FreeResource (unmanagedResource);
    unmanagedResource = null;
  }

  // Other functions use the resource.
}
```

Now, the unmanaged resource will get freed if clients remember to use the **Dispose** idiom. But, that just is not good enough. What if your clients forget to call **Dispose()**? You still have the leak. The only way to guarantee that your resource gets freed is to write a finalizer:

```
class MyClass : IDisposable{
  private HANDLE unmanagedResource = null;
  MyClass () {
    // Call function to acquire the resource.
    unmanagedResource = AcquireResource ();
  }

  ~MyClass () {
    if (unmanagedResource != null)
      FreeResource (unmanagedResource);
    unmanagedResource = null;
  }

  IDisposable.Dispose () {
    if (unmanagedResource != null)
```

```
      FreeResource (unmanagedResource);
    unmanagedResource = null;
  }

  // Other functions use the resource.
}
```

The destructor, or finalizer, simply frees the unmanaged resource, just like the **Dispose( )** method does. Your finalizer should not attempt to make use of any member variables in your class that are managed types. Remember that finalizers run in undetermined order. Any managed variable that also needs finalization may already have been finalized—it may already be gone. The bottom line is that you cannot be sure that any managed resource is still available when your finalizer is called. In practice this is not a problem; finalizers are meant for freeing unmanaged resources.

Visual Basic .NET programmers are accustomed to writing a **finalize** method that calls the base class's finalizer. You do not need to do that in C#. In fact, you cannot call the base class's **finalize** method yourself. The C# compiler uses the C++ destructor syntax, and generates similar code for it. The C# compiler generates a finalizer that automatically calls the base class for you.

Optimizing Finalization

The version in the preceding section does work correctly, but it is nonoptimal. Even when clients diligently call the **Dispose( )** method, you pay the cost of having a finalizer: Your objects live longer and take up computation time in the finalization queue.

The GC has a way to avoid this problem. You can tell the GC that an object does not need to be finalized. In your **Dispose( )** method, you can call the **SuppressFinalize( )** method. This marks your object so that it does not need to be finalized anymore. You call **SuppressFinalize( )** in your **Dispose( )** method:

```
class MyClass : IDisposable{
  // Unchanged methods removed...

  IDisposable.Dispose () {
    if (unmanagedResource != null)
      FreeResource (unmanagedResource);
    unmanagedResource = null;
    GC.SuppressFinalize (this);
  }
```

```
    // Other functions use the resource.
}
```

You will not need to write finalizers, or destructors, often. When you do, remember these steps:

- Write your finalizer using the C++ destructor syntax.

- Your finalizer should perform the same steps as your **Dispose( )** method with respect to unmanaged types. Finalizers should not try to clean up managed types.

- Your **Dispose( )** method should call **GC.SuppressFinalize(this)** to indicate that the object no longer needs finalization.

Working with Weak References

Using a weak reference is quite simple. All you have to do is declare a weak reference to the object you are using and set the strong reference to null. That's it.

To demonstrate a use of a weak reference, I wrote a simple little sample that flips images and lets the user undo the flip. Here is the routine that flips the image vertically. Notice the highlighted line. In order to flip the image, I make a copy of the entire image, which can be used to undo the flip:

```
private void FlipV_Click(object sender, System.EventArgs e) {
    // Make a copy of the bitmap.
    Bitmap b = (Bitmap)ViewImage.Image;
    Bitmap copy = new Bitmap (b);
    // Use the copy to update the current image:
    for (int y = 0; y < b.Size.Height; y++) {
        for (int x = 0; x < b.Size.Width; x++) {
            Color c = copy.GetPixel (x,y);
            int newY = b.Size.Height - 1 - y;
            b.SetPixel (x, newY, c);
        }
    }
    Invalidate (true);
}
```

I could simply keep the extra bitmap around forever. However, that would be a wasteful practice. Instead, I can save the copy as a weak reference. Then, I can try to resurrect the weak reference when needed. First, add a member variable to the class to store the weak reference:

```
private WeakReference theCopy = null;
```

Next, modify the flip function to keep track of the copy in a weak reference. The highlighted line in the following code shows how to initialize a weak reference:

```
private void FlipV_Click(object sender, System.EventArgs e) {
  // Make a copy of the bitmap.
  Bitmap b = (Bitmap)ViewImage.Image;
  Bitmap copy = new Bitmap (b);
  // Use the copy to update the current image:
  for (int y = 0; y < b.Size.Height; y++) {
    for (int x = 0; x < b.Size.Width; x++) {
      Color c = copy.GetPixel (x,y);
      int newY = b.Size.Height - 1 - y;
      b.SetPixel (x, newY, c);
    }
  }
  Invalidate (true);
  theCopy = new WeakReference (copy);
}
```

Finally, you can add the undo function:

```
private void menuItem2_Click(object sender,
  System.EventArgs e) {
  // Put back the copy...
  if (theCopy != null){
    Bitmap b = (Bitmap)theCopy.Target;
    if (b != null)
      ViewImage.Image = b;
    Invalidate (true);
  }
}
```

The highlighted line shows how you turn your weak reference back into a strong reference. Every weak reference contains a *target property*. The target property holds the reference to the real object. When the object is collected, the GC sets this target property to null. The target property is a read/write property; you can redirect a weak reference to point to a new object by simply setting this property.

13. Memory Management and Object Lifetimes

Using the GC Methods

The **System.GC** class is the GC. The GC is a sealed class; you cannot derive your own GC from it. All the methods in the GC class are static methods. I have already shown you the method you will use most often: **GC.SuppressFinalization( )**. This method tells the GC that an object no longer needs to be finalized.

Forcing a Garbage Collection

You can force a garbage collection by using the **GC.Collect( )** method. **GC.Collect( )** is overloaded. You can specify the number of generations to collect:

```
GC.Collect (2); // Collect 0-2 generations of garbage.
```

Or, just the most recent garbage:

```
GC.Collect (0); // Collect only the most recent garbage.
```

If you call the **GC.Collect( )** method with no parameters, the GC collects all the garbage from all generations. You can examine the **GC.MaxGeneration** property to see how many generations the GC is using. In most cases, two is the maximum generation.

Checking Available Memory

You can also see how much memory is available using the **GC.GetTotalMemory( )** method. You can also use this method to force a garbage collection. **GC.GetTotalMemory( )** takes a Boolean parameter. If true, the GC collects garbage before reporting on the amount of memory available.

Customizing Garbage Collection

On the very esoteric side, you can query the generation of an object by using the **GC.GetGeneration( )** method. This method returns an integer that tells you how many garbage collections an object has lived through. This is not necessarily the same as the number of garbage collections that have occurred since the object was created. Remember that once a garbage collection has happened, a 0th-generation object becomes a first-generation object. It will not become a second-generation object until the GC needs to perform a garbage collection on first-generation objects.

Forcing Deterministic Finalization

You can force the finalization of an object with the following code:

```
GC.Collect ();
GC.WaitForPendingFinalizers ();
```

After these two method calls, all garbage has been cleaned up, and the finalizers have been called. But, this is not an efficient piece of code. It will clean up all the garbage and run all the finalizers.

In general, you can call the **WaitForPendingFinalizers( )** method to suspend the execution of your application until all the finalizers in the finalization queue have been called. Your application stops until this process is complete.

Resurrecting Objects

Let me start by saying that this is an advanced topic that you will rarely need. You can write a class so that is supports resurrection. *Resurrection* is the process of re-creating an object after it has been disposed.

Resurrection happens because of finalization. When the GC runs, it finds all "dead" objects. Dead objects that require finalization are placed in the finalizer queue. In a sense, these dead objects are now "live." These objects will have their finalizers called. Well, finalizers are code. Anything can happen. Someone could have written a finalizer to create a live reference to the object again:

```
class MyClass {
  ~MyClass () {
    // I'm not dead:
    Application.obj = this;
    GC.ReRegisterForFinalize (this);
  }
  // Other details omitted.
}
```

The **MyClass** object is now alive, even if not well. It has been resurrected. Notice the call to **ReRegisterForFinalize( )**. You must add this code, if you resurrect an object in a finalizer. Otherwise, the GC will not call the finalizer the next time your object dies.

You can create weak references that track this resurrection property. When you create a weak reference, you can tell it to track resurrection:

```
theCopy = new WeakReference (copy, true);
```

Normally, the target property on a weak reference returns null if the object is in the finalization queue. A weak reference that tracks resurrection does not return null until the object has been finalized. So, using this form of a weak reference, you can retrieve objects that are in the finalization queue.

In practice, this is a dangerous strategy that is effective only in some special situations. Any managed objects that are part of your resurrected object are probably already garbage collected. You will need to add quite a bit of exception-handling code in order to ensure that you can safely resurrect an object, and all the objects it references. You can figure out if the target of a weak reference is alive or in the finalization queue by using the **IsAlive( )** method on the weak reference. If the object is in the finalization queue, any of the objects it references may be gone.

Related solutions:	Found on page:
Catching Exceptions	232
Throwing Exceptions	234

So, any techniques that involve resurrecting objects are very tricky. A lot can go wrong when you start bringing objects back from the dead. You should investigate these techniques only after profiling your application and determining that doing all this extra work would enhance its performance.

Monitoring the GC

The CLR provides a number of performance counters that let you see what the GC is doing while your application is running. To see the GC performance statistics, open the performance monitor under Start|Programs|Administrative Tools. Select the + sign on the toolbar. You will see the dialog box shown in Figure 13.2. Select the .NET CLR Memory object. You can use more than twenty different performance

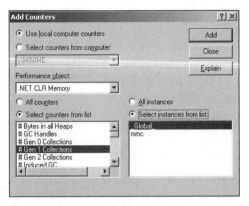

Figure 13.2 You can add performance counters to see how the GC works with your application.

counters. Click on Explain to find out more about each counter's purpose. The ones I use most often are % Time In GC, # Gen 0 Collections, # Gen 1 Collections, and # Gen 2 Collections. From these four statistics, you can get a picture of your application's garbage collection behavior.

Related solution:	*Found on page:*
Creating Performance Counters	419

The .NET designers did not want to build a system that took power away from programmers; they wanted only to make it easier to build applications by building a framework that could do more work for you. The .NET GC exemplifies this goal. Do nothing, and you will get good performance in most cases. However, when your application does atypical things with memory or other resources, you can use the more advanced features in the GC to modify the system behavior. Using those more advanced features requires understanding and quite a bit of research into the performance characteristics of your application.

13. Memory Management and Object Lifetimes

Chapter 14

Unmanaged Programming and Interoperability

In Brief

Even though C# programs run in a managed environment, the C# designers wanted to ensure that you could write code that bypassed the normal managed environment. They envisioned two scenarios. The first is simple performance: In some cases, unmanaged code executes much faster than managed code. The second is native DLL support: C# programs can call native Windows methods through the unmanaged API. This chapter helps you understand when and how to use the unmanaged features in C#.

Defining Unmanaged Programming

Unmanaged programming means accessing memory resources while bypassing the managed runtime. As a result, you give up the convenience of working with the managed runtime. Unmanaged code can overwrite memory or easily crash the system. Because of these dangers, unmanaged code can only be executed in a trusted environment. You must register your code to be able to use unmanaged code.

With these dangers and limitations in mind, you should quickly realize that unmanaged code should not be your first choice for solving a programming problem. You limit the client types your code can be used by when you use unmanaged code, and you increase the chance of the very kinds of errors that the CLR and C# are designed to avoid. Unless you need the special services provided by unmanaged programming to interact with legacy systems or because of special performance needs, you should avoid unmanaged programming. Just like the garbage collector, there is very little syntax involved in unsafe programming. However, you need to understand quite a few concepts to make effective use of unsafe programming.

Unsafe Code Blocks

You can mark code as unsafe, and inside the unsafe code block you can use pointers to access raw memory. The **unsafe** keyword marks a routine or a block of code as unsafe, or not managed by the managed runtime. You can use pointers and other unsafe elements inside unsafe code blocks. You must add the **/unsafe** compiler option to compile code that contains unsafe code blocks.

Marking an unsafe code block notifies the C# compiler that you intend to use pointers or pointer arithmetic inside that block. Trying to use pointers outside of an unsafe code block will generate compiler errors.

Pinned Objects

The garbage collector moves objects when a garbage collection occurs. The .NET runtime updates all references to live objects when a garbage collection moves an object. This will cause unpredictable behavior at best, or some kind of system crash. The **fixed** keyword lets you *pin* an object so that it does not move if a garbage collection happens while you are using unsafe code to read or write an object. The **fix** keyword marks both an object and a block of code. The garbage collector cannot move the fixed object while the block is executing.

Pinning or fixing an object is necessary whenever you are using pointers to the memory occupied by that object. However, fixing an object in one location in memory does have some performance ramifications. The garbage collector cannot compact memory as well when pinned objects are in the way. For this reason, you should strive to fix objects for the shortest period of time that you possibly can. The longer an object is fixed, the more likely the fixed operation will interfere with a garbage collection, and the more likely performance will suffer.

Native Methods

.NET is a totally new environment. Any existing code investment that your organization has is in some other unmanaged language. The .NET design team knew that few organizations could afford to completely discard their current technology investment. Even if they could afford the cost, it would not be effective to completely rewrite an existing program. Knowing these real-world constraints, the .NET team devised ways to convert large projects to .NET over time and leverage existing code while the conversion process takes place.

C# uses attributes to describe the unmanaged method. You need only add the proper attributes on the method declaration, and then you can use the method as though it were a managed method. Visual Studio .NET has tools you can use to import COM objects as well.

DLL Methods

You can call native functions in DLLs using attributes to specify the DLL that contains the function and a prototype for the function. The **DllImport** attribute specifies that a function can be found in a specific DLL. The attribute has one mandatory parameter. You must specify the DLL that contains the method you want to use:

```
[DllImport ("user32.dll")]
public static extern int MessageBoxA(int hWnd, string msg,
  string caption, int mbType);
```

The **DllImport** attribute has several other named parameters you will use to customize the way in which the managed runtime interacts with the unmanaged method:

- The **CallingConvention** parameter lets you specify a different calling convention for the methods in the DLL. The default is **StdCall**, which works for all Win32 methods.

- The **CharSet** parameter lets you specify the character set for string parameters to the method. You can use this parameter to specify ANSI or Unicode strings.

- The **EntryPoint** parameter lets you specify the name or ordinal for the method you are calling. In the preceding example, you could use it to change the name of the **MessageBoxA** function to the more familiar **MessageBox**.

- The **ExactSpelling** parameter lets you specify whether the name of the entry point should match the **CharSet** parameter setting.

- The **PreserveSig** handles how return values are specified. The default for this attribute is true. However, if you have a method that returns an **HRESULT**, you will want to set it to false.

- The **SetLastError** parameter tells the managed runtime whether or not this method will set the last error, and clients can call the Win32 method **GetLastError** to determine the cause of failures.

Thankfully, most of the times the default values for all the parameters work fine. You will often use the **EntryPoint** parameter for methods that have ANSI and Unicode variants. This parameter lets you get the function you want using the more familiar function names. I've rarely found the need to use any other parameters of this attribute.

The **In** and **Out** attributes mark a parameter as an in or out only parameter. Using these attributes lets the runtime optimize away unnecessary copies of these parameters. If not explicitly supplied, the runtime assumes that any reference parameter is an in/out parameter, and value types not passed by reference are in parameters.

Related solution:	Found on page:
Creating Your Own Attributes	219

COM Objects

COM objects take more work than simply calling functions in DLLs. COM objects have their own built-in lifetime support. The lifetime model for COM objects is different than the model used by the .NET runtime. Visual Studio .NET has a tool that creates a proxy .NET assembly to bridge the two worlds. To use a COM object, you need to create this proxy DLL from a type library or a registered COM object. Once you have done that, you can use the COM object just like any .NET assembly. The proxy DLL takes care of all the hard work to perform all the **QueryInterface( )** and **Release( )** calls. The proxy also translates any COM errors into **ComException** objects.

Related solution:	Found on page:
Catching Exceptions	232

You can also use late binding to access COM objects if your COM objects support only the **IDispatch** interface. Using the late binding is a bit more work, and it requires more error checking. In order to use the methods in the interface, you need to use the reflection methods in the **System.Type** class to create the object. Then, you need to use the **System.Type.InvokeMember** function to call the COM method you want. It is not an easy task, but it is possible. Also, calling COM objects from managed programs using late binding has some performance ramifications as well.

Importing and using COM objects is easy for you as a programmer. However, a lot of work is going on inside the generated proxy. Using COM objects in a .NET program also complicates the deployment of your project; you need to deploy the COM object and the COM interface proxy assembly. You should use this COM interoperability only as a way to use COM objects while you convert them to .NET assemblies. Look at the .NET BCL, and you will find that much of the functionality that was formerly available as COM objects is not also available through .NET assemblies.

When to Choose Unsafe Programming

The .NET runtime interacts with existing programming components so that your organization can easily adopt .NET without being forced into a complete rewrite of all its existing functionality. The following section offers some tips for using unsafe programming.

Raw Memory Access

Raw memory access can greatly increase the performance of your application. The downside of raw memory access is that you give up many of the benefits of managed programming. You can overrun memory or write to the wrong location. Also, using raw memory can interfere with the garbage collector. Here are some tips:

- Use raw memory access only after profiling your application to see where the bottlenecks are.

- Limit the length of time you keep memory pinned to avoid interfering with the garbage collector.

- Make sure you don't keep unfixed pointers to raw memory.

Related solution:	Found on page:
Using the Performance Monitor	422

DLL and COM Interoperability

The interoperability mechanisms are meant to bridge the gap between old and new code models. These are best used as a strategy to use existing technology in new C# programs. You can begin creating new C# applications and services by importing existing DLLs and COM objects. Then, over time you can choose to replace this legacy technology with new .NET assemblies. You can choose among other strategies to import existing technology into .NET. Managed C++ is the more useful. You should choose the interoperability strategies discussed here when you are importing COM objects or DLLs that are not class libraries. Managed C++ will be a better strategy for importing class libraries originally written with C++. Consult the .NET documentation for more details.

Immediate Solutions

Remember that there are only a few justifications for using unsafe code in your .NET programs. The sample solutions in this section show you when to use unsafe code as well as how to use it.

Using Unsafe Code

Here is the sample code from last chapter that flipped a bitmap vertically:

```
private void FlipH_Click(object sender, System.EventArgs e) {
  // Make a copy of the bitmap.
  Bitmap b = (Bitmap)ViewImage.Image;
  Bitmap copy = new Bitmap (b);
  // Use the copy to update the current image:
  for (int y = 0; y < b.Size.Height;y++) {
    for (int x = 0; x < b.Size.Width; x++) {
      Color c = copy.GetPixel (x,y);
      int newX = b.Size.Width - 1 - x;
      b.SetPixel (newX, y, c);
    }
  }
  Invalidate (true);
  theCopy = new WeakReference (copy);
}
```

This is actually quite slow. Every call to **GetPixel** and every call to **SetPixel** is bounds-checked. In addition, these methods need to calculate the memory location from the beginning of the image surface. Knowing that you are going to sequentially access every pixel in the image, you can speed it up considerably by using unsafe code and copying the pixels using pointers:

```
using System.Drawing.Imaging;
private void FlipH_Click(object sender, System.EventArgs e) {
  // Make a copy of the bitmap.
  Bitmap b = (Bitmap)ViewImage.Image;
  Bitmap copy = new Bitmap (b);
```

```
Rectangle r = new Rectangle(0,0,b.Width,b.Height);
BitmapData srcImageData = copy.LockBits
  (r,ImageLockMode.ReadOnly, PixelFormat.Format32bppArgb);
BitmapData destImageData = b.LockBits
  (r,ImageLockMode.WriteOnly, PixelFormat.Format32bppArgb);
// Use the copy to update the current image:
unsafe {
  int* pSrc = (int*)srcImageData.Scan0;
  int* pDest = (int*)destImageData.Scan0+destImageData.Width;
  for (int y = 0; y < b.Size.Height;y++) {
    for (int x = 0; x < b.Size.Width; x++) {
      pDest--;
      *pDest = *pSrc;
      pSrc++;
    }
    pDest += 2*destImageData.Width;
  }
}
copy.UnlockBits(srcImageData);
b.UnlockBits(destImageData);
Invalidate (true);
theCopy = new WeakReference (copy);
}
```

This version of the routine uses pointers to copy the pixels from one bitmap to the next. The **LockBits( )** method locks the bitmap in memory and lets you modify the individual bits of the bitmap surface. The **unsafe** keyword creates a block where you can use unsafe code. Inside that block, the pointers are initialized to the start and end of the first scan line in the image. The outer loop handles moving down through the scan lines. The inner loop moves across each scan line in the image. The pointer arithmetic is much faster than repeatedly calling **GetPixel( )** and **SetPixel( )** to find and use a single pixel value.

In order to get this code to compile, you need to add the **/unsafe** compiler option to your build. In Visual Studio .NET, right-click on the project name in the Solution Explorer window and select Properties. Select the Configuration Properties and Build Properties from the listbox on the left. Select True for the Allow Unsafe Code Blocks option as shown in Figure 14.1. Now you can build this project with unsafe code blocks active.

I wanted to show this sample because if you work with bitmaps, you will want to learn to use unsafe code with them. Manipulating image data using unsafe code blocks and pointers is much faster than using managed APIs to manipulate images. Bitmaps are a good real-world

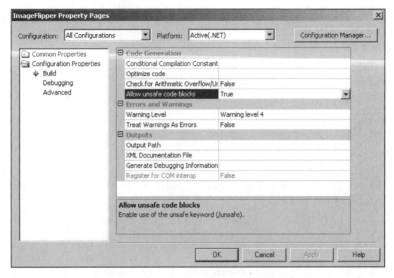

Figure 14.1   Allowing unsafe blocks. You need to allow unsafe code blocks before you can work with unsafe code.

example of the kinds of programming tasks that get the biggest gains from using unsafe code. Bitmaps are large contiguous blocks of memory that represent the pixels of the image. This contiguous block of memory is a matrix of pixels. You can get the address of any adjacent pixel using very simple pointer arithmetic. You will add or subtract one from the pointer to get the adjacent pixel in the same row. You will add or subtract the width of the image to get the adjacent pixel in the previous or next row. Most algorithms that modify or examine images are built around the locality of reference in the image data. You will almost always modify a block of pixels around a single location. You will get the most performance gains using pointers and fixed memory blocks when you are working with large blocks of memory that represent some sequence of objects.

Using Raw Fixed Memory

The example in the preceding section shows a good real-world scenario for using unsafe programming. The .NET team even felt this was common enough that it fixed and unfixed the bitmap in memory for you. When you are working with your own structures, you will need to fix the memory yourself. This simple program generates the first 30 numbers in the Fibonacci sequence (each number in the Fibonacci sequence is generated by adding the previous two numbers together):

```
static void Main(string[] args) {
  int [] numbers = new int [30];
  numbers[0]=numbers[1] = 1;
  unsafe {
    fixed (int* pArray = &(numbers[0])) {
      int* pOldest = pArray;
      int* pLast = pOldest + 1;
      int* pCurrent = pOldest+2;
      for (int index = 2;index < 30; index++) {
        *pCurrent++ = *pLast++ + *pOldest++;
      }
    }
  }

  for (int i=0; i < 30; i++)
    System.Console.WriteLine (numbers[i]);
}
```

This code creates an array of integers and initializes the first two values to 1. Then, it uses an unsafe block to initialize all the remaining numbers. The **fixed** statement initializes a pointer to the numbers object and pins the numbers array in memory.

Inside the **fixed** block, the code uses three pointers to retrieve the values of the previous two numbers and set the current number in the sequence. The advantage of unsafe code here is that you are walking through a reasonably large array in a sequential fashion. Using pointers lets you access the next value much more quickly than calculating it from the beginning of the array each time.

Some of the constructs here are new to C++ programmers and are necessary for unsafe code in C#. The **pArray** pointer cannot be modified. I need to use a different pointer variable to increment and walk through the array. C# does not allow modification of a pinned pointer; you need to assign a different pointer variable to the pinned address in order to manipulate the pointer. Also, you need to ensure that the **fixed** block encompasses all the code that accesses the memory locations; the compiler cannot force it. The following would compile:

```
unsafe {
  int* pOldest;
```

```
fixed (int* pArray = (int*)&(numbers[0])) {
  pOldest = pArray;
}
// The array is no longer fixed. Any of these
// statements could crash, if a GC takes place.
int* pLast = pOldest + 1;
int* pCurrent = pOldest+2;
for (int index = 2;index < 30; index++) {
  *pCurrent++ = *pLast++ + *pOldest++;
}
}
```

Here, the **fixed** block extends only around the assignment to **pOldest**. After that, the **pArray** variable goes out of scope, and the **fixed** block ends. However, **pOldest**, **pLast**, and **pCurrent** are still accessing the array in an unsafe mode. If a garbage collection takes place, the array can move, but the pointers are still pointing to the wrong place. The compiler cannot help you here; you need to make sure that your **fixed** block encompasses all access to a block of memory, not just the fixed pointer. You also need to try to find these bugs by using inspection; they will not cause problems every time. They will only cause bad behavior when a garbage collection happens at the wrong time, and the memory you are accessing moves.

Calling Native Methods

The first step to calling a native method is to declare it and tell the runtime where the method can be found:

```
[DllImport ("user32.dll", EntryPoint="MessageBoxA")]
static extern public int MessageBox (int hWnd, string message,
  string caption, int type);
```

This declaration tells the compiler about the Win32 **MessageBoxA** function. The **MessageBoxA** function is in user32.dll. The optional **EntryPoint** parameter identifies the function as **MessageBoxA**, rather than the default **MessageBox**. Immediately following the attribute is the declaration of the function. You must place the declaration of the external function inside a class. The external function then appears to be a member of that class. As with other DllImport examples, you can use access modifiers on an external method declaration. Any external method must be a static method; you cannot specify an external DLL method as an instance method. After you declare the method, you can call it just like any regular .NET method:

```
MessageBox (0, "Testing Native Methods", "Test", 0);
```

The entire class shows a very simple test of using native methods in your .NET assemblies. Although the example shows a method from the standard Win32 API, you will more likely use this technique to interact with your own DLLs. Most or all of the Win32 functions are now available as .NET BCL functions. Showing this functionality by using a Win32 function is just much simpler. Here is the entire class:

```
using System.Runtime.InteropServices;
class Class1
{
  [DllImport ("user32.dll", EntryPoint="MessageBoxA")]
  static extern public int MessageBox (int hWnd, string message,
    string caption, int type);

  static void Main(string[] args) {
    MessageBox (0, "Testing Native Methods", "Test", 0);
  }
}
```

The MSIL generated for this class shows how native methods inter-act with .NET assemblies (see Figure 14.2). When you load the Disassembler, you can see that the **MessageBox( )** method has been added to the class.

The **MessageBox( )** method generates the following MSIL code. This code shows the prototype and the external declaration for the **MessageBoxA** function:

```
.method public hidebysig static pinvokeimpl("user32.dll" as
  "MessageBoxA" winapi)
  int32  MessageBox(int32 hWnd,
    string message,
    string caption,
    int32 type) cil managed preservesig
{
}
```

The proxy gets added to the assembly metadata so that the imported method appears as a regular method to any .NET code.

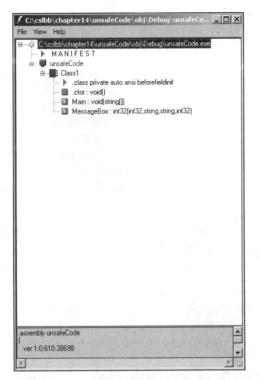

Figure 14.2 MSIL for **Class1**, containing the external method.

You can just as easily make use of the Unicode (or wide character) version of the **MessageBox** function:

```
[DllImport ("user32.dll", EntryPoint="MessageBoxW",
  CharSet=CharSet.Unicode)]
static extern public int MessageBox (int hWnd, string message,
  string caption, int type);
```

The **EntryPoint** parameter has changed to point to **MessageBoxW**, and the **CharSet** parameter now specifies Unicode, instead of the default value of **Auto**. You would perform other customization to the DLL entry point declaration using the other parameters on the **DllImport** attribute.

Using native DLL entry points might seem pretty easy, but you are giving up some of the benefits of running in the .NET-managed environment. There is no compile time checking of the method. You must ensure that you get the method name, its parameters, calling conventions, and character set correct. Any mistakes will generate errors at runtime; the compiler will not catch them. The compiler does not even check for the existence of the DLL you import.

Interacting with COM Objects

I wrote a simple COM object to show you how to use COM objects in your .NET programs. My simple COM object returns a random quote from Yogi Berra (there are so many to choose from). To use the object, make a Windows Forms C# application using Visual Studio .NET. Once you have made the project, right-click on the References tree item in the Solution Explorer and choose the Add Reference command. You get the dialog box shown in Figure 14.3, after you select the COM tab. You select the COM object you want to add. In this case, I picked the **BerraQuotes** type library. Visual Studio .NET will add a wrapper library for you.

Visual Studio .NET creates the wrapper by running the TLBIMP utility. This utility generates a .NET assembly that interoperates with the COM utility (see Figure 14.4). The DLL contains the proxy to work with the COM object.

After you have created the interoperability assembly, you can use the COM object just as you would any normal .NET class. This sample has a button that gets a Yogi quote. Here is the code to get a quote:

```
private void Get_Click(object sender, System.EventArgs e) {
  BerraQuotes.CBerraIsms b = new BerraQuotes.CBerraIsms ();
  Quotes.Text=b.GetQuotes ();
}
```

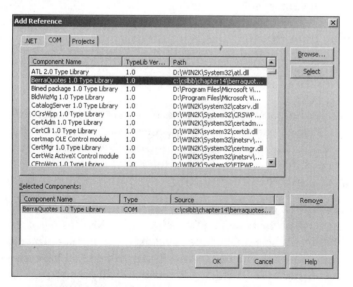

Figure 14.3 Adding COM references to a C# Visual Studio .NET project.

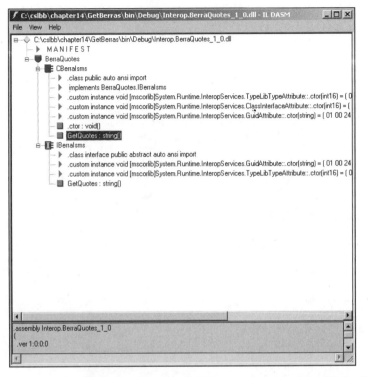

Figure 14.4   MSIL for the interoperability assembly to work with the Berra-Quotes COM object.

The first line of the function creates a new COM object. The interoperability DLL handles all the COM plumbing: **CreateInstance( )**, **QueryInterface( )**, and **Release( )**. The second line invokes the **GetQuotes( )** method on the COM object. That's all there is to it.

My **BerraIsms** object implements just one interface. To work with COM objects that implement multiple interfaces, you simply need to create an interface by casting the object. If the interface does not exist, the cast operation throws an exception.

Multithreaded C# Programming

In Brief

Multithreaded programs have become more common recently to address many other changes in computing. More processing power is available, and programs are often distributed, using a client/server model. The .NET BCL and C# have features that make creating correct multithreaded programs easier. Before going over the techniques provided to work with multithreaded programs, I want to go over some guidelines on when to create multiple threads and when to avoid multithreaded programs.

Multiple threads do not make your program faster. In fact, using multiple threads will add some overhead and will make your program run slightly slower. However, none of the tasks will appear to be completely blocked while waiting for another task to complete. That is the simplest way to express the reason to consider multithreading: You want to give the impression of multiple operations happening simultaneously. Here are some examples of when you want to consider multithreaded applications:

- *Simplified design*—You are writing a server program, and it will service multiple clients simultaneously. In this case, having one thread per client can be advantageous.

- *Performing concurrent tasks*—Your application will need to perform multiple subtasks to complete a user request. Sometimes these multiple tasks can be performed more effectively using threads. Most often, this is when one of the subtasks involves a high-latency communication: database access, external storage access, or communication with an external server.

- *Background processing*—Your application has opportunities for idle time processing. Visual Studio .NET and Microsoft Word both use this strategy. Word uses a background thread to perform spell checking on the current document. Visual Studio .NET parses your code as you type to indicate potential compiler errors. You can create worker threads to perform some processing while your main thread responds to user input.

Creating correct multithreaded programs can be tricky. The more often different threads need to communicate or access shared data, the more complicated working with multiple threads can be. Unless your application exhibits the behaviors from the preceding list or has similar characteristics where you want the appearance of multiple tasks occurring at the same time, you should avoid using multiple threads. Having stated these cautions, let's start learning how to work with threads in .NET using C#.

Related solution:	Found on page:
Adding Performance Conditionals	418

The .NET BCL has a number of classes and structures that support multithreaded programming. The **System.Threading** namespace contains all the classes and structures that you will use to create and work with threads in your application.

Thread Basics

A thread is an object of the **System.Threading.Thread** class. To spawn extra threads in your application, you create an object of the **Thread** class. Once created, you control it by invoking methods on the **Thread** class.

In most cases, you will follow these steps to create and use a new thread in a multithreaded program:

1. Create a new thread by using the **Thread** constructor.
2. Start the thread by invoking the **Thread** class's **Start( )** method.
3. Check to see if the thread is still working.

These three steps are for the simplest case. In many real-world situations, more work is involved. When you create a thread to do some work for you, you will eventually want some notification that the thread finished. Also, somehow, the work that the thread has done will probably change some data structure in your program. You will need to protect the access to those shared data structures from concurrent access.

Completely covering multithreaded programs and all the issues would fill entire books. This chapter tells you about the multithreaded programming support in C# and .NET. If you are already familiar with multithreaded programming techniques, you will be well prepared to use all the multithreaded techniques in C#. If not, this chapter gives you some overview of multithreaded programming with C#. You can examine other sources for more background on multithreaded programming in general.

Creating Threads

Creating a new thread in .NET is easy using C#. You simply create an instance of the **System.Threading.Thread** class. The **Thread** constructor takes a delegate as a parameter. The *delegate* specifies the function the thread should use as its entry point. You need to follow two steps to create a thread. First, you need to create a **ThreadStart** delegate by using a static function in one of your classes. This static method will be the entry point of the thread when you start it. Then, you construct a new thread object using the **ThreadStart** delegate you just created. The new thread is not an object. The thread is not running, it is suspended. That means that the thread is ready to go, but it will not execute until you are ready to start it.

Related solution:	Found on page:
Using Properties for Delegates	147

Starting and Stopping Threads

After you create a thread, you need to start it using the **Thread.Start( )** method. Thread execution begins in the method you specified as the **ThreadStart** delegate, which was discussed in the preceding section. The thread will run until the **ThreadStart** delegate exits. You can think of the **ThreadStart** delegate method as the **Main** method for a thread. After the **ThreadStart** delegate has finished, the thread is dead.

You can control the execution of your subordinate threads by using three different methods. You can stop a thread for a specified amount of time using the **Thread.Sleep( )** method. You can stop and start threads by using the **Suspend( )** and **Resume( )** methods.

Sleep( ) will always stop the current thread. **Suspend( )** will suspend any thread. Also, a thread that is suspended with **Sleep( )** will be resumed by the operating system once it has slept the specified time. A thread that has been suspended with **Suspend( )** can be restarted only with a call to **Resume( )**.

Waiting for Threads

When you start a thread, you will want to know when it has finished its work. You can find out when a thread has finished in two different ways. One is the **Join( )** method in the thread class. The thread that calls **Join( )** will suspend until the target thread dies. **Join( )** is overloaded so that you wait for a period of time and then resume other activities before checking again.

You can also use the **IsAlive( )** method. This returns a Boolean value that tells you whether or not the thread is still alive.

Thread Priority

Multiple threads are scheduled in a round-robin fashion. Basically, each thread gets the same amount of time. You can modify this strategy by raising or lowering a thread's priority. You can change the thread priority at any time after the thread has been created, up until it has finished all its processing.

Changing a thread's priority is a very advanced technique that you should use with caution. This changes the thread scheduling algorithm used by the system. As such, you can easily *starve* a thread so that it does not get any processing time. Starving a thread will mean that it does not get any processing time; the thread will not complete its work.

Killing Threads

You can kill a thread by using the **Thread.Abort( )** method to unconditionally kill it. Calling **Abort( )** raises a **ThreadAbortException** in the target thread. The **Abort( )** call does not block; the calling thread continues execution after the exception is raised.

You cannot catch a **ThreadAbortException**. However, the runtime will execute all **finally** blocks in the target thread before the target thread is completely killed. Because of the **finally** blocks, the target thread may not stop immediately. Any amount of code may need to be executed inside the **finally** blocks. You need to check the thread's status with **IsAlive( )** or call **Join( )** to wait for it to be killed, thereby ensuring that it is gone.

Synchronization

Most of the time that you work with threads, the different threads will somehow be working with the same data. Even simple statements can cause problems. Consider this statement:

```
num = num + 5;
```

The code for this will perform the following steps:

1. Read the value of **num** and store it in a register.
2. Add 5 to the value in the register.
3. Store the new value in the memory location for **num**.

A thread switch can happen between any of these steps. Suppose that a thread switch happens between Steps 1 and 2. Now, the other thread modifies the value of **num**. Then, the system performs another thread switch. Now, 5 is added to the *old* value of **num**. This modified value is stored back in memory. Any changes made by the other thread are lost.

To avoid these kinds of problems, you need to ensure that any code that modifies shared data is *synchronized*. Simply put, you are marking blocks of code so that the system cannot switch threads while shared data is being accessed and modified. Synchronization is one of the most important design issues you will face when creating multithreaded programs. On one hand, you need to make sure that shared data access is synchronized to protect data integrity. On the other hand, the more your code is synchronized, the more your threads execute serially, or one after the other. The more you prevent the system from switching thread contexts, the less benefit you gain from working with multiple threads. Also, a number of classic thread designs discuss deadlock problems. *Deadlock* occurs when two different threads each need a resource owned by the other thread in order to relinquish the shared resource they have. Neither of the two threads will do any work. They are both waiting for the other thread to release a resource.

The dining philosophers shows a classic example of deadlock. Imagine eight philosophers sitting at a round table for a Chinese dinner (see Figure 15.1). The table is set with chopsticks for the dinner. However, instead of a pair of chopsticks for each philosopher, there is one chopstick to the right of each philosopher. During the dinner, each philosopher is thinking, waiting to eat, or eating. When a philosopher decides to eat, he tries to pick up the chopsticks on both sides and starts to eat. If he cannot get both chopsticks, he waits for them. Philosophers are a stubborn bunch, so once a philosopher picks up a chopstick, he does not put it down until he gets to eat.

If each philosopher always grabs with both hands for the chopsticks, there is no problem. But, if each philosopher reaches for the chopstick on his right, you have a deadlock problem. None of the philosophers will relinquish a chopstick, but none of them can get two

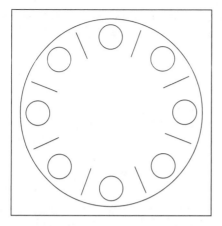

Figure 15.1   The dining philosophers table, with eight settings and a total of eight chopsticks.

chopsticks with which to eat. The only way to avoid deadlock is to structure your code so that a thread gets all or none of the resources it needs to complete a task.

lock and Monitor

The simplest way to serialize access to a shared resource is to use the C# **lock** statement. The **lock** statement implements a critical section. While an object or a class is locked, no other thread can lock the same object. You will typically lock an object as follows:

```
lock (this) {
  // critical code.
}
```

Or, you will lock a class as follows:

```
lock (typeof (MyClass)) {
  // critical code.
}
```

You will lock an object in instance methods and lock a class in static methods. The **lock** statement acquires a lock on the object. If the object cannot be locked, the statement blocks until the lock can be acquired.

Internally, the **lock** statement uses the **System.Threading.Monitor** class. The **System.Threading.Monitor** class has more features than the **lock** statement; the **lock** statement encapsulates the simplest use of the **Monitor** class. Using the **Monitor** class, you can attempt to obtain a lock with a nonblocking call: **Montitor.TryEnter( )**.

Mutex Class

The other method you have to synchronize access to shared data is the **System.Threading.Mutex** class. A mutex has more features than the monitor, and as a result it is slower. The extra power comes from being able to create named mutexes. Named mutexes let you control the synchronized sections of code at a more granular level. Rather than locking an entire class or object, you can create a named mutex for a single method or for all the blocks of code that access one member variable. You can also use mutexes to protect code that crosses different classes or objects.

Thread Safety in .NET Classes

The .NET BCL classes are not thread safe. They should not be made thread safe. You do not want to pay the cost of thread safety in a single-threaded program. You can easily wrap your access to the base class objects in your own classes and add the thread safety primitives in your classes. Making the base classes thread safe would be too much of a burden on the entire class library. Most programs would suffer too much of a performance hit as a result.

Multithreaded Design Guidelines

To get the most from multithreaded applications, you need to design your system so that you can maximize the independent work that each thread can do. The more often different threads interact, the more complicated your design is and the more difficult it will be to get it correct. You want to minimize the amount of communication between threads. Often, if you create a design where different threads need extensive communication, that is indicative of a design flaw. You will not get any improvements if your threads cannot work independently.

Second, you want to minimize the time spent in synchronized code blocks. The more time you spend in synchronized blocks, the more your multithreaded program will resemble a single-threaded application.

Immediate Solutions

Real-world multithreaded programs are often large, complicated programs. Multithreaded programs are difficult enough to understand without trying to understand complicated algorithms as well. So instead, I am going to build a simple application that calculates pi.

You can calculate pi using a Leibnitz series. Pi is $4 * (1 - 1/3 + 1/5 - 1/7 + ...)$. If you carry out the infinite series, it eventually approaches pi. You need to get to the terms $... + 1/10,000,001 - 1 / 10,000,003$ before it gets close. Here is a simple class that calculates pi:

```
public class CalcPi
{
  private double _pi;

  private readonly int iters;

  public CalcPi(int it)
  {
    iters = it;
    // Pi = 1 - 1/3 + 1/5 - 1/7 etc.
    double series = 0;
    double i = 1;
    do {
      series += 1.0/i - 1.0/(i+2);
      i += 4;
    } while (i < iters);
    _pi = series * 4;
  }

  public double pi {
    get {
      return _pi;
    }
  }
}
```

To use the class, you simply create an object and query the property:

```
CalcPi p = new CalcPi (10000000);
double pi = p.pi;
```

15. Multithreaded C# Programming

This class is usable, but it has a big drawback: You will wait in the constructor while it calculates pi. (The math wizards among you will note that there are better ways to calculate pi. The programmer in me wants to tell you that a constant named **Math.PI** saves you from all this work. But, the point of this example is to learn about threads, so this works just fine.) Through the course of these examples, you will see how to move these calculations into their own thread and display a dialog that keeps updating itself to show how the calculations are progressing.

Passing Data to a New Thread

The first step to make the **CalcPi** class multithreaded is to separate the calculations from the creation of the object. When you want to make a class that runs in a different thread, it will have these general entry points:

- A constructor that sets parameters for the work to be performed in the subordinate thread

- An optional set of properties to set any additional parameters for the work to be performed in the subordinate thread

- An entry point to create the thread start delegate, or create the thread

- A set of properties to retrieve the results of the thread's work

The **CalcPi** class needs one other change: The work done by the constructor needs to move into a different function so that it can be performed in another thread:

```
public class CalcPi
{
  private double _pi = 0.0;
  private readonly int TotalIters;

  public CalcPi(int it)
  {
    TotalIters= it;
  }

  public double pi {
    get {
      return _pi;
```

```
      }
  }

  private void calculate () {
    // Pi = 1 - 1/3 + 1/5 - 1/7 etc.
    double series = 0;
    double i = 1;
    do {
      series += 1.0/i - 1.0/(i+2);
      i += 4;
    } while (i < TotalIters);
    _pi = series * 4;
  }
}
```

There are three highlighted changes so far. The function **calculate( )**
performs the actual calculations. Moving the calculations out of the
constructor necessitates creating a new member variable to hold the
number of iterations.

These changes also satisfy the first two bullet points in the list. The
parameters needed to perform the calculations are set in the constructor. The **CalcPi** class does not need extra parameters, so the
constructor is sufficient to set all the parameters needed.

Creating Threads

Now, we need to write the thread starter delegate. The thread start
delegate has no return value and takes no parameters. The **CalcPi**
thread start function will calculate the value of pi:

```
private void ThreadStarter () {
  calculate ();
}
```

Next, you need to add a public function to return a new thread object
using this delegate:

```
public Thread MakeThread () {
  return new Thread (new ThreadStart (this.ThreadStarter));
}
```

Now, the **CalcPi** class can perform all its work in a multithreaded
environment.

Running a Thread

To use this version of **CalcPi**, you need to construct a **CalcPi** object, create the thread, and start it:

```
CalcPi pi = new CalcPi (10000000);
Thread t = pi.MakeThread ();
t.Start ();
```

Returning Data from a Thread

Returning data from a thread is as simple as accessing the property after the thread has finished its work:

```
Thread t = pi.MakeThread();
t.Start ();
while (t.IsAlive)
  Thread.Sleep (1);
this.PiValue.Text = pi.pi.ToString ();
```

The call to **Start( )** begins the calculations in the new thread. The next two lines ensure that the new thread gets to finish its work. The **IsAlive** property of a thread tells you whether the thread is still alive and working, or has died. A thread has *died* when the thread delegate function has finished its work. The call to **Sleep( )** suspends this thread so that the other thread can perform some work.

So far, you have learned the .NET tools to create and start new threads. The rest of these solutions will show you how to implement different solutions to concurrency issues.

Accessing Shared Data

Next, let's add the code so that the display for pi and the display for the number of iterations update as the series keeps getting closer to pi. You still need to add a property and make a few modifications to keep track of how many iterations have happened so far. First, you need to add a private member variable to the **CalcPi** class to store the number of elapsed iterations:

```
private int _iters = 1;
```

Next, you need to add a property to retrieve the number of iterations:

```
public int iters {
  get {
    return _iters;
  }
}
```

Lastly, you need to modify the **calculate()** method to use the new member variable:

```
private void calculate () {
  // Pi = 1 - 1/3 + 1/5 - 1/7 etc.
  double series = 0;
  do {
    series += 1.0/_iters - 1.0/(_iters+2);
    _iters += 4;
  } while (_iters < TotalIters);
  _pi = series * 4;
}
```

All the remaining changes needed are in the form class. Figure 15.2 shows the form used to display the approximation of pi. The form has two edit controls: one for the current number of iterations and one for the current approximation of pi.

The first modification is to stop waiting for the thread to complete when you start the thread. The new version of **Form1_Load** follows:

```
private void Form1_Load(object sender, System.EventArgs e) {
  Thread t = pi.MakeThread();
```

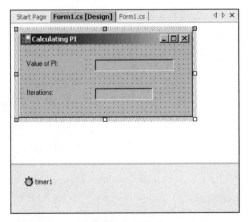

Figure 15.2   The form that displays approximations of pi.

```
    t.Start ();
}
```

This version no longer waits for the thread to finish after starting it. Now, you need to add a timer so that you can check the progress of the calculations and display updated values when the timer goes off. To add a timer, you drag a timer control from the toolbox onto the form. After you have added the timer, right-click on the stopwatch icon and select Properties. Figure 15.3 shows the timer properties page in Visual Studio .NET. You need to enable the timer and set the timer interval to 100 milliseconds.

Finally, you need to write the code that updates the edit controls when the timer event fires. Double-click on the timer icon. Visual Studio .NET adds a timer tick handler to your form:

```
private void timer1_Tick(object sender, System.EventArgs e) {
    this.PiValue.Text = pi.pi.ToString ();
    this.Iteratons.Text = pi.iters.ToString ();
}
```

If you run the sample, the number of iterations and the approximation of pi keep changing until the maximum number of iterations. This simple example has two shared data elements: the member variable storing the current value of pi, and the member variable storing the current number of iterations. The code that reads or writes these shared values needs to be synchronized. The only error for this sample is that the approximation for pi might not represent the value of

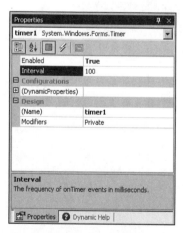

Figure 15.3 Timer properties.

iterations. To fix this error, you need to make sure that a thread switch does not occur when these two values are out of synch.

Reading Shared Data

The **lock** statement synchronizes access to these shared variables so that two threads cannot be executing locked code at the same time. (The two threads are never executing at the same time, so this really blocks a thread from entering a locked section when another suspended thread is already in locked code.)

The goal is to make sure that any code that reads data from another thread cannot be interrupted until all the data copying has been completed. In this application, only two values need to be copied between threads: the number of iterations and the current approximation of pi. To make sure that both values come across at the same time, define a structure to hold both values:

```
public struct PiApproximation {
  private double _pi;
  private int _iterations;

  public double pi {
    get {
      return _pi;
    }
    set {
      _pi = value;
    }
  }

  public int iters {
    get {
      return _iterations;
    }
    set {
      _iterations = value;
    }
  }
}
```

Next, the **CalcPi** class uses one of these values to return the current number of approximations and the current approximation of pi:

```
public PiApproximation PI {
  get {
```

295

```
    PiApproximation pi = new PiApproximation();
    lock (this) {
        pi.pi = _pi;
        pi.iters = _iters;
    }
    return pi;
  }
}
```

Note the highlighted line in the code. It sets a lock on this object. The assignments that copy the current approximation of pi and the current number of iterations happen inside this block. If this thread gets suspended while inside this function, no other thread can execute code that requires locking the same **CalcPi** object until this thread gets awakened and can finish executing the code inside the locked section.

Writing Shared Data

The other lock in the **CalcPi** class is around the code that modifies the values of pi and the number of iterations. That code is inside the **calculate()** function:

```
private void calculate () {
  // Pi = 1 - 1/3 + 1/5 - 1/7 etc.
  double series = 0;
  do {
    series += 1.0/(double)_iters - 1.0/(double)(_iters+2);
    lock (this) {
      _iters += 4;
      _pi = series * 4;
    }
  } while (_iters < TotalIters);
}
```

Here, the lock is created around the code that modifies the iterations and the current value of pi. You need to lock sections of code that read or write shared data areas. The technique used here is an *exclusive lock*: When the data is read or written, no other thread can do either.

Modifying Thread Priority

All threads are created equal, or at least with the same priority in the eyes of the scheduler. This will be the correct behavior almost all the time. If you need to modify the priority of a given thread, you can set the priority property on a thread:

```
private void Form1_Load(object sender, System.EventArgs e) {
  calcThread = pi.MakeThread();
  calcThread.Priority = ThreadPriority.Lowest;
  calcThread.Start ();
}
```

You should use extreme care when you modify the thread priority. You can starve threads by having too low of a priority. *Starving* threads do not get enough processing time to complete their work. Also, each operating system uses a different algorithm to assign processing time to threads based on their priority. Thread priorities that work well on one OS may not work as well on another. In most cases, you should use the normal priority and change thread priorities only after profiling your application.

Pausing and Stopping Threads

The **Thread** class has methods to pause or kill a thread. You can suspend two ways. First, from inside a thread you can call the **Sleep()** class method:

```
Sleep (1);
```

Sleep() suspends the current thread. The parameter gives the number of milliseconds to sleep. **Sleep()** operates on the current thread only; you cannot specify a time value for another thread.

You can also use the thread's **Suspend()** and **Resume()** instance methods to pause or restart another thread. I added a pause/resume button to the sample to demonstrate this feature.

```
private void Pause_Click(object sender, System.EventArgs e) {
  if (this.Pause.Text == "Pause") {
    calcThread.Suspend();
```

```
      this.Pause.Text = "Resume";
   } else {
      calcThread.Resume();
      this.Pause.Text = "Pause";
   }
}
```

The **Pause** and **Resume** methods work like switches: you can start and stop the execution of the thread. A paused thread will not be scheduled for execution. If you call **Suspend( )** on a thread that has already been suspended, it has no effect. If you call **Resume( )** on a thread that is not suspended, it has no effect. When you suspend a thread, you introduce the possibility of deadlock. If the thread gets suspended when it is inside a locked block of code, another thread could wait forever because the suspended thread will never leave the locked block. You need to modify the timer procedure so that it does not try to read the data when the thread is not running:

```
private void timer1_Tick(object sender, System.EventArgs e) {
   // this might cause deadlock if another thread
   // is suspended in the critical section.
   if (this.Pause.Text == "Pause") {
      PiApproximation p = pi.PI;
      this.PiValue.Text = p.pi.ToString ();
      this.Iteratons.Text = p.iters.ToString ();
   }
}
```

You stop a thread by using the **Abort( )** method. Stopping a thread is a rather malicious action. The runtime raises a **ThreadAbort Exception** in the target thread. You cannot catch a **ThreadAbort Exception**, although the target thread does get to execute all **finally** blocks before the thread actually dies. For this reason, you should call **Join( )** on the target thread to wait for confirmation of its death. I added a stop button to the calculate pi sample to show how this works:

```
private void StopButton_Click(object sender,
   System.EventArgs e) {
   StopButton.Enabled = false;
   Pause.Enabled= false;
   timer1.Enabled=false; // No more messages.
   calcThread.Abort ();
   calcThread.Join (); // Wait for death.
   calcThread = null;
}
```

The timer, the pause, and the stop buttons are disabled. Then, the thread is aborted. The **Join( )** call blocks until the thread has finally died. To test this, I added a **finally** clause in the **ThreadStart** delegate function that displays a message box to indicate that all the work has been completed:

```
private void ThreadStarter () {
  try {
    calculate ();
  catch (ThreadAbortException e) {
    System.Windows.Forms.MessageBox.Show ("Caught it");
  } finally {
    System.Windows.Forms.MessageBox.Show ("Dying now!");
  }
}
```

Notice here that you can write code that attempts to catch the exception, but it will never be caught. If you run the sample now, you will see that the "Dying now!" message box pops up when you kill the thread. The "Caught it" message box never appears.

WARNING! There is one interesting gotcha on killing threads: you cannot kill a suspended thread. You can kill a sleeping thread, though. So, the following code will throw a ThreadStateException:

```
calcPi.Suspend ();
calcPi.Abort ();
```

You need to make sure that your main thread is the last thread to exit. If your program ends, and you still have worker threads running, your program never actually finishes. It enters a zombie state where the runtime can't unload your program. See the **Form1_Closed( )** method in the Listing 15.1 for details. Listing 15.2 shows the pi calculating class, with all the added multithreading code.

Listing 15.1   Main thread for the calculate pi sample.

```
using System;
using System.Threading;
using System.Drawing;
using System.Collections;
using System.ComponentModel;
using System.Windows.Forms;
using System.Data;

namespace PiCalc
{
```

```
/// <summary>
/// This form displays the ongoing calculations of PI
/// and the current number of iterations in the series.
/// </summary>
public class Form1 : System.Windows.Forms.Form
{
  private System.Windows.Forms.Label label1;
  private System.Windows.Forms.TextBox PiValue;
  private System.Windows.Forms.Label label2;
  private System.Windows.Forms.TextBox Iteratons;

  private CalcPi pi = new CalcPi(100000000);
  private Thread calcThread = null;
  private System.Windows.Forms.Timer timer1;
  private System.Windows.Forms.Button StopButton;
  private System.Windows.Forms.Button Pause;
  private System.ComponentModel.IContainer components;

  /// <summary>
  /// Default constructor.
  /// </summary>
  public Form1()
  {
    //
    // Required for Windows Form Designer support
    //
    InitializeComponent();
  }

  /// <summary>
  /// Clean up any resources being used.
  /// </summary>
  protected override void Dispose( bool disposing )
  {
    if( disposing )
    {
      if (components != null)
      {
        components.Dispose();
      }
    }
    base.Dispose( disposing );
  }

  #region Windows Form Designer generated code
  /// <summary>
```

```
/// Required method for Designer support - do not modify
/// the contents of this method with the code editor.
/// </summary>
private void InitializeComponent()
{
  this.components = new System.ComponentModel.Container();
  this.label1 = new System.Windows.Forms.Label();
  this.label2 = new System.Windows.Forms.Label();
  this.Pause = new System.Windows.Forms.Button();
  this.PiValue = new System.Windows.Forms.TextBox();
  this.StopButton = new System.Windows.Forms.Button();
  this.timer1 = new System.Windows.Forms.Timer
    (this.components);
  this.Iteratons = new System.Windows.Forms.TextBox();
  this.SuspendLayout();
  //
  // label1
  //
  this.label1.Location = new System.Drawing.Point(8, 24);
  this.label1.Name = "label1";
  this.label1.TabIndex = 0;
  this.label1.Text = "Value of PI:";
  //
  // label2
  //
  this.label2.Location = new System.Drawing.Point(8, 72);
  this.label2.Name = "label2";
  this.label2.TabIndex = 2;
  this.label2.Text = "Iterations:";
  //
  // Pause
  //
  this.Pause.Location = new System.Drawing.Point(24, 112);
  this.Pause.Name = "Pause";
  this.Pause.TabIndex = 5;
  this.Pause.Text = "Pause";
  this.Pause.Click += new System.EventHandler
    (this.Pause_Click);
  //
  // PiValue
  //
  this.PiValue.Location = new System.Drawing.Point(128, 24);
  this.PiValue.Name = "PiValue";
  this.PiValue.ReadOnly = true;
  this.PiValue.Size = new System.Drawing.Size(136, 20);
  this.PiValue.TabIndex = 1;
```

```
this.PiValue.Text = "";
//
// StopButton
//
this.StopButton.Location = new System.Drawing.Point
  (200, 112);
this.StopButton.Name = "StopButton";
this.StopButton.TabIndex = 4;
this.StopButton.Text = "Stop";
this.StopButton.Click += new System.EventHandler
  (this.StopButton_Click);
//
// timer1
//
this.timer1.Enabled = true;
this.timer1.Tick += new System.EventHandler
  (this.timer1_Tick);
//
// Iteratons
//
this.Iteratons.Location = new System.Drawing.Point
  (128, 72);
this.Iteratons.Name = "Iteratons";
this.Iteratons.ReadOnly = true;
this.Iteratons.TabIndex = 3;
this.Iteratons.Text = "";
//
// Form1
//
this.AutoScaleBaseSize = new System.Drawing.Size(5, 13);
this.ClientSize = new System.Drawing.Size(292, 149);
this.Controls.AddRange(new System.Windows.Forms.Control[] {
  this.Pause,
  this.StopButton,
  this.Iteratons,
  this.label2,
  this.PiValue,
  this.label1});
this.Name = "Form1";
this.Text = "Calculating PI";
this.Load += new System.EventHandler(this.Form1_Load);
this.Closed += new System.EventHandler(this.Form1_Closed);
this.ResumeLayout(false);

}
#endregion
```

```csharp
/// <summary>
/// The main entry point for the application.
/// </summary>
[STAThread]
static void Main()
{
  Application.Run(new Form1());
}


/// <summary>
/// Form load handler.
/// </summary>
/// <remarks>
/// This method creates the worker thread to calculate PI.
/// After creating the thread, the priority is lowered, and
/// the worker thread is started.
/// </remarks>
/// <param name="sender">The generator of the event.</param>
/// <param name="e">The event arguments.</param>
private void Form1_Load(object sender, System.EventArgs e) {
  calcThread = pi.MakeThread();
  calcThread.Priority = ThreadPriority.Lowest;
  calcThread.Start ();
}


/// <summary>
/// This is the timer procedure.
/// </summary>
/// <remarks>
/// If the worker thread is running (not suspended),
/// the form fields displaying the approximation
/// of pi get updated.
/// If the thread ran to completion, this method disables
/// further user input.
/// </remarks>
/// <param name="sender">The generator of the event.</param>
/// <param name="e">The event parameters.</param>
private void timer1_Tick(object sender, System.EventArgs e) {
  // this might cause deadlock if the other thread
  // is suspended in the critical section,
  // so, don't update if the thread is paused.
  if (this.Pause.Text == "Pause") {
    PiApproximation p = pi.PI;
    this.PiValue.Text = p.pi.ToString ();
    this.Iteratons.Text = p.iters.ToString ();
  }
```

```
    // Is the thread done?
    if (calcThread.IsAlive == false) {
      StopButton.Enabled = false;
      Pause.Enabled= false;
      timer1.Enabled=false; // No more messages.
      calcThread = null;
    }
  }


  /// <summary>
  /// Stop Button Click handler.
  /// </summary>
  /// <remarks>
  /// This method disables further user input, and kills the
  /// thread that is calculating pi.
  /// </remarks>
  /// <param name="sender">The generator of the event.</param>
  /// <param name="e">The event parameters.</param>
  private void StopButton_Click(object sender,
    System.EventArgs e) {
    StopButton.Enabled = false;
    Pause.Enabled= false;
    timer1.Enabled=false; // No more messages.
    calcThread.Abort ();
    calcThread.Join (); // Wait for death.
    calcThread = null;
  }


  /// <summary>
  /// Pause Button Click Handler.
  /// </summary>
  /// <remarks>
  /// This method suspends or resumes the calculating
  /// thread. Killing suspended threads is invalid, so
  /// when the thread is paused, this method disables
  /// the stop button.
  /// </remarks>
  /// <param name="sender">The generator of the event.</param>
  /// <param name="e">The event arguments.</param>
  private void Pause_Click(object sender, System.EventArgs e) {
    if (this.Pause.Text == "Pause") {
      calcThread.Suspend();
      this.Pause.Text = "Resume";
      this.StopButton.Enabled = false;
    } else {
      calcThread.Resume();
      this.Pause.Text = "Pause";
```

```
        this.StopButton.Enabled = true;
      }
    }

    /// <summary>
    /// Closed notification handler.
    /// </summary>
    /// <remarks>
    /// Exiting a program with worker threads
    /// running results in a hung process. So,
    /// this method kills the worker thread, if
    /// it is still running.
    /// </remarks>
    /// <param name="sender">The generator of the event.</param>
    /// <param name="e">The event arguments</param>
    private void Form1_Closed(object sender, System.EventArgs e) {
      if (calcThread != null) {
        calcThread.Abort ();
        calcThread.Join (); // Wait for death.
      }
    }
  }
}
```

Listing 15.2   The calculate pi class, ready for multithreading.

```
using System;
using System.Threading;

namespace PiCalc
{
  /// <summary>
  /// Simple struct to store the current
  /// approximation of PI and the number
  /// of iterations.
  /// </summary>
  public struct PiApproximation {
    private double _pi;
    private int _iterations;

    /// <summary>
    /// The current value of PI.
    /// </summary>
    public double pi {
      get {
        return _pi;
      }
```

```
      set {
        _pi = value;
      }
    }

    /// <summary>
    /// The number of iterations used to calculate
    /// this value.
    /// </summary>
    public int iters {
      get {
        return _iterations;
      }
      set {
        _iterations = value;
      }
    }
  }


/// <summary>
/// The pi calculation class.
/// </summary>
public class CalcPi
{
  private double _pi;
  private int _iters;
  private readonly int TotalIters;

  /// <summary>
  /// Constructor.
  /// </summary>
  /// <remarks>
  /// This function stores the number of iterations
  /// used to create this value.
  /// </remarks>
  /// <param name="it">The total number of iterations.</param>
  public CalcPi(int it)
  {
    _iters = 1;
    _pi = 0;
    TotalIters = it;
  }

  /// <summary>
  /// The current approximation of PI.
  /// </summary>
```

```
public PiApproximation PI {
  get {
    PiApproximation pi = new PiApproximation();
    lock (this) {
      pi.pi = _pi;
      pi.iters = _iters;
    }
    return pi;
  }
}


/// <summary>
/// Create a thread using the thread delegate.
/// </summary>
/// <returns>
/// A thread that will calculate pi using this object.
/// </returns>
/// <remarks>
/// This function creates a new thread to calculate pi.
/// The returned thread has not been started yet.
/// </remarks>
public Thread MakeThread () {
  return new Thread (new ThreadStart (this.ThreadStarter));
}


// This function uses the Leibnitz series to
// calculate pi:
// Pi = 1 - 1/3 + 1/5 - 1/7 etc.
private void calculate () {
  double series = 0;
  do {
    series += 1.0/(double)_iters - 1.0/(double)(_iters+2);
    lock (this) {
      _iters += 4;
      _pi = series * 4;
    }
  } while (_iters < TotalIters);
}


// This is the function used to start the worker thread.
// It calls the calculate () function to calculate pi.
// The finally clause displays a message box to let
// you test the Join () function.
private void ThreadStarter () {
  try {
    calculate ();
  } finally {
```

```
        System.Windows.Forms.MessageBox.Show ("Dying now!");
      }
    }
  }
}
```

Using the **Monitor** Class

The C# compiler uses the **System.Threading.Monitor** class to implement the **lock** statement. This statement

```
lock (this) {
  // code here...
}
```

is equivalent to this statement:

```
System.Threading.Monitor.Enter (this);
// code here...
System.Threading.Monitor.Exit (this);
```

The **Monitor** class has other static methods that give you more flexibility. Most often, you will want to use the **TryEnter()** method to attempt to get a lock, and continue performing other work if you do not get the lock. The second parameter specifies the time to wait, in milliseconds:

```
if (true == Monitor.TryEnter (this, 100)) {
  // code here.
  Monitor.Exit ();
} else {
  // Can't get the lock, move on.
}
```

Using the Producer/Consumer Idiom

One of the more common uses of the **Monitor** class is to create a pair of threads that work as a producer and a consumer. The producer/consumer idiom involves the **Wait()** and **Pulse()** methods of the **Monitor** class. This idiom involves three classes:

- The *storage* object holds the value(s) being transferred from the producer to the consumer.

- The *producer* object creates the value(s) and stores them in the storage object.

- The *consumer* object reads the value(s) from the storage object.

The producer runs in one thread and writes values to the storage object. The consumer runs in another thread and reads values from the storage object. The storage object contains code that runs in both threads and handles the sequence of write/read/write/read and so on. Let's go through another example calculating pi and printing the values out. The first piece to understand is the **Main** function, which creates three classes for the application, starts the threads, and waits for the threads to exit (see Listing 15.3).

Listing 15.3   Main test function for the producer/consumer idiom.

```
static void Main(string[] args)
{
  // Create the storage object.
  PiApproximation pi = new PiApproximation();

  // Create the producer.
  PiProducer prod = new PiProducer(pi, 100000);
  Thread producerThread = prod.CreateProducerThread();

  // Create the consumer
  PiConsumer cons = new PiConsumer(pi, 100000);
  Thread consumerThread = cons.CreateConsumerThread();

  // Start the threads.
  producerThread.Start();
  consumerThread.Start ();

  // Wait for both threads to end:
  producerThread.Join();
  consumerThread.Join ();
}
```

Next, let's examine the producer class (see Listing 15.4). When you construct the producer class, you give it a reference to the storage object. The **CreateThread()** function, replaced here by **CreateProducerThread()**, should be familiar by now: It creates the thread using a private function as the thread entry point. The **calculate()** function simply writes each successive approximation of pi to the storage object. The only interesting change here is the conspicuous absence of any synchronization code. All the synchronization code is in the storage object.

Listing 15.4   The producer class.

```
/// <summary>
/// Producer class.
/// </summary>
/// <remarks>
/// Create the successive values for the approximation.
/// </remarks>
class PiProducer {
  private PiApproximation _pi;
  private int TotalIters;

  /// <summary>
  /// Constructor.
  /// </summary>
  /// <param name="pi">The storage object.</param>
  /// <param name="iterations">The number of iterations.</param>
  public PiProducer (PiApproximation pi, int iterations) {
    _pi = pi;
    TotalIters = iterations;
  }

  /// <summary>
  /// Thread creation function.
  /// </summary>
  /// <returns>The producer thread.</returns>
  public Thread CreateProducerThread () {
    return new Thread (new ThreadStart(this.calculate));
  }

  /// <summary>
  /// Calculation function.
  /// </summary>
  /// <remarks>
  /// Notice that there are no synchronization
  /// blocks here. All the synchronization code is
  /// in the storage class. This function simply
  /// calls the WriteData () function that
  /// handles all synchronization.</remarks>
  private void calculate () {
    double series = 0;
    int iters = 1;
    do {
      // Calculate the next value:
```

```
      series += 1.0/(double)iters - 1.0/(double)(iters+2);
      iters +=  4;
      _pi.WriteData(iters, series * 4);
    } while (iters < TotalIters);
  }
}
```

The consumer class is constructed in a similar fashion (see Listing 15.5). The thread function in the consumer class reads the data from the storage object and prints it to the console. As with the producer, this class does not contain any synchronization blocks.

Listing 15.5 The consumer class.

```
/// <summary>
/// Consumer Object.
/// </summary>
/// <remarks>
/// This class creates a thread to read values
/// from the storage object and print them to
/// the console.
/// </remarks>
class PiConsumer {
  private PiApproximation _pi;
  private int TotalIters;

  /// <summary>
  /// Constructor.
  /// </summary>
  /// <param name="pi">The storage object.</param>
  /// <param name="iterations">The number of iterations.</param>
  public PiConsumer (PiApproximation pi, int iterations) {
    _pi = pi;
    TotalIters = iterations;
  }

  /// <summary>
  /// Thread creation function.
  /// </summary>
  /// <returns>The consumer thread.</returns>
  public Thread CreateConsumerThread () {
    return new Thread (new ThreadStart (this.printValues));
  }

  /// <summary>
  /// Output function.
  /// </summary>
  /// <remarks>
```

```
/// Notice that there are no synchronization
/// blocks here. All the synchronization code is
/// in the storage class. This function simply
/// calls the ReadData () function that
/// handles all synchronization.</remarks>
private void printValues () {
  int iters = new int ();
  double pi = new double ();
  do {
    _pi.ReadData (out iters, out pi);
    System.Console.WriteLine("Iters: {0}\tPi: {1}",
      iters.ToString (), pi.ToString ());
  } while (iters < TotalIters);
  }
}
```

The storage object manages the sequence of operations in the **ReadData()** and **WriteData()** methods (see Listing 15.6). The **PiApproximation** object contains three data members: the value of pi, the number of iterations, and a flag that indicates whether a data value is ready in the object or not. The **ReadData()** and **WriteData()** methods toggle this flag. These two methods work together to handle the data transfer through this object. Both functions are entirely in locked blocks. The **ReadData()** function starts by looking at the value of the **_valueReady** flag. If no value is ready, it calls **Monitor.Wait()**, which is a blocking call. It suspends the current thread until another thread pulses the same object. After the pulse, this function reads the data that is now available. After reading the data, it sets the **_valueReady** flag to false. Finally, it calls **Monitor.Pulse()** to notify the producer that data can be written.

The producer works the same. If a value is already available, it calls **Monitor.Wait()**. The reader wakes up the producer thread when it has finished reading the current value. After waking up, the producer writes the next value, sets the **_valueReady** flag, and pulses the consumer thread.

The end result is that the producer writes a value and effectively wakes up the reader thread. The consumer reads a value and effectively wakes up the producer. You can use this technique anytime you create a series of values in one thread and use them in another. Using **Pulse()** and **Wait()** ensures that the consumer is awakened as soon as the value is ready, and the producer is awakened as soon as the value has been read. Also, neither the consumer nor producer spend processor cycles waiting for the other thread.

Listing 15.6   Storage class for the readers and writers idiom.

```
/// <summary>
/// Simple class to store the current
/// approximation of PI and the number
/// of iterations.
/// </summary>
public class PiApproximation  {
  private double _pi = 0.0;
  private int _iterations = 0;
  // Write first.
  private bool _valueReady = false;

  /// <summary>
  /// Writer function.
  /// </summary>
  /// <param name="iterations">
  /// The number of iterations
  /// </param>
  /// <param name="val">
  /// The current approximation.
  /// </param>
  public void WriteData (int iterations, double val) {
    lock (this) {
      if (_valueReady) {
        // Wait.
        Monitor.Wait (this);
      }
      // Done waiting:
      _pi = val;
      _iterations = iterations;
      _valueReady = true;
      Monitor.Pulse(this); // Signal.
    }
  }

  /// <summary>
  /// Reader Function.
  /// </summary>
  /// <param name="iterations">
  /// The number of iterations.
  /// </param>
  /// <param name="val">
  /// The current approximation.
  /// </param>
  public void ReadData (out int iterations, out double val) {
    lock (this) {
      if (!_valueReady) {
```

```
        // Wait.
        Monitor.Wait (this);
      }
      // Done waiting:
      val = _pi;
      iterations = _iterations;
      _valueReady = false;
      Monitor.Pulse(this); // Signal.
    }
  }
}
```

Using the **ReaderWriterLock** Class

If you look back at all the samples shown so far, they involve one thread that creates data and one thread that consumes data. The code shown in those examples is inefficient for applications that have one writer and multiple readers. Clearly, multiple readers can access the same data at the same time without introducing any ill effects. The .NET library provides a class that handles multiple readers and a single writer correctly: the **ReaderWriterLock** class.

To use the **ReaderWriterLock**, you create a new **ReaderWriterLock** object:

```
ReaderWriterLock rwLock = new ReaderWriterLock ();
```

To acquire a read lock, use the **AcquireReaderLock()** method. This method blocks until a reader lock is available. When you are done reading the data, you release the lock using the **ReleaseReaderLock()** method:

```
rwLock.AcquireReaderLock ();
// read goes here.
rwLock.ReleaseReaderLock ();
```

Writing data works the same. Use **AcquireWriterLock()** and **ReleaseWriterLock()**:

```
rwLock.AcquireWriterLock ();
// write goes here.
rwLock.ReleaseWriterLock ();
```

There is one trick to using the **ReaderWriterLock**: You can dead-lock a thread by acquiring a read lock and then trying to get the write lock:

```
// Bad code, this will deadlock:
rwLock.AcquireReaderLock ();
// do some reads.
// Discover you need to write.
// This will never return:
rwLock.AcquireWriterLock ();
// Can't get here. You haven't released the read lock.
```

The way you avoid this problem is to upgrade the reader lock to a writer lock. You can downgrade it again afterward:

```
rwLock.AcquireReaderLock ();
// do some reads.
// Discover you need to write.
System.Threading.LockCookie wr =
  rwLock.UpgradeToWriterLock ();
// Do the writes.
// Now, downgrade the lock:
rwLock.DowngradeFromWriterLock (ref wr);
// Read some more data.
// Release the read lock:
rwLock.ReleaseReaderLock ();
```

The **ReaderWriterLock** is almost as simple to use as the **lock** statement. And, it gives you the flexibility to support multiple readers working on a dataset concurrently.

Using Mutexes

All the examples up to this point have shown the **Monitor** class as the method of synchronizing data access between threads. The **Monitor** class is the simpler of the two synchronization objects; you should use it whenever you can. However, the **Monitor** class is not as powerful as the **Mutex** class. The **Mutex** class (Mutex stands for *Mutual Exclusion*) provides different functionality than the simple **Monitor** class.

Now, it's time to finally let those philosophers eat (refer back to the "Synchronization" section to review the philosophers' example). The problem occurs because in order for a philosopher to eat, he needs to get both of the chopsticks next to him. The deadlock problem occurs when each philosopher grabs one chopstick. None of them will let go of a chopstick, so no one gets two chopsticks, and no one gets to eat.

The **Monitor** class, and the **lock** statement, only waits for one resource to become available. The **Mutex** class supports waiting for more than one object at a time. Using a mutex and the **WaitAll()** function is the key to avoiding the deadlock. I wrote a sample program to show you the table where the diners are eating (see Figure 15.4).

The philosopher class represents a single diner. The constructor takes two mutex objects, representing the chopsticks on either side of the diner. The code that works to avoid deadlock is in the **threadProc()** function. The **Mutex.WaitAll()** static function waits for all the objects to be available before any of them are locked:

```
Mutex.WaitAll (Chopsticks);
```

Much of the rest of the sample should be familiar to you by now. The entire sample is shown in Listing 15.7. The main window paints the plates in front of the philosophers different colors depending on the philosopher's activity. Thinking philosophers have green plates (black), waiting philosophers have yellow plates (light gray), and eating philosophers have red plates (dark gray).

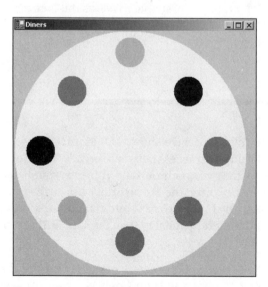

Figure 15.4   The diners sample in action.

The **Mutex** class is the most complicated, but the most full featured, mechanism for synchronizing threads. As in this sample, the mutex supports waiting for multiple mutexes to be available. None of the resources are locked until all are available. You can also create named mutexes:

```
Mutex myLock = new Mutex (false, "MyMutex");
```

The first parameter indicates whether you want to lock the mutex as part of creating it. You can create named mutexes to provide synchronization between different processes. Different programs can try to lock the same named mutex.

Finally, in addition to waiting for *all* mutex objects to be available, you can wait for any one of a set of objects:

```
Mutex.WaitAny (mutexArray);
```

Mutexes are more powerful than monitors, but they are also much more performance-intensive. Any multithreaded code that you can fully protect with monitors will be faster.

Listing 15.7 **The philosopher class shows how to wait for multiple objects. The diners class is the form for the sample.**

```
using System;
using System.Threading;
using System.Drawing;
using System.Collections;
using System.ComponentModel;
using System.Windows.Forms;
using System.Data;

namespace dining
{
  /// <summary>
  /// The philosopher represents one guest
  /// at the table.
  /// </summary>
  public class Philosopher
  {
    // Seed the random number generator differently
    // for each philosopher.
    static int seed = 0;

    /// <summary>
    /// The current action of the philosopher.
```

```
/// </summary>
public enum State {
  WAITING,
  EATING,
  RESTING }

// Store references to the two mutex objects
// that represent the two chopsticks.
private Mutex[] Chopsticks = new Mutex[2];

// Let callers know what I am doing.
private State whatImDoing = State.WAITING;

/// <summary>
/// Construct a philosopher.
/// </summary>
/// <param name="left">The mutex for left chopstick.</param>
/// <param name="right">The mutex for the right
/// chopstick.</param>
public Philosopher(Mutex left, Mutex right)
{
  Chopsticks[0] = left;
  Chopsticks[1] = right;
}

/// <summary>
/// Report our current action.
/// </summary>
public State Activity {
  get {
    return whatImDoing;
  }
}

/// <summary>
/// Create the thread to emulate a philosopher.
/// </summary>
/// <returns>
/// The new thread.
/// </returns>
public Thread createThread () {
  return new Thread (new ThreadStart (threadProc));
}

/// <summary>
/// The thread procedure for the philosophers.
/// </summary>
```

```
/// <remarks>
/// This function emulates the philosophers.
/// Philosophers try to eat, finish eating,
/// then ponder life.
/// To avoid deadlock, a philosopher does not
/// grab a chopstick, unless he can get both of
/// them.
/// </remarks>
private void threadProc () {
  Random n = new Random(seed++);
  while (true) {
    // Try to get the chopsticks.
    whatImDoing = State.WAITING;
    Mutex.WaitAll (Chopsticks);
    // eat for random period.
    whatImDoing = State.EATING;
    Thread.Sleep(n.Next (1000, 15000));
    // put down chopsticks.
    whatImDoing = State.RESTING;
    Chopsticks[0].ReleaseMutex();
    Chopsticks[1].ReleaseMutex();
    // rest for random period.
    Thread.Sleep (n.Next (1000, 15000));
  }
 }
}


/// <summary>
/// Form class for the Diners sample.
/// </summary>
public class Diners : System.Windows.Forms.Form
{
  // Set the table for 8.
  private const int NUMBER = 8;

  // 8 Philosophers, 8 chopsticks, and 8 threads:
  private Philosopher [] People = new Philosopher [NUMBER];
  private Mutex [] Chopsticks = new Mutex [NUMBER];
  private Thread [] threads = new Thread [NUMBER];

  private System.Windows.Forms.Timer timer1;
  private System.ComponentModel.IContainer components;

  public Diners()
  {
    //
    // Required for Windows Form Designer support
```

15. Multithreaded C# Programming

```
    //
    InitializeComponent();
}


/// <summary>
/// Clean up any resources being used.
/// </summary>
protected override void Dispose( bool disposing )
{
    if( disposing )
    {
        if (components != null)
        {
            components.Dispose();
        }
    }
    base.Dispose( disposing );
}


#region Windows Form Designer generated code
/// <summary>
/// Required method for Designer support - do not modify
/// the contents of this method with the code editor.
/// </summary>
private void InitializeComponent()
{
    this.components = new System.ComponentModel.Container();
    this.timer1 = new System.Windows.Forms.Timer
        (this.components);
    //
    // timer1
    //
    this.timer1.Interval = 1000;
    this.timer1.Tick += new System.EventHandler(this.Tick);
    //
    // Diners
    //
    this.AutoScaleBaseSize = new System.Drawing.Size(5, 13);
    this.ClientSize = new System.Drawing.Size(392, 373);
    this.Name = "Diners";
    this.Text = "Diners";
    this.Load += new System.EventHandler(this.Diners_Load);
    this.Closed += new System.EventHandler(this.OnClosed);
    this.Paint += new System.Windows.Forms.PaintEventHandler
        (this.OnPaint);
```

```
}
#endregion

/// <summary>
/// The main entry point for the application.
/// </summary>
[STAThread]
static void Main()
{
    Application.Run(new Diners());
}

/// <summary>
/// Load the form.
/// </summary>
/// <param name="sender">The generator of the event</param>
/// <param name="e">The event args.</param>
/// <remarks>
/// This function creates the initial application
/// objects. 8 Mutex objects are created for the
/// chopsticks. 8 philosophers are created to represent
/// the philosophers. Finally, the 8 threads are created and
/// started.
/// </remarks>
private void Diners_Load(object sender, System.EventArgs e){
    int i = 0;
    // Create 8 mutexes for the chopsticks.
    for (i=0;i<NUMBER; i++)
        Chopsticks[i]=new Mutex();

    // Create 8 philosophers and 8 threads.
    for (i=0;i<NUMBER;i++)
        People[i] = new Philosopher(Chopsticks[i],
            Chopsticks[(i+1)% NUMBER]);

    // Create the threads:
    for (i=0;i<NUMBER; i++) {
        threads[i] = People[i].createThread();
        // Start them:
        threads[i].Start ();
    }
    timer1.Enabled = true;
}

/// <summary>
/// Closed handler.
```

```
/// </summary>
/// <param name="sender">The generator of the event.</param>
/// <param name="e">The event args.</param>
/// <remarks>
/// Before the program can exit, all the threads must be
/// stopped. This method stops them and waits for
/// notification of their exits.
/// </remarks>
private void OnClosed(object sender, System.EventArgs e) {
  // Abort and destroy all threads.
  for (int i = 0; i < NUMBER; i++) {
    threads[i].Abort ();
    threads[i].Join ();
  }

}


/// <summary>
/// Paint all the philosophers.
/// </summary>
/// <param name="sender">The generator of the event.</param>
/// <param name="e">The event parameters</param>
private void OnPaint(object sender,
  System.Windows.Forms.PaintEventArgs e) {
  Point[] locations = {new Point  (175, 10),
                       new Point (275, 75),
                       new Point (325, 175),
                       new Point (275, 275),
                       new Point (175, 325),
                       new Point (75, 275),
                       new Point  (20, 175),
                       new Point (75,  75)};

  Graphics g = e.Graphics;
  // Draw the table:
  g.FillEllipse(Brushes.Beige,0,0,400,400);

  for (int i = 0; i < NUMBER; i++) {
    Rectangle r = new Rectangle (locations[i],
      new Size (50,50));
    switch (People[i].Activity){
    case Philosopher.State.RESTING:
      // paint a green rectangle.
      g.FillEllipse(Brushes.Green, r);
      break;
    case Philosopher.State.WAITING:
```

```
      // paing a yellow rectangle.
      g.FillEllipse(Brushes.Yellow,r);
      break;
    case Philosopher.State.EATING:
      g.FillEllipse(Brushes.Red,r);
      // paint a red rectangle.
      break;
    }
  }
}


/// <summary>
/// Tick method.
/// </summary>
/// <param name="sender">The generator of the event.</param>
/// <param name="e">The event args.</param>
/// <remarks>
/// This method simply updates the display to show which
/// philosophers are eating, which are waiting, and which
/// are resting.
/// </remarks>
private void Tick(object sender, System.EventArgs e) {
  Invalidate ();
}
  }
}
```

Chapter 16

Collections

In Brief

Many programming tasks will involve working with multiple items of the same or similar types. You will need some kind of collection to store these multiple items and work with them. The .NET BCL contains classes and interfaces that model many of the classic data structures available for collections: vectors, lists, queues, hash tables, and dictionaries. All the collections perform the same basic functions; you can add and remove elements, iterate all the elements, and search for a particular element. The difference between collections is the performance characteristics for different operations. As such, the collection classes make extensive use of interfaces to factor out common behavior. Using some care, you can write functions that will work with multiple collection classes by coding to the interface instead of the class.

The .NET BCL also provides functions that work with elements in a collection. All these algorithms depend on your class implementing particular interfaces. You will want to implement functionality such as ordering and copying using these interfaces to get the most out of the collection classes.

Arrays

The array is the simplest collection. It is the most limited, and it is the fastest. It is the fastest because it provides the least dynamic data structure. You must declare the number of dimensions and the size of the array when you create it. Any array you create is derived from the **System.Array** abstract class. The array is the simplest collection structure. It is the only collection class that is part of the **System** namespace, instead of the **System.Collections** namespace.

Using an array is quite simple and natural. Several of the examples in previous chapters have used arrays for data structures. Arrays have two properties that make them different than any other collection type:

- *Arrays are completely type-safe*—Arrays are declared with a particular type. Only that type may be added to an array. All other collections store references to **System.Object** objects.

- *Arrays cannot change size once declared*—Once you declare an array, you cannot grow the array to store more elements than you had originally planned.

These two restrictions help to make the array faster than other collection classes. You do not need to check types when you examine elements in an array. Also, there is much less work for the runtime to manage the memory in an array. The array is also unique in that you can declare arrays with multiple dimensions or jagged arrays.

Single Dimension Arrays

To declare a *single dimension,* you specify the type stored in the array and the rank of the array. You also can optionally construct the array:

```
int [] firstArray; // Not initialized
int [] myArray = new int [10]; // created.
// None of the elements are initialized.
```

Notice that the size of the array is not part of the variable type. The following is legal C#:

```
int [] myArray = new int [10]; // 10 elements.
MyArray = new int [20]; // 20 elements now.
```

You also can initialize the elements that go in the array:

```
// create an array with 10 elements, containing 0-9.
int [] myArray = {0,1,2,3,4,5,6,7,8,9};
// Explicitly declare the size:
int [] myArray = new int [10]{0,1,2,3,4,5,6,7,8,9};
```

When you specify the size of the array, as in the second example, the number of elements in the initializer must match the size of the array. Neither of the following will compile:

```
// Neither work correctly:
int [] myArray = new int [9]  {0,1,2,3,4,5,6,7,8,9};
int [] myArray = new int [11]  {0,1,2,3,4,5,6,7,8,9};
```

Once you create the array, you can access the elements by using the array index:

```
int i = myArray[3]; // Get the 4th element.
```

This example sets *i* to the value of the fourth element in the array. The lowest index in all C# arrays is 0. If you try to access the array outside of its declared bounds, the runtime throws an **IndexOutOfRangeException**:

```
int i = myArray[12]; // Throws an IndexOutOfRangeException.
```

Internally, any array declared in C# is derived from **System.Array**. You can use any of the methods that are declared in **System.Array** with any of the arrays you create. The **Array** class also implements four different interfaces: **ICloneable**, **IList**, **ICollection**, and **IEnumerable**. For example, the C# **foreach** statement expects the collection to support the **IEnumerable** interface:

```
foreach (int i in myArray) {
  System.Console.WriteLine (i.ToString ());
}
```

Multiple Dimension Arrays and Jagged Arrays

C# has support for multiple dimension arrays, of which there are two different styles: *multiple dimension* arrays and *jagged* arrays. Multiple dimension arrays contain more than one index:

```
// create a 4X2 matrix.
int [,] matrix = new int [4,2];
```

This statement creates an array containing eight elements. Multiple dimension arrays are also referred to as *rectangular* arrays. This distinguishes them from jagged arrays:

```
int [][] arrayOfArrays = new int [4] [];
arrayOfArrays[0] = new int [5];
arrayOfArrays[1] = new int [3];
arrayOfArrays[2] = new int [7];
arrayOfArrays[3] = new int [4];
```

Jagged arrays are actually arrays of arrays. Each element in *arrayOfArrays* is an array of integers. This gives jagged arrays the ability to have different rows containing different numbers of elements. Multiple dimension arrays have fixed numbers of elements for each dimension.

These simple examples show arrays with two dimensions. You can, however, use any number of dimensions in an array. In fact, you can even mix jagged arrays and multiple dimension arrays.

16. Collections

TIP: *The extra overhead means that multiple dimension arrays are more efficient than jagged arrays. You should use multiple dimension arrays instead of jagged arrays unless you need to have different lengths for the different rows in your jagged array.*

Collection Classes

The simple array can handle many of the cases where you need more than one object of a particular type. When you need more sophisticated data storage, the .NET BCL contains many classes you can use for different data structures. I go through the collection classes in order from the most general to the most specific. All the collection classes store references to **System.Object** objects. Therefore, any time you work with the elements in the collection, you will need to explicitly cast the object in the collection to the specific type of object you actually stored in the collection.

Examining the Collection Classes

In this section, I discuss only a few of the collections. These collections are part of the **System.Collections** namespace. Other collection classes are more specialized and are derived from these collections. For example, collection classes in the **System. Windows.Forms** namespace are used for managing controls on forms, and collection classes in the **System.Data** namespace work with database elements.

ArrayList

The **ArrayList** stores a sequence of elements. The **ArrayList** differs from the **Array** class in that you can change the storage capacity of an **ArrayList** dynamically. Internally, the **ArrayList** class uses an array to store the objects in the collection. The performance characteristics of the **ArrayList** and the array are very similar. The dynamic memory management of the **ArrayList** will affect the performance of this data structure. You can control these effects by using the **Capacity** property of the **ArrayList**.

TIP: *You should choose the **ArrayList** to get the best performance for an unsorted sequence of elements that must change size dynamically. The **ArrayList** also gets better performance for sorted operations when you can control the frequency of insert and remove operations.*

HashTable

The **HashTable** stores key/value pairs. **HashTable**s cannot contain multiple copies of the same key value. The **HashTable** provides the fastest performance for a collection that examines elements by lookup, rather than iterating values. The **HashTable** is not sorted in the normal sense. Rather, the **HashTable** stores items in buckets based on the value returned by the hash function. The elements are ordered based on the value of the hash function. If you iterate all the elements in a **HashTable**, you will not get the elements in order. However, if you search for a specific element, you will get the best performance using a **HashTable**.

*TIP: You should use the **HashTable** when most of your element access is searching for elements, not iterating the collection. The **HashTable** is also faster than the **SortedList** when elements are frequently added to the collection.*

SortedList

The **SortedList** stores key/value pairs, just like the **HashTable** does. The **SortedList** differs from the **HashTable** in how it stores values in the collection. A **SortedList** stores two arrays internally, one for the keys and one for the values. Using the **SortedList**, you can search for keys in the structure, just like you can with the **HashTable**. When you iterate a **SortedList**, you will get the keys in sorted order. Every insert operation moves elements in the internal arrays; each new object gets inserted in sorted order. Insertions and lookups are slower than with the **HashTable**, but you do get to iterate all the items in order.

*TIP: You should use the **SortedList** when you need key/value pairs in sorted order. It is slower than the **HashTable**, but you can control the iteration order.*

Stack

The **Stack** is a special purpose collection. The **Stack** provides a limited interface to support the specific interface of a stack: Items are pushed onto and popped off of a stack. You can enumerate all the items in the stack by using the **IEnumerable** interface.

*TIP: You should use the **Stack** only when you need the particular characteristics of a last-in, first-out stack container.*

Queue

The **Queue** is also a special purpose collection. It provides a limited interface to support adding items to the end of the queue and removing them from the front of the queue. The **Queue** does support the **IEnumerable** interface, so you can examine all the items in the queue.

TIP: You should use the **Queue** only when you need the particular characteristics of a first-in, first-out queue container.

BitArray

The **BitArray** is a special structure that stores bits to represent an array of Boolean values. The **BitArray** trades space for speed. The **BitArray** supports Boolean logic operations on the bits in the **BitArray**. You can perform **AND**, **OR**, **NOT**, and **XOR** operations on all the bits in two different **BitArray** containers.

TIP: You should use the **BitArray** when your design creates Boolean data structures that model large numbers of Boolean values.

Choosing a Collection

Choosing one of the special purpose collections should be fairly obvious. If you need the special properties in the **Queue**, **Stack**, or **BitArray**, that is what you use. You should choose one of the general collection classes based on the performance characteristics of the collection and which operations you will perform most often. Here are a few selection tips:

- Use an array of the specified type if you do not need to resize the collection often. This will give you the best performance.

- Use the **ArrayList** structure when you need to resize the collection. This is the most common collection to use when you need or want the dynamic memory management provided by the runtime.

- Use the **HashTable** when you need to store keys and values, and the majority of your access is searching for a specific key.

- Use the **SortedList** when you need to store keys and values, and you need to enumerate those values in order.

Boxing and Unboxing

The collection classes all store references to **System.Object** objects. You will often want to store value types in your collections. When you store value types in your collections, they are boxed when you add them to the collection. Conversely, they are unboxed when you remove them from the collection. The end result of this conversion is that you cannot modify a value type inside a collection. You will always replace a value type with another object of the same type in the collection.

16. Collections

The boxing and unboxing operations take time and memory. You do pay a performance penalty when you put value types in collections. You can avoid this penalty by storing your value types in arrays, rather than the more sophisticated collection classes.

Collection Interfaces

The collection classes are distinguished primarily by their performance characteristics. You can write code that works correctly with multiple different collection classes by coding to the interfaces defined by the collection classes.

The .NET design team separated the collection classes from the interfaces that collections implement for two different reasons. In addition to allowing you to create methods that can work with different collection classes, it can help you write your own collection classes. By implementing these interfaces, you can create a specialized collection class that will work with any methods that work with the standard collections in the .NET BCL. The collections that are outside of the **System.Collections** namespace implement many of these interfaces so that those specialized collections work seamlessly with the .NET BCL.

ICollection

The **ICollection** interface provides methods that are implemented by all classes that store more than one object. All the collection classes listed in the "Collection Classes" section, including arrays, implement **ICollection**. The **ICollection** interface contains a property for the number of objects in the collection. The only method in the **ICollection** interface supports copying the collection to an array.

IEnumerable

The **IEnumerable** interface contains one method: **GetEnumerator ()**. All the collections support this interface. In addition, many classes that can act like a collection support this interface. For example, the **string** class supports this interface so that you can enumerate the characters in the string.

IEnumerator

You use an object that supports the **IEnumerator** interface to enumerate all the elements in a collection. The **IEnumerator** interface has methods to move forward in the collection and to reset the enumerator to the beginning of the collection. Every collection returns an object that supports **IEnumerator** through its **IEnumerable** interface.

The **HashTable** and **SortedList** classes support a special kind of enumerator called the **IDictionaryEnumerator**. The **IDictionary-Enumerator** contains extra methods to return either the key or the value in a dictionary.

IDictionary

The **IDictionary** interface is derived from both the **ICollection** and **IEnumerable** interfaces. It adds those methods that are specific to collections that store key/value pairs and support lookup based on the keys. The **IDictionary** interface is implemented by the **HashTable**, the **SortedList**, and many other special purpose collections outside of the **System.Collections** namespace. The **IDictionary** interface lets you add and remove key/value pairs or enumerate the keys or values separately.

IList

The **IList** interface contains methods that should be supported by any collection that stores a sequence of values. **IList** methods let you add and remove elements, find elements by value, and retrieve values based on their index in the collection. The common methods used by all collections are actually part of the **IList** interface.

Interfaces Used by Collections

The .NET collections need some functionality provided by the objects in a collection to provide their functionality. Your objects should provide two interfaces—**IComparer** and **IHashCodeProvider**—to allow them to work more easily with the .NET libraries. You should consider implementing these interfaces for classes that you will put in collections.

IComparer

The **IComparer** interface is used by the **Sort ()** methods in the **ArrayList** and **SortedList** collections to sort the objects that are stored in the collection. You implement the **IComparer** interface to provide an ordering in your class. If your class does not naturally support an ordering function, you need not implement this interface. If your class does not support an ordering function, simply don't support this interface; the collections still work, except that you cannot sort the elements.

16. Collections

IHashCodeProvider

The **IHashCodeProvider** provides a custom hash function for different objects. Overriding the **Object.GetHashCode ()** is generally a better way to implement the hash function. However, when you are putting objects in a **HashTable** that do not support **GetHashCode** (), or the **Object.GetHashCode ()** function does not provide the distribution you need, you can provide your own hash function by using an object that implements the **IHashCodeProvider** interface.

Immediate Solutions

The key point to remember as you look at these examples is that the .NET collections are designed so that similar or identical constructs work with different collections.

Using Arrays

Many of the samples written so far have included some form of array. The **System.Array** and instantiations of that class are by far the most common simple collection you will use.

Initializing Single Dimension Arrays

When you create a single dimension array, you must declare the size of the array. You cannot resize the array later, although you can re-create it with a different size. You can initialize a single dimension array when you declare the array:

```
Point[] locations = new Point [8] {new Point (175, 10),
  new Point (275,  75),
  new Point (325, 175),
  new Point (275, 275),
  new Point (175, 325),
  new Point ( 75, 275),
  new Point ( 20, 175),
  new Point ( 75,  75)};
```

That construct is shorthand for declaring each array element individually after creating the array:

```
Point[] locations = new Point [8]; // Elements are null.
locations [0] = new Point (175, 10);
locations [1] = new Point (275,  75);
locations [2] = new Point (325, 175);
locations [3] = new Point (275, 275);
locations [4] = new Point (175, 325);
locations [5] = new Point ( 75, 275);
locations [6] = new Point ( 20, 175);
locations [7] = new Point ( 75,  75);
```

16. Collections

Initializing Multiple Dimension Arrays

You create a multiple dimension array in a similar manner to the single dimension array. When you declare the array, you must declare how many dimensions are in the array. The number of dimensions is also referred to as the *rank* of the array.

```
int [,] twoDArray; // 2 Dimensions
int [,,] threeDArray; // 3 Dimensions.
int [,,,,,] sixDArray; // 6 Dimensions.
```

When you create the array, you must specify the length of each dimension:

```
twoDArray = new int [3,4];
// Now, you can intialize the elements:
twoDArray[0,0] = 0;
twoDArray[0,1] = 1;
twoDArray[0,2] = 2;
twoDArray[0,3] = 3;
twoDArray[1,0] = 4;
twoDArray[1,1] = 5;
twoDArray[1,2] = 6;
twoDArray[1,3] = 7;
twoDArray[2,0] = 8;
twoDArray[2,1] = 9;
twoDArray[2,2] = 10;
twoDArray[2,3] = 11;
```

Like single dimension arrays, you can initialize the array when you create it, or even when you declare the array:

```
int twoDArray [,] = new int [3,4] {
   {0,1,2,3},
   {4,5,6,7},
   {8,9,10,11}};
```

The outer brackets specify the leftmost, or outermost, dimension. Each inner set of brackets specifies a more inner dimension, or more to the right, in the array initialization.

Initializing Jagged Arrays

You must initialize jagged arrays differently than single or multiple dimension arrays. Jagged arrays are implemented as an array of arrays. As such, you create each element in the outer dimensions using an array creation statement:

```
int [][] JaggedArray; // 2 D jagged array.
JaggedArray = new int [3][]; // Create an array
// of single dimension arrays.
JaggedArray[0] = new int [4]; // Create an array
JaggedArray[1] = new int [3]; // Second Array.
JaggedArray[2] = new int [5]; // Third Array.

// Create elements:
JaggedArray[0][0] = 0;
JaggedArray[0][1] = 1;
JaggedArray[0][2] = 2;
JaggedArray[0][3] = 3;

// Next array:
JaggedArray[1][0] = 4;
JaggedArray[1][1] = 5;
JaggedArray[1][2] = 6;

// Last array:
JaggedArray[2][0] = 7;
JaggedArray[2][1] = 8;
JaggedArray[2][2] = 9;
JaggedArray[2][3] = 10;
JaggedArray[2][4] = 11;
```

You can combine all these initializers into a single construct:

```
int [][] JaggedArray = new  int [][] {
  new int [] {0,1,2,3},
  new int [] {4,5,6},
  new int [] {7,8,9,10,11}
};
```

Enumerating Single Dimension Array Elements

The **foreach** statement is the best way to enumerate all the elements in your array:

```
foreach (Point p in locations) {
  // Draw the points.
}
```

The **foreach** construct provides you with two very important benefits:

- The elements being retrieved from the array are typechecked. Any incompatible elements in the array are skipped. In fact, the **InvalidCastException** gets caught and handled, without you needing to write any extra code.

16. Collections

337

- The **foreach** statement properly handles the length of the array. You do not need to remember the size of the array.

This same statement works correctly for all sequence containers.

Related solution:	Found on page:
Catching Exceptions	232

Enumerating Multiple Dimension Array Elements

You can enumerate a multiple dimension array the same as a single dimension array:

```
int twoDArray [,] = new int [3,4] {
  {0,1,2,3},
  {4,5,6,7},
  {8,9,10,11}};

foreach (int i in twoDArray)
  Console.WriteLine (i.ToString());
```

This will print all the numbers in the array. The innermost dimension increases first, the outermost dimension last. For example, the preceding statement will print 0 through 11, in order. If you want to enumerate the rows and columns separately, you will need to use the **GetLength ()** method of the array class:

```
for (int x= 0; x < twoDArray.GetLength (0); x++) {
  for (int y = 0; y < twoDArray.GetLength (1);y++) {
    Console.Write ("{0}, ", twoDArray[x,y].ToString());
  }
  Console.WriteLine ();
}
```

*WARNING! Do not use the **Rank** or **Length** properties to enumerate the array. The **Rank** property tells you how many dimensions are in the array. The **Length** property gives the total length of the array, not the length of a single dimension.*

Enumerating Jagged Array Elements

Jagged arrays are arrays of arrays. Enumerating all the elements in a jagged array involves nested loops. Once again, **foreach** will work to iterate the arrays that make up the jagged array. An inner **foreach** loop will iterate each element in each array:

```
int [][] JaggedArray = new int [][]
  { new int [] {0,1,2,3},
    new int [] {4,5,6},
    new int [] {7,8,9,10,11}};

foreach (int [] a in JaggedArray ) {
  foreach (int i in a) {
    Console.Write ("{0}, ", i);
  }
  Console.WriteLine ();
}
```

Using Array Methods

The **System.Array** class also contains methods that manipulate the elements, or the order of elements, in an array. Remember that the array is actually a specific instance of **System.Array**. The **System.Array** class supports the **ICloneable**, **ICollection**, **IList**, and **IEnumerable** interfaces. Any of those interface methods are part of the array class. You can use the **Sort ()** method to sort a single dimension array. The **BinarySearch ()** method will find an element in an array. The **Reverse ()** method will reverse the order of elements in an array. These methods are covered in the next section on sequence containers.

Working with **ArrayList**

Arrays are the right data structure when you rarely change the size of the container once it is created. When you need to dynamically change the size of a container, the **ArrayList** container will be easier to use and much more efficient than the vector. Vectors cannot change size. If you need to resize them, you must recreate them. The **ArrayList** grows dynamically when you add an element or a range of elements:

```
ArrayList l = new ArrayList ();
l.Add (2); // Add one element.
l.AddRange (twoDArray); // Add a range of elements.
// Any kind of collection can be added:
l.AddRange (JaggedArray);
```

The **ArrayList** stores a single sequence of elements, and you can add and remove those elements anytime in your program. The **Remove ()** method lets you remove an element either by index or by value:

```
1.Remove (5); // remove the fifth element.
1.Remove ((object) 3); // remove the first '3' in the collection.
```

The second version performs a linear search through the collection to find a particular value. You will see later that there are quicker ways to remove an element from a sorted collection.

Reserving Space

The **ArrayList** has two properties that let you manage the storage in the **ArrayList** container: **Capacity** and **Count**. **Capacity** stores the amount of space reserved in the collection for elements. **Count** returns the number of elements actually in the collection. You can control the way in which the collection grows by manipulating the **Capacity** before a large insert operation:

```
ArrayList 1 = new ArrayList ();
1.Add (2); // Add one element.
1.Capacity += twoDArray.Length; // Reserve Space.
1.AddRange (twoDArray); // Add a range of elements.
```

Anytime you are adding large groups of elements to a collection, you can use this method to increase the capacity in one call, rather than taking repeated performance hits to increase the capacity multiple times as the collection grows. Similarly, you can use this property to trim excess capacity from an **ArrayList** when you know you will not be adding more elements:

```
1.Capacity = 1.Length; // Trim excess capacity.
1.TrimToSize (); // Does the same thing.
```

Trim the **ArrayList** with caution, because the next **Add ()** will cause the **ArrayList** to grow, with the associated time cost.

Enumerating Collections

These collections all contain indexers that return a reference to the individual elements in the collection:

```
int val = (int)1[3]; // Get the fourth element.
1[3] = ++val; // modify the fourth element.
```

All the sequence collections—**ArrayList**, **Queue**, and **Stack**—support the **IEnumerable** interface. The **foreach** statement uses the **IEnumerable** interface. So, to enumerate an **ArrayList**, **Queue**, or **Stack**, use the **foreach** statement shown before:

```
ArrayList 1 = new ArrayList ();
1.Add (2); // Add one element.
1.AddRange (twoDArray); // Add a range of elements.
foreach (int i in 1) {
  Console.WriteLine (i.ToString ());
}
```

The **foreach** statement means you do not have to make the cast when you retrieve objects from your collections. However, the **foreach** statement does perform the same cast. If the wrong type of object is in your collection, an **InvalidCastException** gets thrown, and the remainder of the collection does not get enumerated.

Searching and Sorting

The **ArrayList** collection contains methods to sort the collection and to search for an element in a collection. The **Sort ()** and **Search ()** methods use the method defined in the **IComparable** interface. Here is a simple class that stores CD titles and artists:

```
class Album : IComparable {
  private string _Title;
  private string _Artist;

  public Album (string artist, string title) {
    _Artist = artist;
    _Title = title;
  }

  public string Title {
    get {
      return _Title;
    }
    set {
      _Title = value;
    }
  }

  public string Artist {
    get {
      return _Artist;
    }
    set {
      _Artist = value;
    }
  }
```

16. Collections

341

```
public override string ToString () {
  return _Artist + ",\t"+ _Title;
}

public int CompareTo (object o) {
  Album other = o as Album;
  if (other == null)
    throw new ArgumentException ();
  if (_Artist != other._Artist)
    return _Artist.CompareTo (other._Artist);
  else
    return _Title.CompareTo (other._Title);
}
}
```

(handwritten annotation: ∴ <dynamic-cast>)

The class simply stores two strings: the artist and the title of the album. The last method, **CompareTo ()**, provides the ordering function for the **Album** class. The **CompareTo ()** method should return −1 if this object is less than the reference object, 0 if the objects are equivalent, and 1 if this object is greater than the reference object. If the other object is not of the correct type, the **CompareTo ()** method should throw an **ArgumentException**.

Now you can sort the collection:

```
ArrayList arr = new ArrayList ();

arr.Add (new Album ("Grateful Dead", "American Beauty"));
arr.Add (new Album ("Bare Naked Ladies", "Gordon"));
arr.Add (new Album ("Smashmouth", "Astro Lounge"));
// etc.

// Sort:
arr.Sort ();
// Print all the albums:
foreach (Album a in arr) {
  Console.WriteLine (a);
}
```

But, what if you want to sort the albums by title? Well, an overloaded version of the **Sort ()** method takes another parameter: an object that supports the **IComparer** interface. **IComparer** has one method, **Compare ()**, which compares two objects of the same type. The return value for **Compare ()** follows the same convention as the **CompareTo ()** method in the **Icomparable ()** method. Here is a simple class to compare the albums based on the title:

```
class TitleComparer : IComparer {
  public int Compare (object l, object r) {
    Album left = l as Album;
    Album right = r as Album;
    if ((left == null) || (right == null))
      throw new ArgumentException ();
    if (left.Title != right.Title)
      return left.Title.CompareTo (right.Title);
    else
      return left.Artist.CompareTo (right.Artist);
  }
}

// Using it is simple:
// Sort by title:
arr.Sort (new TitleComparer());
foreach (Album a in arr) {
  Console.WriteLine (a);
}
```

Searching the collection is equally simple. The **BinarySearch ()** method searches an **ArrayList** to find a particular value. The default version searches for the value, using the **IComparable.CompareTo ()** method on the objects being sought:

```
Album l = new Album ("Bare Naked Ladies", "Gordon");
// Default Sort:
arr.Sort ();
// Default search (returns 0)
int index = arr.BinarySearch(l);

// Sort by title.
arr.Sort (new TitleComparer());
// Search by title (returns 2):
index = arr.BinarySearch (l, new TitleComparer ());
Console.WriteLine (index.ToString ());
```

WARNING! *If you do not use the same* **Compare ()** *functions for both the Sort () and BinarySearch () functions, you get undefined results. Searching on an unsorted collection also yields undefined behavior.*

The **ArrayList** collection contains many other methods that let you manipulate the collection. These methods let you copy ranges of the **ArrayList**, remove or replace elements, or access individual elements.

Working with Dictionaries

The .NET BCL has two kinds of dictionary collections: the **HashTable** and the **SortedList**. Both of these collections store key/value pairs. Because these collections store pairs of values, the interface is a bit different from the sequence containers. When you enumerate these values, you get a special type of object that contains the key/value pair. The observable difference between these two types of collections is the order of the elements in the collections. When I refer to a "dictionary" in any of the following discussions, the discussion is valid for both the **SortedList** and the **HashTable**. The performance of the collections differs as well. Searching for a specific key in a **HashTable** is a *constant time operation*—it completes in the same amount of time, no matter how many objects are in the collection. Searching for a specific key in a **SortedList** is a logarithmic operation. The time to find an element grows with the logarithm of the number of elements in a collection.

You create a **SortedList** or a **HashTable** by constructing the collection:

```
HashTable h = new HashTable ();
SortedList l = new SortedList ();
```

The **HashTable** and **SortedList** both store **System.Object** references for both the keys and values. So, you need to manage a few details to make sure that your dictionaries work correctly. Internally, the dictionaries—both the **HashTable** and the **SortedList**—use the **IComparer** interface or the **Object.GetHashCode ()** method to compare and organize objects. If you make a mistake and use the wrong type of elements as the keys, your dictionary will not work correctly. You will not be able to find elements because the keys cannot be compared properly.

Adding and Removing Elements

You add elements to a dictionary by using the **Add ()** method. You supply both the key and a value:

```
Hashtable h = new Hashtable();
h.Add ("Gordon", "Bare Naked Ladies");
h.Add ("Astro Lounge", "Smashmouth");
h.Add ("American Beauty", "Grateful Dead");
h.Add ("Abraxus", "Santana");
```

```
h.Add ("Wheels of Fire", "Cream");

SortedList list = new SortedList();
list.Add ("Gordon", "Bare Naked Ladies");
list.Add ("Astro Lounge", "Smashmouth");
list.Add ("American Beauty", "Grateful Dead");
list.Add ("Abraxus", "Santana");
list.Add ("Wheels of Fire", "Cream");
```

The **HashTable** and the **SortedList** have different performance characteristics for the **Add ()** method. The **HashTable** adds elements in constant time. The **SortedList** takes logarithmic time to add elements; it must search for the correct location in the collection for the new element.

You remove elements from any dictionary by using the **Remove ()** method. You also can use the **RemoveAt ()** method for a **SortedList**:

```
h.Remove ("Abraxus"); // Find and remove.

list.Remove("Abraxus"); // Find and remove.
list.RemoveAt (2); // Remove the 3rd element.
```

The **RemoveAt ()** method is faster than the **Remove ()** method for a **SortedList** collection. The **Remove ()** method must find the element before it can remove it. **Remove ()** is a constant time operation for a **HashTable**.

Finding Elements

The dictionary classes contain indexers that let you find values in the collection by the key. These give you a very natural syntax to access and change elements:

```
artist = (string) list["American Beauty"];
```

These indexers return a reference to the value associated with the specified key. If the key is not in the collection, the indexer returns null. The value returned must be cast to the proper type; the method returns a reference to a **System.Object** object. Just like other methods that need to search for elements in a dictionary, the **HashTable** version is faster. The **HashTable** retrieves an element in constant time; the **SortedList** needs logarithmic time to find and retrieve an element.

Enumerating Elements

As with other collections, you can use the **foreach** statement to enumerate all the elements in a dictionary. There are some differences for dictionaries, though. The dictionary classes provide a more specialized **IEnumerator**. The dictionary enumerator returns a **DictionaryEntry** object that contains properties for both the key and value. In this way, you can work with both the key and value when you enumerate a dictionary:

```
foreach (DictionaryEntry d in h) {
  Console.WriteLine ("{0}, {1}", d.Key, d.Value);
}

foreach (DictionaryEntry d in list) {
  Console.WriteLine ("{0}, {1}", d.Key, d.Value);
}
```

Up to this point, every section has shown you that the **HashTable** is faster than the **SortedList**. Enumerations are the one area where the **SortedList** may be more appropriate. The **SortedList** does keep the collection in sorted order, based on the keys. The **HashTable** enumerates the collection based on the value returned by the hash function. That order is most likely meaningless to you and your users.

In Brief

The .NET library contains more than 1,500 classes. I cannot possibly cover all of them in any reasonably in-depth fashion. Much of the development tasks will be familiar to anyone who has written Windows programs in the past. Two new packages require more discussion: WebForms, designed to create rich Web applications using .NET, and WebServices, designed to create software components accessible via the Internet. Finally, one key benefit to the .NET architecture is interlanguage programming. You need to program to a subset of the C# language that is CLS (common language specification) compliant. I will cover these key areas of the .NET libraries and point you to the SDK documentation for more information on other areas of the libraries.

Windows Development

The Windows development tools encompass several namespaces. The **System.Windows** namespace has many subordinate namespaces for specific Windows development tasks. For example, the **System. Windows.Forms** namespace contains many classes to work with dialogs, forms, and controls. The classes in this namespace will be familiar to anyone who has created Windows programs. These classes include controls, window classes, and other higher-level constructs. The **Forms** and **Controls** classes have more rapid application development (RAD) constructs. Those who have used VB will be familiar with the development paradigms used. These new controls support design time properties that make it much simpler to create Windows programs.

The **System.Drawing** and other subordinate namespaces (**System. Drawing.Drawing2D**, **System.Drawing.Imaging**, **System. Drawing.Printing**, and **System.Drawing.Text**) contain a new GDI+ library. GDI+ is an updated version of the GDI library that is more object-oriented. The GDI+ library also contains a better model for colors, bitmaps, and image controls.

If you have done any Windows programming, these new tools will be familiar to you. The new classes are similar or improved versions of previous versions that you have already used. These new classes are easier to use; in keeping with other .NET classes, these objects use cleanup resources automatically. These classes use resources other than memory, so they do support the **IDisposable** interface.

WebForms

WebForms is a new library that you can use for developing Web applications. These classes are part of the ASP .NET initiative. ASP .NET is a new updated version of the ASP programming model. The goal of ASP .NET is to provide a way to develop Web applications using the familiar Windows programming model. ASP .NET contains new classes that model HTML controls. ASP .NET also contains several other controls that do not map to simple HTML controls, but rather are built-in code using standard HTML constructs. For example, the **System.Web.UI.WebControls.DataGrid** class displays database data in a grid. The grid is built using HTML tables, but you program the **DataGrid** control at a much higher level. All the WebForms classes support an event model that makes it easier to respond to user input in a Web application. This event model is similar to the current Windows event model.

WebForms provides many services that make designing and creating Web applications similar to creating Windows applications. You design forms, set properties on the controls and forms, and define event handlers for the events the form and controls can fire. The same steps you use to create Windows applications are used for Web applications. The controls and forms even make use of the HTTP session services to provide you with state services in the controls and forms in your applications.

Web Services

Web Services provide a consistent protocol for wide area network distributed applications. Web Services use HTTP as a transport protocol between client and server. Web Services use SOAP-encoded XML to transport data between client and server. Web Services are a way of providing access to components across the Internet. The .NET library contains classes that make it much easier to create and consume these widely distributed services. The **System.Web.Services** namespace contains classes and attribute classes that make creating Web Services as simple as creating any class. The .NET Framework SDK and Visual Studio .NET provide tools that automatically generate proxy classes for you.

You need to be cognizant of the speed, latency, and overhead when you design Web Services. You need to create an interface to your Web Service that works well with this kind of connection. To do this, you need to make sure that you minimize the number of method calls that are made to your Web Service. You need to try to design your Web Service so that you retrieve a reasonable amount of data in each message.

CLS Compliance

One of the key design goals for the .NET Framework is language interoperability. Programmers can use many languages to create .NET assemblies and programs. Each language has particular advantages and disadvantages. Programmers will want to use different languages for different purposes. The .NET Framework contains a specification called the common language specification. The CLS provides the definition for you to follow that ensures that all the constructs and interfaces in your assembly can be accessed by any other assembly, even if it was created using another language.

Each language supports constructs that are not CLS-compliant, and C# is no exception. It is unlikely that any developer will always remember the subset of C# that is CLS-compliant. You use the **CLSCompliantAttribute** to mark assemblies, classes, methods, or properties as compliant or not compliant. The compiler generates errors for non-CLS-compliant code inside a definition marked as CLS-compliant. By default, code without this attribute is considered not CLS-compliant. As examples, unsigned values (**UInt16**, **UInt32**, and so on) are not CLS-compliant.

Immediate Solutions

The .NET library provides many different ways to deliver your functionality. You can create Windows applications, Web applications, and WebServices. You also can create binary components that can be used by programs written in other languages. Through these samples, you will learn how to create each of those different types of programs and how to ensure that your assemblies are CLS-compliant. This chapter builds a CLS-compliant component and shows you how to make sure that your components provide the expected interfaces for users of your components. Once you create the component, you will create different applications that use the component.

The component is a simple class that calculates the payment schedule for a simple interest loan. The equation is the present value equation from any economics textbook:

Payment=Principal×(MonthlyInterestRate×(1+DailyInterestRate) ^Months)/(((1+MonthlyInterestRate)^Months)–1)

After calculating the payment, you add the interest each month then subtract the payment to get the remaining balance.

Creating CLS-Compliant Code

The first step is to create a CLS-compliant assembly that performs the calculations outlined in the preceding section. Start Visual Studio .NET and select File|New|Project (see Figure 17.1). Name the new project **LoanCalc**. Visual Studio .NET creates the new project for you.

This project should be a CLS-compliant assembly, which means limiting it to a subset of C# syntax that is compliant with the CLS. These restrictions include the following:

- Unsigned types (such as **UInt16**, **UInt32**, and so on) cannot be part of the public interface of a class.

- Unsafe types, such as pointers, cannot be part of the public interface to a class.

- Identifiers must be unique, even if case-insensitive.

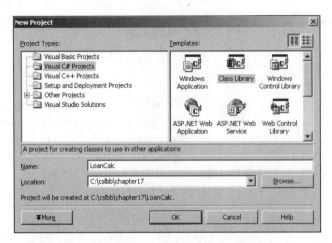

Figure 17.1 Create a new C# class library project.

The first two restrictions affect only the public interface of the class; you can use unsigned and unsafe types internally. The last restriction affects the entire class; you must make sure that all identifiers, even private identifiers, are unique, even if case-insensitive. Sometimes, these restrictions are difficult to remember. Thankfully, there is an attribute that tells the compiler to check your code for CLS compliance. The first step is to mark this entire assembly as CLS-compliant. Open up the AssemblyInfo.cs file and add the following line:

```
[assembly: CLSCompliant (true)]
```

Now, the assembly is marked for CLS compliance. You need to mark each type that is intended to be CLS-compliant as well. Next, take care of my largest annoyance in Visual Studio .NET, the generic name your files and classes get when you create a new project. Change the name of **Class1.cs** to **LoanCalc.cs**. Next, open **LoanCalc.cs** and change the name of the class to **PaymentCalculator**. Finally, add the **CLSCompliant** attribute to the **PaymentCalculator** definition:

```
[type:CLSCompliant (true)]
public class PaymentCalculator
```

Next, let's create the core logic for the **PaymentCalculator** class (see Listing 17.1). The constructor takes the parameters necessary to calculate the payment schedule, and then it calculates and stores the monthly payment and the remaining balance after each month. All the other methods are simple properties and an indexer that allows client code to access the payment value, the term of the loan, and the remaining balance after any given month.

Listing 17.1 **PaymentCalculator** class, first version.

```
/// <summary>
/// Summary description for PaymentCalculator.
/// </summary>
/// <remarks>
/// This is a CLS Compliant class that calculates
/// the payment schedule for a simple interest loan.
/// This class was created as a sample to show how
/// to create a class that implements the expected
/// interfaces so that it can be easily used
/// with other .net classes.
/// </remarks>
[type:CLSCompliant (true)]
public class PaymentCalculator {
  /// <summary>
  /// The payment necessary to fulfill the
  /// loan obligation.
  /// </summary>
  private decimal payment;

  /// <summary>
  /// The array of remaining balances in the loan.
  /// </summary>
  /// <remarks>
  /// The remaining balance after n months
  /// is stored in Values[n].
  /// </remarks>
  private decimal [] Values;

  /// <summary>
  /// The term of the loan, in Months.
  /// </summary>
  private int Months;

  /// <summary>
  /// Construct a new PaymentCalculator.
  /// </summary>
  /// <param name="principal">
  /// The original principal for the loan.
  /// </param>
  /// <param name="interestRate">
  /// The interest rate, as a decimal number, not
  /// a percentage. For example, 0.029 is a
```

```
/// 2.9% interest rate.
/// </param>
/// <param name="numMonths">
/// The term of the loan, in months.</param>
public PaymentCalculator(double principal,
  double interestRate, int numMonths) {
  Months = numMonths;
  Values = new decimal[numMonths];
  double rate = interestRate / 12.0;
  double express = Math.Pow (1.0+rate, numMonths);
  double numerator = rate * (express);
  double denominator = express-1.0;
  payment = (decimal)(principal * numerator / denominator);
  for (int i=0; i < numMonths; i++) {
    principal += principal * rate;
    principal -= Math.Min ((double)payment, principal);
    Values[i] = (decimal)principal;
  }
}


/// <summary>
/// Read-only indexer to retrieve the remaining
/// balance in the loan, after a specified
/// number of months.
/// </summary>
public decimal this [int month] {
  get {
    return Values[month];
  }
}


/// <summary>
/// Read-only Property to retrieve the monthly
/// payment necessary to pay off the loan in the
/// specified number of months.
/// </summary>
public decimal Payment {
  get {
    return payment;
  }
}


/// <summary>
/// Read-only property to return the length of
/// the loan.
```

```
/// </summary>
public int Time {
  get {
    return Months;
  }
}
}
```

Supporting Enumerations

This class can now be used by any other .NET assembly. The **CLSCompliant** attribute told the compiler to check our code for noncompliant constructs. However, you need to do some more work. First, client code will want to iterate the payment schedule by using the **foreach** statement. As this class stands, it can't. The code generated by **foreach** uses the **IEnumerable** interface to create an enumerator, and it enumerates the objects. You need to perform two tasks to add this capability. First, you need to create a nested class inside the **PaymentCalculator** that supports the **IEnumerator** interface. This nested class implements the **IEnumerator** interface to return subsequent balances to other objects.

The **IEnumerator** interface has three different methods that must be supported:

- **MoveNext ()** advances the enumerator to the next element. It returns true if the enumerator points to a valid object or false if the enumerator has moved past the end.

- **Reset ()** moves the enumerator back to the beginning of the collection.

- **Current ()** returns the object that the enumerator refers to.

Finally, the enumerator needs a constructor that takes the object that this particular enumerator will reference. After you create the nested class, you need to modify the **PaymentCalculator** class to support the **IEnumerable** interface. The **IEnumerable** interface has one method: **GetEnumerator ()** (see Listing 17.2). This method creates and returns a new enumerator object that can enumerate this **PaymentCalculator**. Now, the **PaymentCalculator** can be used with common .NET and C# idioms.

Related solution:	Found on page:
Programming with Interfaces	198

17. .NET Library

Listing 17.2   Enumerator class for the PaymentCalculator. This class, which is nested inside the PaymentCalculator, enumerates the entire collection.

```
/// <summary>
/// Nested class to enumerate the values
/// in the PaymentCalculator.
/// </summary>
/// <remarks>
/// The class accesses the properties in the
/// PaymentCalculator to move through the
/// objects in the collection and return
/// the value at the current point in the
/// collection.
/// </remarks>
[type:CLSCompliant (true)]
class LoanEnumerator : IEnumerator {
  /// <summary>
  /// The object being enumerated.
  /// </summary>
  private PaymentCalculator calc;

  /// <summary>
  /// The current index. This is a pointer
  /// into the object.
  /// </summary>
  private int index;

  /// <summary>
  /// Constructor.
  /// </summary>
  /// <param name="p">
  /// The object to enumerate.
  /// </param>
  public LoanEnumerator (PaymentCalculator p) {
    calc = p;
    index = -1;
  }

  /// <summary>
  /// Move Forward.
  /// </summary>
  /// <returns>
  /// true if the enumerator
  /// still points to a valid object.
  /// false if the enumerator moves past
  /// the end of the collection.
```

```
/// </returns>
public bool MoveNext () {
  ++index;
  if (index >= calc.Time)
    return false;
  else
    return true;
}


/// <summary>
/// Reset to the start of the
/// object.
/// </summary>
public void Reset () {
  index = -1;
}


/// <summary>
/// Get the object at this point
/// in the collection.
/// </summary>
public object Current {
  get {
    return calc[index];
  }
}
} // End of Enumerator
```

Supporting **ICollection**

There is one more step to make this component more usable with the different .NET classes. The DataBound controls expect to work with objects that support the **ICollection** interface. One way to add this capability to this object is to create a **System.Data.DataView** object that contains the information this collection returns, formatted for display:

```
/// <summary>
/// Read-only property that returns an ICollection
/// interface for the entire list of balances
/// during the duration of the loan.
/// </summary>
public ICollection Balances {
  get {
    DataTable dt = new DataTable ();
    DataRow dr = null;
```

```
dt.Columns.Add (new DataColumn ("Months",
  typeof (System.Int32)));
dt.Columns.Add (new DataColumn ("Remaining Balance",
  typeof(System.String)));
for (int i = 0; i < Months; i++) {
  dr = dt.NewRow ();
  dr[0] = i;
  // pass "C" to ToString to print the values
  // in currency format.
  dr[1] = Values[i].ToString ("C");
  dt.Rows.Add (dr);
}
DataView dv = new DataView (dt);
return dv;
}
}
```

This simple property creates a data table, and then it adds two columns to it. The loop adds a row to the data table for every monthly payment necessary to pay off the loan. Finally, the routine creates a data view on the table and returns the new data view.

The finished object is CLS-compliant, so it can be used by components created in other languages. In addition, it supports the **IEnumerable** and **ICollection** interfaces so that it can be easily incorporated into other .NET programs. The completed class is shown in Listing 17.3.

Listing 17.3   The finished **PaymentCalculator** class.

```
using System;
using System.Collections;
using System.Data;

namespace LoanCalc {
  /// <summary>
  /// Summary description for PaymentCalculator.
  /// </summary>
  /// <remarks>
  /// This is a CLS-compliant class that calculates
  /// the payment schedule for a simple interest loan.
  /// This class was created as a sample to show how
  /// to create a class that implements the expected
  /// interfaces so that it can be easily used
  /// with other .net classes.
  /// </remarks>
  [type:CLSCompliant (true)]
```

17. .NET Library

```
public class PaymentCalculator : IEnumerable {
  /// <summary>
  /// Nested class to enumerate the values
  /// in the PaymentCalculator.
  /// </summary>
  /// <remarks>
  /// The class accesses the properties in the
  /// PaymentCalculator to move through the
  /// objects in the collection and return
  /// the value at the current point in the
  /// collection.
  /// </remarks>
  [type:CLSCompliant (true)]
    class LoanEnumerator : IEnumerator {
    /// <summary>
    /// The object being enumerated.
    /// </summary>
    private PaymentCalculator calc;

    /// <summary>
    /// The current index. This is a pointer
    /// into the object.
    /// </summary>
    private int index;

    /// <summary>
    /// Constructor.
    /// </summary>
    /// <param name="p">
    /// The object to enumerate.
    /// </param>
    public LoanEnumerator (PaymentCalculator p) {
      calc = p;
      index = -1;
    }

    /// <summary>
    /// Move Forward.
    /// </summary>
    /// <returns>
    /// true if the enumerator
    /// still points to a valid object.
    /// false if the enumerator moves past
    /// the end of the collection.
    /// </returns>
    public bool MoveNext () {
```

```
        ++index;
        if (index >= calc.Time)
          return false;
        else
          return true;
      }

      /// <summary>
      /// Reset to the start of the
      /// object.
      /// </summary>
      public void Reset () {
        index = -1;
      }

      /// <summary>
      /// Get the object at this point
      /// in the collection.
      /// </summary>
      public object Current {
        get {
          return calc[index];
        }
      }
    }

    /// <summary>
    /// The payment necessary to fulfill the
    /// loan obligation.
    /// </summary>
    private decimal payment;

    /// <summary>
    /// The array of remaining balances in the loan.
    /// </summary>
    /// <remarks>
    /// The remaining balance after n months
    /// is stored in Values[n].
    /// </remarks>
    private decimal [] Values;

    /// <summary>
    /// The term of the loan, in Months.
    /// </summary>
    private int Months;

    /// <summary>
```

```
/// Construct a new PaymentCalculator.
/// </summary>
/// <param name="principal">
/// The original principal for the loan.
/// </param>
/// <param name="interestRate">
/// The interest rate, as a decimal number, not
/// a percentage. For example, 0.029 is a
/// 2.9% interest rate.
/// </param>
/// <param name="numMonths">
/// The term of the loan, in months.</param>
public PaymentCalculator(double principal,
  double interestRate, int numMonths) {
  Months = numMonths;
  Values = new decimal[numMonths];
  double rate = interestRate / 12.0;
  double express = Math.Pow (1.0+rate, numMonths);
  double numerator = rate * (express);
  double denominator = express-1.0;
  payment = (decimal)(principal * numerator / denominator);

  for (int i=0; i < numMonths; i++) {
    principal += principal * rate;
    principal -= Math.Min ((double)payment, principal);
    Values[i] = (decimal)principal;
  }
}


/// <summary>
/// Read-only indexer to retrieve the remaining
/// balance in the loan, after a specified
/// number of months.
/// </summary>
public decimal this [int month] {
  get {
    return Values[month];
  }
}


/// <summary>
/// Read-only Property to retrieve the monthly
/// payment necessary to pay off the loan in the
/// specified number of months.
/// </summary>
public decimal Payment {
  get {
```

```
        return payment;
    }
}


/// <summary>
/// Read-only property to return the length of
/// the loan.
/// </summary>
public int Time {
  get {
    return Months;
  }
}


/// <summary>
/// Return the enumerator for this object.
/// </summary>
/// <returns>
/// The IEnumerator object that can enumerate
/// this object.
/// </returns>
public IEnumerator GetEnumerator () {
  return new LoanEnumerator (this);
}


/// <summary>
/// Read-only property that returns an ICollection
/// interface for the entire list of balances
/// for the duration of the loan.
/// </summary>
public ICollection Balances {
  get {
    DataTable dt = new DataTable ();
    DataRow dr = null;
    dt.Columns.Add (new DataColumn ("Months",
      typeof (System.Int32)));
    dt.Columns.Add (new DataColumn ("Remaining Balance",
      typeof(System.String)));
    for (int i = 0; i < Months; i++) {
      dr = dt.NewRow ();
      dr[0] = i;
      // pass "C" to ToString to print the values
      // in currency format.
      dr[1] = Values[i].ToString ("C");
      dt.Rows.Add (dr);
    }
```

```
        DataView dv = new DataView (dt);
        return dv;
      }
    }
  }
}
```

Creating Windows Forms Applications

Now that you have created the component, it's time to use it. The first way to test out this component is to create a Windows application to use the component. Create a new Windows application project using Visual Studio .NET. Create a new solution for the new project. Once you have created the new solution, add the **LoanCalc** project to it. Do this by right-clicking the Solution node in the Solution Explorer and selecting Add|Existing Project.

Next, you need to add the **LoanCalc** assembly to the list of references in the build for this new project. Right-click the References node (see Figure 17.2) in the **LoanCalcApp** project. Select Add Reference. Choose the Projects tab and double-click the **LoanCalc** project. Now, the LoanCalc.dll assembly has been added to the list of linked assemblies. By adding the project to the solution, you get an

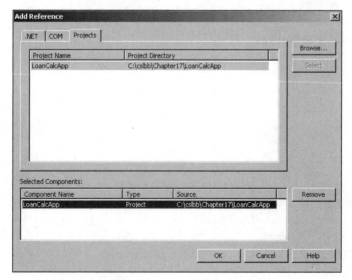

Figure 17.2 The Add Reference dialog box.

important benefit: Visual Studio .NET knows to specify the debug version of LoanCalc.dll in debug builds and the release version in release builds.

Creating the Form

Next, we add some controls to the form. You edit the form using the same paradigm as in previous versions of Visual Basic. You drag controls onto the form. The docked window on the lower-right of Visual Studio .NET shows the design properties of the control as you edit it. Some properties are common to all controls: the name of the control, the position, and size to name a few. Each control has its own distinct properties as well.

All the controls that you will be adding are part of the **System. Windows.Forms** namespace. However, you will not be spending much time editing the code for the forms. The Visual Studio .NET IDE lets you modify the design time properties of the controls. You can create and edit most of the controls to your forms and dialogs using this IDE.

I made a form with a subpanel for input controls and a list view control for the output from the component. The first task is to add a panel to the form. The panel does not look like much, but it aids in the form display as we add more controls. After you add the panel, you need to change one property of the panel: Dock the panel to the left of the form (see Figure 17.3).

Figure 17.3 Docking the panel to the left of the form.

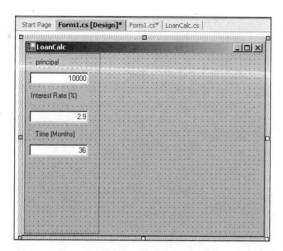

Figure 17.4 Add edit controls and labels for the input fields.

Next, add edit controls and labels for the principal, interest rate, and the time of the loan, as shown in Figure 17.4. Drop these controls on top of the panel you just added. You drag the controls from the toolbox to the form, just as you did in previous Windows development tools.

Next, drag a button and another edit control to the form. The user will click the button to calculate the loan values over time. The edit control will display the payment value once the loan has been calculated. Change the read-only property for this edit control to True. Change the text property on the button to Calculate.

Next, drag a **ListView** onto the form. Place the **ListView** control in the area of the form that is not covered by the panel. Finally, change the **Dock** property on the **ListView** to Fill. Now the **ListView** fills all the area of the form not contained by the panel.

Last, modify the names of the controls that you will be using to program the behavior of the application. Select each of the edit controls and change the name to something more meaningful than **edit1**, **edit2**, and such. I chose **Principal**, **Interest Rate %**, and **Time (Months)**. Also, I placed meaningful values in the three edit controls to help users figure out how to use it. To do this, modify the **Text** property of each of the three edit controls. Figure 17.5 shows the completed form.

Adding Behaviors

We need one more function to finish this application. Double-click the Calculate button. Double-clicking any control adds a handler for the default action on the control—a click handler in the case of a

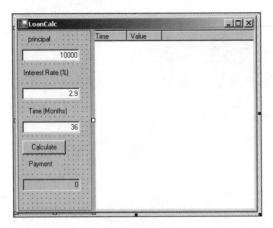

Figure 17.5   The finished form.

button. The click handler retrieves values from the edit controls and tries to parse the text in the edit controls as double values. If the values are invalid, the application shows a message box and does not try to calculate anything. After parsing the values, this routine creates a **PaymentCalculator** object and initializes it. After creating the object, the last block of code sets the payment value in the Payment edit box. Finally, the **foreach** loop at the end of the function adds all the values to the **ListView**:

```
private void button1_Click(object sender, System.EventArgs e) {
  double princ = Double.Parse (principal.Text);
  if (princ <= 0) {
    MessageBox.Show
      ("Principal must be a number greater than 0");
    return;
  }

  double rate = Double.Parse (InterestRate.Text);
  if (rate <= 0) {
    MessageBox.Show("Rate must be a number greater than 0");
    return;
  }
  int time = int.Parse (Months.Text);
  if (time <= 0) {
    MessageBox.Show("months must be a number greater than 0");
    return;
  }
  // Change percentage (easier for users) to
  // decimal (used in calculation). That is the
```

```
// reason for the /100.
LoanCalc.PaymentCalculator calc = new
  LoanCalc.PaymentCalculator(princ, rate/100, time);
payment.Text = calc.Payment.ToString("C");
Data.Items.Clear ();
int month = 0;
foreach (decimal balance in calc) {
  Data.Items.Add (month.ToString());
  Data.Items[month].SubItems.Add (balance.ToString ("C"));
  ++month;
}
}
```

Related solution:	Found on page:
Handling Events	153

Let me describe the code that adds the balances to the **ListView**. The data control is the **ListView**. The first line inside the **foreach** loop adds a new item to the **ListView**. The second line adds the second column of the row. The call to **ToString ("C")** displays the value as currency. The C# compiler generates code that uses the **IEnumerable** interface in the **PaymentCalculator** class. That's all there is. Now, just build the application and run it.

Creating Web Applications

You use ASP.NET to create Web applications using .NET. ASP.NET contains two sets of controls that you can use to create Web forms and Web applications. The **System.Web.UI.HtmlControls** namespace contains classes that loosely map to HTML controls. These are thin wrappers around the functionality provided by standard HTML controls. The other, more powerful namespace is **System.Web. UI.WebControls**. These are rich controls that have much more code behind the control. These controls contain code that determines the user's browser, and they adjust the behavior of the control based on the browser. For example, if you have turned off JavaScript in your browser, the control will generate HTML code that does not use JavaScript, but rather will use server-side logic to affect the behavior of the control.

Before you create a Web application, you need to be running a Web server. Visual Studio .NET creates the source on your local Web server.

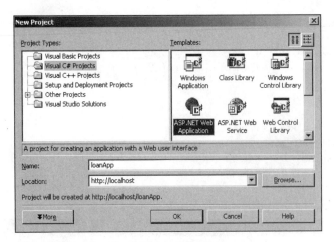

Figure 17.6 Creating a Web application.

Your project's source is actually stored on the Web server. Your first step is to create a new project. Select File|New|Project in Visual Studio .NET (see Figure 17.6). Notice that the location of the application is now **http://localhost** and that the name of the application is "loanApp".

Visual Studio .NET creates two files for every page in an ASP .NET application: a .aspx file and a .aspx.cs file. The .aspx file contains the HTML code, along with some extra attributes. The .aspx.cs file contains the code that drives the page. These two files are linked by a set of attributes at the top of the .aspx file:

```
<%@ Page language="c#" Codebehind="WebForm1.aspx.cs"
  AutoEventWireup="false" Inherits="loanApp.WebForm1" %>
```

Despite the line breaks shown here, this appears on one line. The language attribute sets the language for the code in the page. The **Codebehind** attribute points to the source file that drives the page.

One main goal of ASP .NET is that you can create a Web application as easily as you have been able to create Windows applications. Creating the form is very similar to the way you create forms and dialogs in Windows. To create the form, you drag and drop controls onto the form. The **WebControls** namespace contains a large number of controls—covering all of them would fill a book on its own. I cover two different controls in particular because one points to the differences between local and Web applications, and the other shows some of the power of the Web controls (see Figure 17.7).

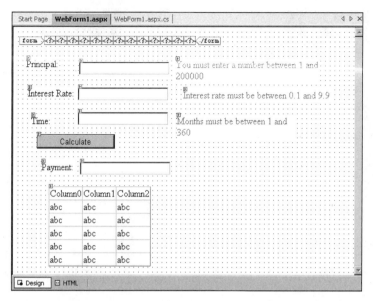

Figure 17.7 The Web form for the Web loan calculator.

The desktop application uses the **MessageBox ()** method to inform the user of invalid values in the edit control. **MessageBox ()** is not available in Web applications. Also, opening a new window would require a round trip to the server. The **RangeValidator** control links to another control and displays an error message when the value is not in the range specified. This way, you can catch invalid user input before the user sends any information to the server. You configure the range validator by using the same tools that you would use for any other control. Simply drag the validator onto the form and modify the appropriate properties. The properties you will use most often are **MinimumValue**, **MaximumValue**, **ErrorMessage**, and **ControlToValidate**. You edit these properties in the properties window of the Visual Studio .NET IDE, just like the properties of a control in a Windows application. Figure 17.8 shows the validation control in action.

The bottom of the form contains a **DataGrid** control, which is a powerful control designed to display information from a database. To display database information, the **DataGrid** control uses the **ICollection** interface, so you can use the **DataGrid** control to display data from any object that supports the **ICollection** interface. The **PaymentCalculator. Balances** property returns a view on the data that supports the **ICollection** interface. You need to bind the **DataGrid** control to the collection provided by the **PaymentCalculator**.

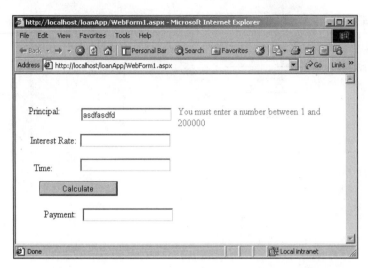

Figure 17.8 The range validator makes itself visible when the user enters invalid data in the control.

To add the logic to finish the application, double-click the Calculate button in Visual Studio .NET. This adds a method to your .aspx.cs file to handle the click event on the button. The event handler varies from control to control—double-clicking always adds a handler for the default event. The logic in the click handler is shown in the following code. Once again, you parse the text in the input controls, create a new **PaymentCalculator** object, and retrieve the values from the payment calculator. The last two calls set the data source for the grid and bind the data source to the grid.

```
private void Button1_Click(object sender, System.EventArgs e) {
    double principal = Double.Parse(Principal.Text);
    double percentage = Double.Parse(Rate.Text);
    int time = Int32.Parse(NumMonths.Text);
    LoanCalc.PaymentCalculator calc = new
        LoanCalc.PaymentCalculator (principal,
        percentage/100, time);
    payment.Text=calc.Payment.ToString ("C");
    DataGrid1.DataSource = calc.Balances;
    DataGrid1.DataBind ();
}
```

Lastly, you build and run the application. You enter the values in the form; the range validators ensure that the input data is reasonable. Click the Calculate button to see the results (see Figure 17.9).

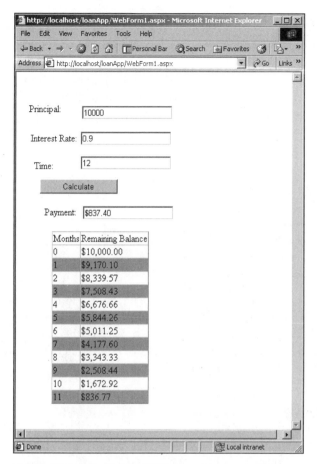

Figure 17.9 The finished Web-based loan calculator.

Creating Web Services

The last major type of project to discuss is the Web Service. A Web Service is a component that client programs access using the HTTP protocol. You can use Web Services on an intranet or across the Internet.

To create a Web Service, choose the ASP .NET Web Service as the project type when you create a new project in Visual Studio .NET. Visual Studio .NET creates the Web site on your local machine, and it installs a number of files on the site. The source for your Web Service is in Service1.asmx.cs. Just like a Web application, two files are created here: Service1.asmx, which contains the HTML code, and Service1.asmx.cs, which contains the ASP code.

Writing a Web Service using C# is amazingly simple: You simply add code in the **WebService** class. Methods that are part of the Web Service interface are marked with the **[WebMethod]** attribute. The loan calculator contains two methods to return the information about the loan. The first is a method to get the monthly payment:

```
[WebMethod]
public decimal GetPayment(double principal,
  double rate, int numMonths) {
  LoanCalc.PaymentCalculator calc = new
    LoanCalc.PaymentCalculator (principal,
    rate/100, numMonths);
  return calc.Payment;
}
```

This looks like any other C# method. The only addition is the **[WebMethod]** attribute. The next method demonstrates the technique to create a class that can be serialized across the Web. The **GetPaymentSchedule ()** returns an array of nodes that contain the elapsed months and the remaining balance:

```
[WebMethod]
public LoanNode [] GetPaymentSchedule (double principal,
  double rate, int numMonths) {
  LoanCalc.PaymentCalculator calc = new
    LoanCalc.PaymentCalculator (principal,
    rate/100, numMonths);

  LoanNode [] balance = new LoanNode[numMonths];
  for (int i=0;i<numMonths;i++) {
    balance[i] = new LoanNode();
    balance[i].Month= i;
    balance[i].Balance = calc[i];
  }
  return balance;
}
```

Related solution:	*Found on page:*
Declaring Web Methods	217

Serializing Objects

Like the last method in the preceding section, this one is marked with the **[WebMethod]** attribute. You need to add two different attributes to the **LoanNode** class so that you can serialize those objects across the Web (see Listing 17.4). The **XmlRoot** attribute defines a class as serializable. The unnamed parameter defines the name of the object when serialized as an XML file. The **XmlAttribute** attribute defines the name of the particular property in the XML file.

Listing 17.4 A class that can be serialized in a Web Service. The highlighted lines show the attributes necessary to serialize an object.

```
[XmlRoot ("Balance", Namespace="loanCalcService")]
public class LoanNode {
  private int TheMonth = 0;
  private decimal TheBalance = 0.0M;

  [XmlAttribute ("Month")]
  public int Month {
    get {
      return TheMonth;
    }
    set {
      TheMonth = value;
    }
  }

  [XmlAttribute ("Balance")]
  public decimal Balance {
    get {
      return TheBalance;
    }
    set {
      TheBalance = value;
    }
  }
}
```

Finally, build and run the service. ASP .NET provides some extra functionality that lets you test your Web Service using Internet Explorer. Start your Web Service in Visual Studio .NET (press Ctrl+F5), and you see the window shown in Figure 17.10.

17. .NET Library

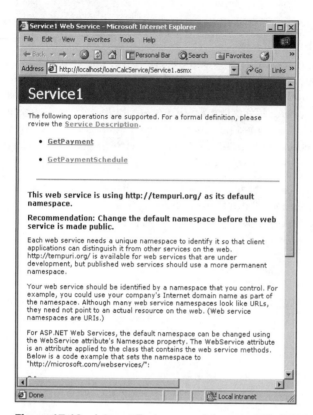

Figure 17.10 Internet Explorer can drive your ASP .NET Web Service.

Click the link for GetPaymentSchedule. Internet Explorer displays a
window that lets you enter parameters to test the method (see Figure
17.11). Enter the parameters and click Invoke. Internet Explorer creates a new window with the results from the method (see Figure 17.12).

17. .NET Library

Figure 17.11   Internet Explorer lets you enter the parameters and invoke your Web Service.

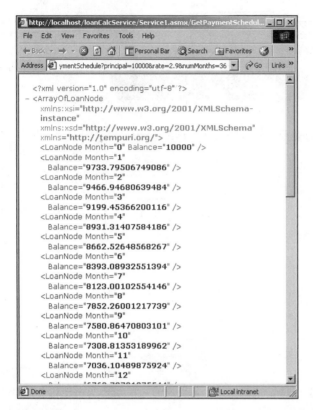

Figure 17.12   The results of invoking **GetPaymentSchedule** across the Web.

Consuming Web Services

In time, you also will need to consume a Web Service. Visual Studio .NET provides a simple tool to create the proxy classes necessary to consume a Web Service. Right-click on the References node in your project and select Add Web Reference. Visual Studio .NET displays a dialog that lets you select a Web Service (see Figure 17.13). The dialog contains links to Microsoft's test Web Services and the links on your local server. If you need a different service, and you know the address, you can type it in the address bar. Once you select the server, you can select the particular service on that site. Finally, click the Add Reference button.

After you have added the Web reference, Visual Studio .NET contacts the Web Service and creates a proxy class that can invoke the Web

Service (see Figure 17.14). You call the proxy class just like you would call any other object in your solution. If you are developing both the Web Service and the Web Service client, Visual Studio .NET gives you a way to update the Web reference. Right-click the host node under the Web References and select Update Web Reference. This will generate a new proxy and replace the existing proxy.

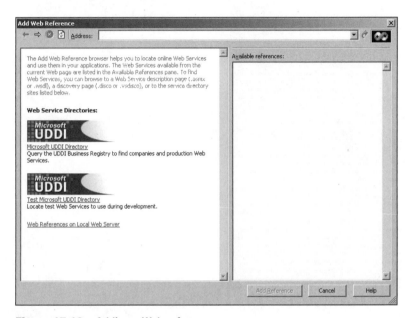

Figure 17.13   Adding a Web reference.

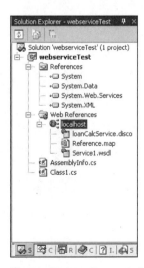

Figure 17.14   Your solution now contains a proxy class to access the selected Web Service.

Chapter 18

Reflection and Metadata

In Brief

Every .NET assembly contains *metadata* that describes that assembly. The metadata contains information about the assembly as a whole, each type defined in the assembly, and all the methods, properties, and data members inside each type. You can use this information in many different ways. Visual Studio .NET uses this information to provide IntelliSense support for .NET assemblies you use in your program. Other tools use the metadata information to load and invoke methods in .NET assemblies.

With all metadata, you can query any of the attributes in the object you are using. You can search for a particular attribute, or you can get all the custom attributes that are attached to a particular entity. You can use these attributes to mark different assemblies, classes, methods, or properties.

Assembly Metadata

You get a **System.Reflection.Assembly** object by loading an assembly from disk. Once you have created the **Assembly** object, you can use its methods and properties to determine quite a bit about that particular assembly. Different methods let you determine what modules, types, and files are part of the assembly. You also can use methods in the **Assembly** to create instances of the objects in the assembly.

The **Assembly** object is the first entry point into the reflection APIs to learn information about any of the types in the assembly file. Once you have learned what types are in the assembly, you can delve further into the assembly by using the **Type** metadata.

NOTE: The **Assembly** *object contains information about all types in an assembly, regardless of access level. You can see all the types in an assembly, even those that are internal to the assembly.*

Type Metadata

The **System.Type** class stores the metadata about a single type. A type may be any one of a class, struct, interface, or enum. Once you have the **Type** object, you can determine quite a bit about a particular type. You can find all the elements in the type, including the private types. You can find constructors, and you can even invoke constructors to create an object. You can invoke static methods once you have loaded the type information. Once you have created an object, you can invoke any of the methods or properties on the object.

You also can determine which interfaces a particular type supports. The **GetInterfaces ()** method returns an array of **Type** objects, one for each interface that an object supports. You can use this information to work with these objects in standard ways, once you have created the object.

Types can contain nested types. Using methods in the **Type** class, you can get a list of all nested types inside a particular type. Those are, rather obviously, **Type** objects. You can now access and work with all the nested types inside a particular type.

The **Type** object APIs do not contain methods that let you query and access any members of the type that are not public members.

MemberInfo Metadata

Way back in Chapter 1, you learned that C# is a strong object-oriented language, and all code and data must be defined and declared inside some type. There are no global functions, no global data, no global anything. So, you can find anything inside a **Type** object. All the data, functions, properties, and events are somewhere inside the class that a **Type** object refers to. In general, the methods that return member information do not return information about members declared in base classes. However, you can get a **Type** object for the base class and continue your efforts by querying that object.

The **System.Reflection.MemberInfo** class is the base class for all members of a type. These members may be fields, properties, events, or methods. The **MemberInfo** class contains the information that is common to all members of a type: the name of the member, the **Type** that contains this member, and the kind of member.

ConstructorInfo Metadata

The **ConstructorInfo** class contains information about a particular constructor for a type. In particular, you can retrieve all the parameters used for each constructor. The **ConstructorInfo** object also contains an **Invoke ()** method that invokes the particular constructor. You can use this information to create a new instance of the class being queried.

18. Reflection and Metadata

381

MethodInfo Metadata

The **MethodInfo** class is closely related to the **ConstructorInfo** class. It contains information about a public method that is part of a type. In addition to the parameter information and the **Invoke ()** method, the **MethodInfo** metadata object tells you the return type of the method, the name of the method, and whether the method is virtual or sealed. You also can determine if the method is a static method. There is also a flag that can tell you if a method is an abstract method.

FieldInfo Metadata

The **FieldInfo** class provides you with information about the fields inside a type. You can get the type of the field and the name of the field. You also can determine if the field is **readonly**, or even **const**. You can determine if the field is static or an instance variable. The **FieldInfo** class also includes **GetValue ()** and **SetValue ()** methods that let you read or write the value of the field.

PropertyInfo Metadata

The **PropertyInfo** class has an interface that looks very similar to the **FieldInfo** class. Remember that properties are meant to look like fields to the outside world. Even in metadata, they look like the metadata for data members. Indexers in a class will be returned as properties. You will see a **PropertyInfo** member of the metadata that represents any indexers in your class. As with the **FieldInfo** metadata, you can determine the type of the property and invoke the **get** and **set** methods. You can determine if a property supports **set** accessors before you try to change the value of a property.

EventInfo Metadata

The **EventInfo** metadata has the most members of any of the metadata returned from a type. The **EventInfo** object can tell you what method would add and remove an event handler. You can find the method that raises an event. The **EventInfo** object also has a method that lets you directly add an event handler.

When to Use Metadata

The **Reflection** classes and the **Reflection** APIs are useful for one simple purpose: late binding. You can write code that can interact with classes that get written after your components.

In practice, you can use this kind of feature to create a scripting engine. You can load assemblies in a given directory and query the interfaces in the assembly. Once you have learned the capabilities of those assemblies, you can call the methods in the assemblies and let them perform work on your behalf.

Immediate Solutions

To demonstrate the **Reflection** APIs, this chapter creates a simple application that loads an assembly and displays all the types in it. Once a type is found, all the public methods and members inside are queried and displayed. This shows you how to find all the information you need to create and use the types in any assembly.

This sample shows you the more common elements you can find using **Reflection**. There are other, more esoteric elements in the **Reflection** API. You can look in the documentation for more ways to use reflection. The sample output comes from loading the **LoanCalc** assembly developed in the last chapter.

Loading an Assembly

The first step to working with metadata and reflection is to load the assembly. For this sample, I load the assembly in the constructor for the class. The constructor takes a single string argument, the file containing the assembly:

```
class ClassLoader
{
  private Assembly LoadedAsm;

  public ClassLoader (string asmName) {
    LoadedAsm = Assembly.LoadFrom (asmName);
  }
}
```

Querying Assembly Metadata

Now you have a handle to an assembly. The next step is to print the metadata about this assembly:

```
public void ListAssemblyInfo () {
  // Get the public name:
  Console.WriteLine(LoadedAsm.FullName);
  // Is it global?
  if (LoadedAsm.GlobalAssemblyCache == true) {
```

```
      Console.WriteLine ("\tThis is a Global Assembly");
   } else {
      Console.WriteLine ("\tThis is a Local Assembly");
   }
   // Get the EntryPoint
   MethodInfo entry = LoadedAsm.EntryPoint;
   if (entry != null) {
      Console.WriteLine ("\tAssembly EntryPoint:\t{0}",
        entry.Name);
   } else {
      Console.WriteLine ("\tThis Assembly has no Entry point.");
   }
   // Get all the Custom Attributes:
   object [] attrs = LoadedAsm.GetCustomAttributes(true);
   if (attrs.Length == 0) {
      Console.WriteLine ("\tNo Custom Attributes Found");
   } else {
      Console.WriteLine ("\tFound Attributes:");
      foreach (object o in attrs) {
        Console.WriteLine ("\tFound Attribute\t{0}",
          o.ToString ());
   } }
}
```

The first item in this function prints the full name of the assembly.
The **FullName** property in the **LoanCalc** assembly prints this value:

```
LoanCalc, Version=1.0.628.28954, Culture=neutral,
  PublicKeyToken=null
```

Next, the **GlobalAssemblyCache** property tells whether this assembly is a global or a local assembly. The **LoanCalc** assembly is a local assembly.

This routine next looks for an entry point in the assembly. If the assembly is a DLL, there is no entry point. However, if the assembly is an executable, the **EntryPoint** property returns a **MethodInfo** object that points to the entry point. The entry point will be the **Main ()** function defined in that build.

Finally, this routine prints the attributes found in the assembly. The **LoanCalc** assembly has quite a few attributes, especially when you make a debug build:

```
Found Attributes:
  System.Reflection.AssemblyCopyrightAttribute
```

18. Reflection and Metadata

```
System.Diagnostics.DebuggableAttribute
System.Reflection.AssemblyKeyNameAttribute
System.Reflection.AssemblyKeyFileAttribute
System.Reflection.AssemblyDelaySignAttribute
System.Reflection.AssemblyTrademarkAttribute
System.Reflection.AssemblyProductAttribute
System.Reflection.AssemblyCompanyAttribute
System.Reflection.AssemblyConfigurationAttribute
System.Reflection.AssemblyDescriptionAttribute
System.Reflection.AssemblyTitleAttribute
System.CLSCompliantAttribute
```

You saw earlier that you also can search for specific attributes and query the attributes for particular values. When you then cast the attribute to the proper type, you can query the attribute for all its properties.

Related solution:	Found on page:
Finding Attributes Using Reflection	220

Finding Types in an Assembly

The **GetTypes ()** method returns all the types defined in an assembly. The array of **Types** contains all types—public or not. In addition, all nested types are contained in this array. Here is the routine in the **AssemblyLoader** class that finds and prints the types defined in an assembly:

```
public void PrintTypes () {
    Type [] LoadedTypes = LoadedAsm.GetTypes();
    if (LoadedTypes.Length == 0) {
        Console.WriteLine ("\tNo Types!");
    } else {
        Console.WriteLine("\tFound Types:");
        foreach (Type t in LoadedTypes) {
            Console.WriteLine ("\t\t{0}", t.FullName);
        }
    }
}
```

The **LoanCalc** assembly produces the following output:

```
Found Types:
  LoanCalc.PaymentCalculator
  LoanCalc.PaymentCalculator+LoanEnumerator
```

The **FullName** property gives you the type name, along with any namespaces that are part of the fully qualified name. Notice that the nested type generates a name with the containing type, a plus sign (**+**), and the nested type.

Refining Type Information

The **Type** class has many different properties that can help you learn more about a particular type. For example, you can tell if a type is a top-level public type by using the **IsPublic** property. You can find nested types by using the **IsNestedPublic** property. The array of types also returns a **Type** object for each enum and struct, in addition to the information returned for all the classes defined in the assembly. Using these properties, here is a more robust version of the **PrintTypes ()** function:

```
public void PrintTypes () {
  Type [] LoadedTypes = LoadedAsm.GetTypes();
  if (LoadedTypes.Length == 0) {
    Console.WriteLine ("\tNo Types!");
  } else {
    Console.WriteLine("\tFound Types:");
    foreach (Type t in LoadedTypes) {
      if (t.IsPublic) {
        Console.Write ("\t\tPublic ");
      } else if (t.IsNestedPublic) {
        Console.Write ("\t\tPublic Nested ");
      } else {
        Console.Write ("\t\tNot Public ");
      }
      if (t.IsEnum) {
        Console.Write ("Enum: ");
      } else if (t.IsValueType) {
        Console.Write ("Struct: ");
      } else {
        Console.Write ("Class: ");
      }
      Console.WriteLine ("{0}", t.FullName);
    }
  }
}
```

Finding Constructors

Now that you found the types, you can find more information about the type. The obvious choice is to find the constructors. The **Type** class contains a method that returns information about every public constructor defined in the type. The method returns an array of **ConstructorInfo** objects. This array includes information on a type constructor or static constructor. This routine takes a type and prints all the information about each constructor:

```
private void PrintConstructorInfo (Type t) {
  ConstructorInfo [] ctors = t.GetConstructors();
  foreach (ConstructorInfo c in ctors) {
    // Print the params.
    ParameterInfo [] pList = c.GetParameters();
    if (pList.Length == 0) {
      if (c.IsStatic)
        Console.WriteLine ("\tFound static Constructor.");
      else
        Console.WriteLine ("\tFound default consructor.");
    } else {
      // Print the params:
      Console.WriteLine ("\tParameter List:");
      foreach (ParameterInfo p in pList) {
        // Print each parameter.
        Console.WriteLine ("\t\t{0} {1}",
          p.ParameterType.FullName, p.Name);
      }
      Console.WriteLine ();
    }
  }
}
```

Creating Instances

You use the **ConstructorInfo** class's **Invoke ()** method to create an instance of the object. You pass all the parameters to the particular constructor as an array of objects, and the **Invoke ()** method returns a reference to the new object, cast as an object:

```
object [] parms = new object[3];
parms[0] = new int (5);
parms[1] = new double (32.0);
parms[2] = new string ("The default string");
object o = c.Invoke (parms);
// o is the new object.
```

Finding Methods

You use a similar strategy to find methods in a type. You need to consider a couple of new nuances when you reflect on methods. You now get the name of the method and the return type. Also, there are two different versions of the **GetMethods ()** function. The version with no parameters returns all methods available to this type, including all inherited methods. Often, you will want only the methods that are defined in this type, not in its base classes. Here is the function that prints all the information about regular methods in a **Type**:

```
private void PrintMethodInfo (Type t) {
  MethodInfo [] methods = t.GetMethods
    (BindingFlags.DeclaredOnly | BindingFlags.Public |
    BindingFlags.Instance | BindingFlags.Static);
  foreach (MethodInfo m in methods) {
    // Print the name.
    if (m.IsStatic)
      Console.WriteLine("Static Method: {0}", m.Name);
    else
      Console.WriteLine ("Method: {0}", m.Name);
    // Print the return value.
    Console.WriteLine ("\tReturns {0}", m.ReturnType.FullName);
    // Print the params.
    ParameterInfo [] pList = m.GetParameters();
    if (pList.Length == 0) {
      Console.WriteLine ("\tNo Parameters");
    } else {
      // Print the params:
      Console.WriteLine ("\tParameter List:");
      foreach (ParameterInfo p in pList) {
        // Print each parameter.
        Console.WriteLine ("\t\t{0} {1}",
          p.ParameterType.FullName, p.Name);
      }
      Console.WriteLine ();
    }
  }
}
```

Pay special attention to the **GetMethods ()** parameters. The **BindingFlags.DeclaredOnly** flag indicates that only the methods declared or overridden in this **Type** are returned. However, if you do not include any other flags, you do not get any methods at all. You need to add the **Instance**, **Static**, and **Public** flags to get the information you want.

Also, notice that you can retrieve a flag to see if a parameter is an **out** parameter. However, you cannot find out if a parameter is a **ref** parameter. The **ParameterInfo** class has properties for **IsIn, IsOut**, and **IsRetval**. You can use these flags to determine how to retrieve information from the methods you find using reflection.

Invoking Methods

The **MethodInfo** class also has an **Invoke** member to call that particular method on the particular object. The **MethodInfo** version of the **Invoke ()** method has one extra parameter: the object on which to invoke the method:

```
object o;
// o was initialized by invoking a
// ConstructorInfo.Invoke () method.
object [] parms = new object[3];
parms[0] = new int (5);
parms[1] = new double (32.0);
parms[2] = new string ("The default string");
object rval = m.Invoke (o, parms);
// rval has the return value
```

Finding Properties

The **Type** information lets you retrieve all the properties supported. The **GetProperties ()** method gives you a collection of the properties in the **Type**. Additionally, all indexers are returned in the **GetProperties ()** method. When you examine the **PropertyInfo**, you can find any index parameters, the type of the property, and whether the property is read-only, write-only, or read/write:

```
private void PrintPropertyInfo (Type t) {
  PropertyInfo [] props= t.GetProperties
    (BindingFlags.DeclaredOnly | BindingFlags.Public |
    BindingFlags.Instance | BindingFlags.Static);
  foreach (PropertyInfo p in props) {
    // Print the name.
    Console.WriteLine ("Property: {0}", p.Name);
    // Print the return value.
    Console.WriteLine ("\tType {0}", p.PropertyType.FullName);
    if (p.CanRead)
      Console.WriteLine ("Readable property.");
    if (p.CanWrite)
```

```
      Console.WriteLine ("Writable property.");
    // Print the index parameters.
    ParameterInfo [] pList = p.GetIndexParameters();
    if (pList.Length == 0) {
      Console.WriteLine ("\tNo Parameters");
    } else {
      // Print the params:
      Console.WriteLine ("\tParameter List:");
      foreach (ParameterInfo parm in pList) {
        // Print each parameter.
        Console.WriteLine ("\t\t{0} {1}",
          parm.ParameterType.FullName, parm.Name);
      }
      Console.WriteLine ();
    }
  }
}
```

Invoking Properties

Invoking properties is much easier than invoking methods. The **PropertyInfo** class contains two methods, **GetValue ()**, and **SetValue ()**, that you can use to **get** and **set** a property:

```
object o;
// o was initialized by invoking a
// ConstructorInfo.Invoke () method.
object rval = p.Invoke (o,null);
// rval has the "get" value of the property.
object newVal;
// initialize "newVal".
p.Invoke (o, newVal, null);
// the property now has the value "newVal".
```

The null parameter would be replaced by an array containing the index parameters to **get** or **set** an indexer.

Chapter 19

Versioning

In Brief

The versioning APIs and the versioning strategy in .NET solve one problem: New components do not break old programs. You have undoubtedly had this problem some time in the past with your existing programs and applications. Some new application updates a DLL, maybe even a totally different DLL that just happens to have the same name. More subtle versioning problems also exist. What happens when you want to update a component and you find that some new version of the component has a member with the same name you are already using? Depending on the release schedule, you may not want to rework your entire application to change the name of the function and every call to that function.

All the tools and updates described in this chapter apply to global assemblies only. Private assemblies do not participate in versioning. When you deploy an application, you decide whether the components you use are private or global. Global components must be installed in the global cache. Private components are copied somewhere in the directory where the application is installed.

Component Versions

Every .NET assembly has a version associated with it. The version contains four different components:

- Major version number
- Minor version number
- Build number
- Revision number

You store the version number in an attribute. Whenever you create a new project, that attribute is written in your AssemblyInfo.cs file:

```
[assembly: AssemblyVersion("1.0.*")]
```

The asterisk specifies that the build number and revision number get default values. The build number specifies the number of days since January 1, 2000. The default revision number is the number of seconds since midnight local time. Whenever you are creating or updating an assembly that will be installed in the global cache, you should explicitly set all four parts of the version for it.

Compatible Version Changes

When you build an application, the compiler generates a manifest of all the assemblies your application references. Included in this manifest is the version number for each of these assemblies. When you run a .NET program, the CLR examines this manifest to load all the referenced assemblies. The CLR will load the newest compatible version of all shared assemblies that your application references. Compatible versions all share the same major and minor version number. The build number and revision number must be the same as specified, or newer. You can examine the manifest by using the .NET Disassembler. Figure 19.1 shows the location of the manifest for the **LoanCalc** application developed in Chapter 17. If you double-click on the Manifest node, you see all the referenced assemblies, including the versions:

```
.assembly extern System.Windows.Forms
{
  .publickeytoken = (B7 7A 5C 56 19 34 E0 89 ) // .z\V.4..
  .ver 1:0:2411:0
}
.assembly extern System
{
  .publickeytoken = (B7 7A 5C 56 19 34 E0 89 ) // .z\V.4..
  .ver 1:0:2411:0
}
.assembly extern mscorlib
{
  .publickeytoken = (B7 7A 5C 56 19 34 E0 89 ) // .z\V.4..
  .ver 1:0:2411:0
}
.assembly extern System.Drawing
{
  .publickeytoken = (B0 3F 5F 7F 11 D5 0A 3A ) // .?_....:
  .ver 1:0:2411:0
}
.assembly extern LoanCalc
{
  .ver 1:0:628:28954
}
// [ more deleted]
```

Compatible changes must not change the public or protected interfaces to any public type defined in the assembly. In addition, the observable changes should be limited to bug fixes. You want to be very careful to ensure that a change in the behavior of the component will not break an existing application.

19. Versioning

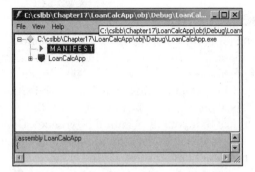

Figure 19.1   Every assembly contains a manifest that describes the
assemblies referenced by this assembly.

Incompatible Version Changes

Throughout the lifetime of a component, you will enhance and extend the functionality of a component. When you make these incompatible updates, you should update your assembly version number to change the major or minor revision number. No stated guidelines exist for making the distinction between a major and a minor revision change. You need to use your own judgment as to the scope of changes for a major revision update.

Application Updates

You need to work with two different scenarios to handle new component versions in your applications. The first scenario is when you need to use a specific version of a shared component, even when a newer compatible version is installed. The second scenario is when you have updated to a new incompatible version and find that the necessary code changes are greater than you expected.

Modifying Version Policy

You can modify the default versioning policy to specify a specific version or force an application to use the version of an assembly used to build the application. When the CLR loads an application, it looks in the same directory as the application for a file with the same base name as the application and the .config extension. For example, the configuration file for myApp.exe would be myApp.exe.config. This file is an XML file that can contain different configuration properties for that particular application. You can also specify system-wide configuration settings in the machine.config file.

The most common modification would be to request a specific version of a specific assembly. To do this, you would use the **bindingRedirect** XML node. The attributes in this node specify which revision of a particular assembly should be substituted for an updated version:

```
publicKeyToken="c7063449adc3ec1f" />
<bindingRedirect oldVersion="1.0.1.1"
   newVersion="1.0.0.0" />
```

Basically, this node says that whenever a version of **LoanCalc** is requested, it will be load version 1.0.0.0, regardless of the latest version or even the version specified in the manifest of the application.

Hiding Functions

This particular issue is a developer issue only. Let's suppose that you created a new class that is derived from a class defined in some other assembly. Then, you update that other assembly. Suddenly, the referenced assembly contains a method that conflicts with a method defined in your class. This causes a problem if the function added is a virtual function. The C# compiler expects that any function declared with the **virtual** keyword represents the root virtual function. Virtual functions that override base class declarations are marked with the **override** keyword. You can get the correct runtime behavior by specifying your existing virtual function as **new**. The compiler now knows that your new function should not override the function of the same name in the base class:

```
class B {
  public virtual void foo ();
}

class D {
  public virtual new void foo ();
}
```

This feature does far more than simply suppress a warning. Any code inside **class B** that calls **foo ()** makes a virtual function call. The compiler knows that **D.foo ()** is not an override of **B.foo ()**. Therefore, any code in **B** that calls **foo ()** calls **B.foo ()**, not **D.foo ()**.

Notice that you have effectively made it impossible for any class derived from **D** to override **B.foo ()**. You should consider the use of

new as a short-term fix, if at all possible. When development schedules allow, you should try to change the name, which can be a very difficult task, especially if the function is in a binary component that your clients make use of. The **new** keyword is not a perfect solution, but it is better than anything that came before.

Immediate Solutions

To demonstrate how the versioning strategy works, I create a simple component that has one property to display the version of the component.

Versioning Shared Components

Start Visual Studio .NET and create a class library. Add one static method to the library to report on the complete version of the component:

```
using System;

namespace VersionTest
{
  public class VersionReporter {
    public static string version {
      get {
        return "1.0.0.0";
      }
    }

    public VersionReporter() {
    }
  }
}
```

Next, open the AssemblyInfo.cs file and add a corresponding version attribute. You will find an existing attribute that uses the default setting. Modify the **AssemblyVersion** attribute so that is has an explicit version:

```
[assembly: AssemblyVersion("1.0.0.0")]
```

Related solution:	Found on page:
Finding Attributes Using Reflection	220

Creating a Strong Name

The next step is to create a strong name for this assembly so that it can be used by this component. The .NET Framework contains a tool named **sn** that builds strong names for assemblies. To create a new key for this component, open a command window, go to the directory where you created your library, and type "sn /k versiontest.key". This command creates a file called versiontest.key. Next, you need to edit AssemblyInfo.cs to reference the new key file. At the bottom of the file, you will find this line:

```
[assembly: AssemblyKeyFile("")]
```

Change this attribute to reference the new key file:

```
[assembly: AssemblyKeyFile("..\\..\\versiontest.key")]
```

The path to the key file must be relative to the output directory for the output file. That is why the ..\\..\\ part of the path is included. Build the assembly. Now your assembly is signed, and you can add it to the global cache.

Installing a Global Assembly

You install an assembly in the global cache by using another command-line tool that is part of the .NET Framework SDK: **gacutil**. At the command prompt, change to the directory with the built VersionTest.Dll file and type "gacutil /I VersionTest.Dll". Your new assembly is now installed in the global cache. If you start Explorer and look in the Assembly folder under your Windows installation folder, you will see the **VersionTest** assembly (see Figure 19.2).

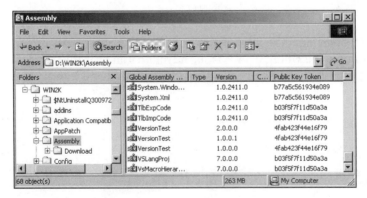

Figure 19.2   Viewing assemblies in Explorer.

Managing Version Numbers

Creating a new version involves one simple step: Modify the **AssemblyVersion** attribute in the AssemblyInfo.cs file. In this sample, you also need to update the **static** property that returns the version to match the built version.

To demonstrate the different ways you can specify versions, create two new versions of the component: 1.0.0.1 and 2.0.0.0. So that you can build test programs that use the different versions of the component, copy the different DLLs to different local directories so that you can build the test program using different versions of the component. After you create each, update the global assembly to add these new versions. Simply run the **gacutil** command as you did in the preceding section. Look at the global cache in Explorer, and you can see that all three versions are installed in the .NET global cache.

Using Versions

The next simple sample shows you how .NET manages versions, and how you can modify that behavior to use different versions of a component. Create a console application. Add the following code to display the version from the version test component:

```
using System;

namespace versionUser
{
  class VersionOutput {
    static void Main(string[] args) {
      string ver = VersionTest.VersionReporter.version;
      Console.WriteLine ("Using version {0}", ver);
    }
  }
}
```

To build and use this component, you need to reference the **VersionTest** component. Right-click on the References node in the Solution Explorer. Select Add Reference. Click on Browse to find the component. Select the 1.0.0.0 file for the **VersionTest** DLL. Now, build the executable. When you run the executable, you see the following message:

```
Using version 1.0.0.0
```

Because you built with version 1.0.0.0, you get that version. Even though the newer version is supposed to be compatible, you get the version you built with.

Specifying Specific Versions

Finally, you can modify the configuration file so that you use a specific version of a particular component. The following file shows how to specify that you want to use version 2.0.0.0, regardless of the version used to build the application or the default version policies.

```
<?xml version="1.0" encoding="UTF-8"?>
<configuration>
  <runtime>
    <assemblyBinding xmlns="urn:schemas-microsoft-com:asm.v1">
      <dependentAssembly>
        <assemblyIdentity name="VersionTest"
        publicKeyToken="d1f168d931f3dbbc" />
        <bindingRedirect oldVersion="1.0.0.0"
        newVersion="2.0.0.0" />
      </dependentAssembly>
    </assemblyBinding>
  </runtime>
</configuration>
```

The **assemblyIdentity** node specifies the particular assembly to modify. The **publicKeyToken** attribute specifies the key. (The exact key used is specific to my machine; your key will be different.) The **bindingRedirect** node specifies the specific old and new versions to use in this application. Now, if you run the application, you get the following:

```
Using version 2.0.0.0
```

Chapter 20

Defensive Programming

In Brief

Defensive programming techniques are meant to help you find bugs more quickly and easily. The purpose of these techniques is to halt the program as close as possible to the point where an error is introduced. The remainder of the "In Brief" section describes the techniques you can use to catch these errors. The "Immediate Solutions" section describes the C# syntax that supports these techniques.

Invariants

An *invariant* is some condition that is always true. These invariants may be either *class* invariants or *object* invariants. Class invariants describe the static conditions that are always true for a class. Object invariants describe the state of a single object. These invariants represent those conditions that must be true for the object to be usable. As an example, consider the string class. The memory storage allocated for the string must be at least as large as the length of the string. If not, the string is invalid.

A *static* invariant represents conditions that are true for the class. For example, the **Console** class needs to have a valid output stream. The output stream needs to point to a valid output device.

When you design a class, you will want to decide what the invariants for the class—and each object of the class—are. Consider these questions:

- Can any fields have null values after the object is created?
- What fields are initialized in constructors?
- What ranges of values are valid for each field?
- What static fields are defined in the class?

These types of questions will lead you to determine exactly what invariants you expect for your class. Once you have defined these properties, you can write a function that tests these assumptions.

TIP: The class and object invariants describe those conditions that you always expect to be true whenever any method in your class is invoked. These invariants describe the expected state of an object. You should test these assumptions when you enter every public method in your class.

Parameter Validation

Many of your public functions and properties will take parameters. You probably have some expectations about those parameters. These questions are the same as the first two questions for your object invariants:

- What parameters must not be null?
- What ranges of values are valid for each parameter?

After you have defined for yourself what assumptions you have placed on each parameter, you can test those assumptions when you enter the function.

TIP: *You should test the validity of each parameter when you enter a function. These validations ensure that your function logic will work as you expect.*

Functions and Object State

Every function does something. Sometimes functions change the internal state of an object; sometimes they don't. You can describe a function (or a property) in terms of its *preconditions* and *post conditions*. The preconditions describe the state of the object before the function starts. The post conditions describe the state of the object after the function has executed.

Preconditions

The preconditions describe the state of the object when you enter the function. Here are some examples of preconditions:

- The object's invariants are valid.
- The parameters to the function are valid.

You may have other preconditions for a particular function. Some functions may be called only once; some functions may need to be called in a particular order. Some functions may have more stringent conditions than others. For example, consider an object that may allow some fields to be null. Some of the functions may expect this field to be null. Others may expect the field to be initialized already. These represent other preconditions in the object.

TIP: *Preconditions describe the assumptions for the state of an object when a function is entered. The preconditions are a superset of the object invariants.*

Post Conditions

The post conditions describe a set of conditions you expect from the object after the function has completed all its work. Once again, the post conditions are usually a superset of the class and object invariants. In addition, the post conditions will describe either that the internal state of the object did not change, or they will describe exactly how the object did change. The post conditions should also describe any changes to **ref** or **out** parameters. The post conditions also are affected by the weak or strong exception guarantee. The strong guarantee says that if an exception will be thrown by the function, the internal state of the object will not change.

TIP: *Post conditions describe the state of an object and the changes to any parameters after the function has completed its work. Post conditions are a superset of the object invariants, and are part of the definition of the work performed by the function.*

Debug Output

The .NET Framework also contains APIs that let you print either performance, or debug statements to the console. The **System. Diagnostics.Debug** and **System.Diagnostics.Trace** classes provide static methods that you can use to print output to the debug console. Both of these classes have methods that are similar to the methods in the **Console** class: **Write ()**, and **WriteLine ()**. Additionally, they have methods named **WriteIf ()**, and **WriteLineIf ()**. These can be used to conditionally generate output.

When you run the application, these statements typically get sent to the console window. When you execute your program using the Visual Studio .NET IDE debugger, the Debug output gets sent to the Output window in Visual Studio .NET.

Defensive Programming and Performance

All of this extra work takes time and cycles. Also, the defensive programming techniques are intended to stop the program immediately as soon as some assumption is no longer true. Stopping the programming immediately helps you find the cause of these problems with a minimum of effort, but it maximizes the discomfort of your users. Users don't like it when your program just stops, with no chance to save any work or finish the current task.

Every language contains special keywords and ways to add these extra defensive steps to debug builds and exclude them from release builds. C# provides both attributes and preprocessor directives to ensure that these defensive techniques are only included in debug builds. Your challenge is to ensure that these tests do not affect that behavior of your program. You do not want different behavior between your release and debug builds.

Immediate Solutions

In this section, I update the producer/consumer sample from Chapter 15 to illustrate the syntax support in the C# language for defensive programming.

Enabling Debug Output

All the classes you need for this chapter are defined in the **System.Diagnostics** namespace. Add that declaration to the top of your source files:

```
using System.Diagnostics;
```

You use the **System.Diagnostics.Debug** class to control the output from any of the classes in this namespace. The **Debug** class contains a collection of listeners that receives output from all of the objects that print messages to the console. By default, there is one listener in the collection. That listener responds only to the **Debug.Assert** message. It responds by displaying a dialog box and letting you debug or close the program (see Figure 20.1). None of the other messages will be displayed anywhere. To see any of your other error messages, you need to add other listeners:

```
// Turn on the debug consoles:
//Debug.Listeners.Clear (); uncomment to continue on errors.
Debug.Listeners.Add (new TextWriterTraceListener
    (Console.Error));
```

Figure 20.1   This dialog box shows your error message and where the assertion failed.

Notice the commented-out line. You can remove the default listener—doing so means that any of your **Assert** statements will not stop execution of the program. Rather, the output from the **Assert** message will simply be written to any of the other listeners.

Writing Invariant Functions

You write the invariant function for each class by using the **Conditional** attribute. This makes your invariant function available only in debug builds. The compiler also uses the **Conditional** attribute to remove calls to that method if the conditional is not defined. Here is the invariant function for the **PiApproximation** class:

```
[Conditional ("DEBUG")]
private void VerifyValid ()
{
  // The PI Approximation must not be null.
  Debug.Assert((_pi != null), "PiProducer Error",
    "The pi approximation object is null");

  // TotalIters must be a positive number.
  Debug.Assert ((TotalIters > 0), "Pi Producer Error",
    "The total iterations is invalid.");
}
```

This method exists only when the conditional symbol **DEBUG** has been defined (see Figure 20.2). By default, the **DEBUG** symbol is defined in debug builds for all projects created with Visual Studio .NET. **DEBUG** is not defined in release builds.

You can call the **VerifyValid ()** method anywhere in your class. If the **DEBUG** preprocessor symbol is defined, the function call is generated. If the **DEBUG** symbol is not defined, the function call is not emitted by the compiler.

You should call the **VerifyValid ()** method as the first and last statement in all public methods and public property accessors.

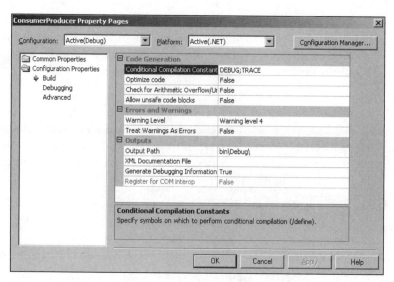

Figure 20.2 Setting the conditional compilation symbols in Visual Studio .NET.

Validating Parameters

After instrumenting the code to check your invariants at the beginning and ending of each function, you want to add checks on all the parameters in each of your functions. Here are the tests for the **PiApproximation.WriteData ()** method:

```
public void WriteData (int iterations, double val) {
  VerifyValid ();
  Debug.Assert ((iterations > 0), "PiApproximation.WriteData",
    "iterations is not greater than 0");
  Debug.Assert ((val > 2.0), "PiApproximation.WriteData",
    "val is not greater than 2.");
  Debug.Assert ((val < 4.0), "PiApproximation.WriteData",
    "val is greater than 4.");
  lock (this) {
    if (_valueReady) {
      // Wait.
      Monitor.Wait (this);
    }
    // Done waiting:
    _pi =   val;
    _iterations =   iterations;
```

```
      _valueReady =    true;
      Monitor.Pulse(this); // Signal value.
    }
    VerifyValid ();
  }
```

I have added two calls to **VerifyValid ()** at the beginning and the end of the function. In addition, I have added three different calls to **Debug.Assert ()**, which are highlighted. These calls ensure that the data being written to the approximation of pi are in the valid range. You should add similar **Assert** statements to check the validity of all the parameters in all public methods in your classes.

Testing Preconditions and Post Conditions

Testing preconditions and post conditions involves understanding the work that should be done by each method in your class. An obvious example in this application is the code that creates the thread in the **PiProducer** class:

```
public Thread CreateProducerThread () {
  VerifyValid ();
  Thread rVal = new Thread (new ThreadStart(this.calculate));
  Debug.Assert ((rVal != null), "PiProducer.CreateProducerThread",
    "Could not create thread");
  VerifyValid ();
  return rVal;
}
```

This function creates a new thread for the **PiProducer** object. If, for some unknown reason, the thread creation fails, this function did not meet its post conditions successfully. So, in addition to the **VerifyValid ()** calls that exist at the beginning and the end of this function, there is now an additional **Assert** statement to ensure that the thread was successfully created.

NOTE: *The samples shown here are somewhat simplified. In fact, all the **Assert** statements used in these examples would be caught by exceptions slightly later in the code. These techniques become far more beneficial when you are creating more complex classes with more complex capabilities. The more complicated the state of a particular object, the more useful these techniques are.*

Printing Output

You can use two different classes to print messages to all the debug listeners: **System.Diagnostics.Debug** and **System.Diagnostics. Trace**. These two classes have exactly the same interface. The difference is that debug output is controlled by the presence or absence of the **DEBUG** preprocessor symbol, and the trace output is controlled by the presence or absence of the **TRACE** preprocessor symbol. By default, the **DEBUG** symbol is defined for debug builds only; the **TRACE** symbol is defined for both debug and release builds. I have added **Debug** and **Trace** statements to print the actions of the reader:

```
public void ReadData (out int iterations, out double val) {
  VerifyValid ();
  lock (this) {
    if (!_valueReady) {
      Debug.WriteLine ("Reader is Waiting");
      // Wait.
      Monitor.Wait (this);
    }
    // Done waiting:
    Debug.Assert ((_valueReady == true),
      "PiApproximation.ReadData Error",
      "value ready false when it should have been written.");
    Trace.WriteLine ("Reading Value");
    val =   _pi;
    iterations = _iterations;
    _valueReady =   false;
    Debug.WriteLine ("Done Reading");
    Monitor.Pulse(this); // Signal.
  }
  VerifyValid ();
}
```

Trace statements are included in release builds and therefore affect performance adversely. You should use them more judiciously than **Debug** statements.

Controlling Output More Closely

Finally, there are many other methods that you can use with these two classes to filter the output from **Trace** and **Debug** based on other conditions. The **WriteIf** or **WriteLineIf** methods write output only if a particular Boolean expression is true. You can use different expressions to filter debug or trace to only some classes or objects.

The other method lets you modify the output of **Debug** and **Trace** statements using environment variables or the Registry. Two different classes allow you to control output: **BooleanSwitch** and **TraceSwitch**. You can use **TraceSwitch**, despite the name, to control **Debug** statements as well as **Trace** statements. You can set the value of either of these switch types using either an environment variable or in the Registry.

For discussion purposes, I show you how to use the **TraceSwitch**. The **BooleanSwitch** is almost the same. The only difference is that the **BooleanSwitch** can have values of enabled or disabled, rather than an enumeration of different levels.

Your first step is to create a static variable that holds the **TraceSwitch**:

```
static TraceSwitch myTraceSwitch = new TraceSwitch
  ("myTraceSwitch", "The test switch");
```

You use the switch by checking different properties on the switch to determine if a particular trace level has been enabled. Each higher level implies all lower levels:

Value	Output	Meaning
0	Off	No output
1	Error	Print error messages
2	Warning	Print warning messages
3	Info	Print informational messages
4	Verbose	Print all diagnostic messages

You can toggle different **Debug** and **Trace** statements on or off by using these properties:

```
Debug.WriteLineIf (myTraceSwitch.TraceError, "Done Reading");
```

The preceding statement prints the **Done Reading** message if the trace switch is set to Error, Warning, Info, or Verbose. You can set the value of the switch using a .config file for the application:

```
<configuration>
  <system.diagnostics>
    <switches>
```

```
            <add name="myTraceSwitch" value="3" />
        </switches>
    </system.diagnostics>
</configuration>
```

The preceding config file would set the switch to Info.

Using this technique, you can specify different switches to control different parts of your program's output. This can help you pinpoint the location of any errors and find them quickly.

The capability to set **Trace/Boolean Switches** via the Registry and by environment variables is no longer available. Now, you must use a .config file to do this.

Chapter 21

Profiling C# Applications

In Brief

The .NET Framework creates and uses Windows 2000 or Windows NT performance counters to analyze the runtime performance of your application. The .NET Framework creates many categories that you can use to monitor the performance of the .NET Framework. In addition, you can create your own custom counters to log performance data. In both cases, you read the performance data using the Perform tools. You can use these tools to monitor your application's performance and determine what areas of your application to concentrate on to increase performance.

The use of the standard Windows performance counters gives you some great advantages: You can use the Perform tools to find relationships among different measurements on the performance of your application.

.NET Performance Counters

Nine different categories of performance counters are defined by the .NET runtime. These counters display the performance characteristics of the .NET CLR. You can view these standard counters to determine how well your application interacts with the .NET runtime.

The category you will use most often is the *Memory* category. The Memory category lets you see what the garbage collector does when your application is running. I use the % Time In GC and the heap sizes for Generation 0 through Generation 2 counters most. Those counters help me watch how often my application interacts with the garbage collector. Those counters will help you understand when your application needs more memory, how quickly it allocates memory, and when it slows down for garbage collection operations.

The other categories are more specialized. If you are writing an application with many different threads, the *Threading* category can help you determine how often threads try unsuccessfully to acquire locks. You can also determine how much time the CLR spends scheduling threads, rather than letting your application do its work.

The *Loading* category helps you determine how much executing time your application spends finding and loading assemblies. You can use the counters described in this section to see any performance implications in your application that are related to having the CLR find and load assemblies you reference.

Custom Performance Counters

In addition to using the standard .NET performance counters, you can create your own custom counters and write values to the system log. The **System.Diagnostics** namespace contains several classes that let you read standard values, create and write custom values, and create and write computed values.

Like all performance-measuring tools, you need to exercise some restraint when you collect performance data. The more data you try to collect, the more the act of collecting data interferes with the actions of your program. Performance profiling takes a number of iterations to get correct, especially for large programs. Your first task will be to isolate where your program spends the most time. You can start this task by finding the number of calls per second in interesting methods. This will tell you which methods in your application are being called the most often.

Immediate Solutions

To show you how you can monitor your applications, I add some performance counters to the multithreaded pi calculator application written for Chapter 15. Specifically, I add a performance counter to monitor the number of iterations performed per second.

Adding Performance Conditionals

To do performance testing, you want a new build configuration that copies the release build settings but that adds a new conditional symbol to control performance metric generation. To create a new build configuration, select Build|Configuration Manager. Select <New...> from the combo box. Next, you need to create a new configuration that copies the current release build settings. Enter PERFORMANCE for the configuration name, and select the release build as the source from which to copy settings (see Figure 21.1).

After you have created the new configuration, select the PERFORMANCE build as the active configuration. Right-click on the Solution node in the Solution Explorer and select Properties. Add a new conditional compilation symbol PERFORMANCE (see Figure 21.2). Now, this new build will include code selected for conditional compilation based on the PERFORMANCE symbol. You will want to associate all the code that performs performance tracking with this symbol.

Figure 21.1   Copying build settings to make a new build configuration.

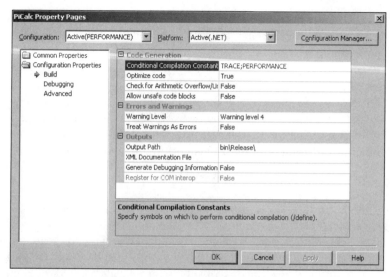

Figure 21.2 Adding conditional symbols to control performance-tracking code.

Creating Performance Counters

You need to follow several steps to create a performance counter. You need to create a category of performance counters. The function that creates a category takes a collection of counters that are added to the category. So, the first step is to create a collection of categories:

```
CounterCreationDataCollection counters = new
  CounterCreationDataCollection ();
```

Next, you add the counter creation data object to the collection:

```
CounterCreationData cnt = new CounterCreationData(
  "Iterations per Sec",
  "The number of iterations per second",
  PerformanceCounterType.RateOfCountsPerSecond32);
counters.Add (cnt);
```

The **CounterCreationData** object describes the data stored in the counter. The first two parameters are the name and the description of the counter. The third parameter describes the type of counter. The

419

RateOfCountsPerSecond32 is by far the most common counter that you will use. It calculates the rate of change to the counter and reports the rate of change of this counter over time. Next, you need to create the category:

```
PerformanceCounterCategory c = null;
if (PerformanceCounterCategory.Exists("AppPerformance")) {
  PerformanceCounterCategory.Delete ("AppPerformance");
}
c = PerformanceCounterCategory.Create("AppPerformance",
  "Iteration Counters", counters);
```

This block of code removes the category if it exists, and then re-creates it. I generally structure the code that creates the category this way because it is more resilient to change. If you try to create a category that already exists, it will fail. However, you may very well want to add and remove performance counters during the course of performance analysis. So, with each run I simply remove the category and re-create it with the set of counters that I feel are necessary now.

Finally, you need to get a handle to any of the counters you need and make them writeable, as follows:

```
perfCounter = c.GetCounters()[0];
perfCounter.ReadOnly = false;
```

Here, **perfCounter** is a member variable that holds a reference to the performance counter. By default, all performance counters are read-only. (You can also write applications that read existing performance counters without creating their own performance counters. I don't cover that here, however.) By setting the **ReadOnly** property to false, you indicate that your application is writing this performance counter instead of reading it. Listing 21.1 shows the entire function, including the attribute to control the compilation.

Listing 21.1   Creating a performance counter to track performance.

```
// Added for performance counters:
#ifdef PERFORMANCE
private PerformanceCounter perfCounter;
#endif

[Conditional ("PERFORMANCE")]
private void CreatePerfCounter () {
  // Create the collection:
  CounterCreationDataCollection counters = new
    CounterCreationDataCollection ();
```

```
// Create the counter data:
CounterCreationData cnt = new CounterCreationData(
  "Iterations per Sec",
  "The number of iterations per second",
  PerformanceCounterType.RateOfCountsPerSecond32);
counters.Add (cnt);

// Re-initialize the category:
PerformanceCounterCategory c = null;
if (PerformanceCounterCategory.Exists("AppPerformance")) {
  PerformanceCounterCategory.Delete ("AppPerformance");
}
c = PerformanceCounterCategory.Create("AppPerformance",
  "Iteration Counters", counters);

// Make the counter writable:
perfCounter = c.GetCounters()[0];
perfCounter.ReadOnly = false;
}
```

Related solution:	Found on page:
Controlling Conditional Compilation	212

Writing to Performance Counters

Writing the counter is simple: You use the **Increment()** or **IncrementBy()** method to change the value of the counter:

```
[Conditional ("PERFORMANCE")]
private void UpdatePerfCounter (int incBy) {
  perfCounter.IncrementBy (incBy);
}
```

I wrap the code that modifies a counter inside a function for two reasons. First, if you are using more than one counter, one function can perform all the updates to the counters. Second, I prefer the **Conditional** attribute to the preprocessor statements. You can only apply the **Conditional** attribute to functions, not to blocks or individual statements.

Finally, you need to call the **UpdatePerfCounter** function in your thread method, as shown in the following code:

```
// This function uses the Leibnitz series to
// calculate pi:
// Pi = 1 - 1/3 + 1/5 - 1/7 etc.
private void calculate () {
  double series = 0;
  do {
    series += 1.0/(double)_iters - 1.0/(double)(_iters+2);
    lock (this) {
      _iters += 4;
      _pi = series * 4;
      UpdatePerfCounter (1);
    }
  } while (_iters < TotalIters);
}
```

Using the Performance Monitor

To manage the performance, you run the application, which makes the performance counter category and counters for the first time. Next, run the performance monitor. You will find it in the Start menu under Administrative Tools. Alternatively, you can type "perfmon" from the Run command on the Start menu.

Next, click on the plus (+) icon on the toolbar. Doing so allows you to add a counter (see Figure 21.3). Select the AppPerformance performance object. This category has only one counter: the iterations per second. Select it and click on Add. After you have added all the counters you want to watch, click on Close.

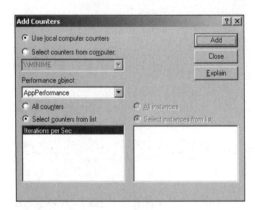

Figure 21.3   Adding a performance counter.

Next, start the application. Pause the thread as often as you like. You will get a graph that resembles the one shown in the rightmost part of Figure 21.4.

In larger applications, you will be examining the relationships between different performance counters. You can add standard .NET performance counters to interact with the counters you have made. Then you can analyze the interaction between different variables in the application.

All of this examination may require more analysis than you can do by simply watching Perfmon. In these cases, you can create logfiles from performance data that Perfmon collects. These logfiles are CSV files that you can import into Excel or any other spreadsheet program to analyze after collecting data.

To create a logfile, open the Performance Logs And Alerts node in the tree view. Select the Counter Logs. Right-click in the rightmost pane and select New Log Settings. Create a new log file and add the performance counters you want to measure. You can create logfiles that are constantly generating, which is useful for measuring services, or you can manually start and stop the logfile. After running the logs, you can import the logfile data into your favorite spreadsheet program

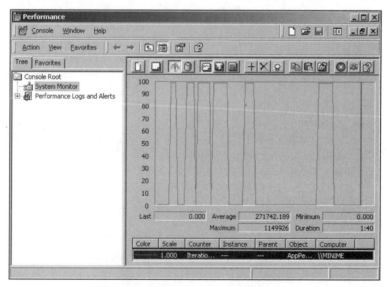

Figure 21.4   Monitoring performance calculating pi.

(again, Excel is an excellent choice) for any type of statistical analysis you need to perform to determine where the bottlenecks are in your application.

I demonstrated only one type of performance counter in this chapter. There are several others. The .NET Framework documentation shows how to create and interact with these different counters. The main key is to collect data that helps you isolate the performance bottlenecks in your application.

Preprocessor Directives

The purpose of this appendix is to provide you with a brief description of the C# preprocessor directives. You can find information on all the preprocessor directives in the C# language documentation that is part of the .NET Framework or Visual Studio .NET. If you are like me, however, you won't think of searching for some particular preprocessor directive to solve a particular problem. So, here is a brief description of each C# preprocessor directive with which you can work, and of what each one does.

Managing Preprocessor Symbols

You can use the **#define** preprocessor directive to define a conditional symbol:

```
#define TEST_BUILD
```

You can also remove a symbol using **#undef** preprocessor directive:

```
#undef TEST_BUILD
```

You create the same kind of symbols using the **/define** or **/d** compiler option. Symbols created with **#define** or **/d** are a type of Boolean value: The symbol either exists or it does not exist. Unlike C and C++, you cannot create variables with **#define**. These symbols can be used only with either the **Conditional** attribute or with **#if** preprocessor directives.

Conditional Compilation

You use the **#if**, **#elif**, **#else**, and **#endif** preprocessor directives to compile code conditionally:

```
#if TEST_BUILD
  // test code.
#elif RELEASE_BUILD
  // release algorithms.
#else
  // other code.
#endif
```

You can also combine symbols using **&&** (AND) or II (OR). You can also use **!** to represent NOT:

```
#if (TEST_BUILD || DEBUG)
  // test code.
#endif

#if (!DEBUG && TRACE)
    // trace, but not debug code.
#endif
```

These preprocessor directives differ from the **Conditional** attribute in that the **Conditional** attribute can be applied only to methods (functions or properties), not to individual code blocks.

Generating Messages

The **#warning** and **#error** preprocessor directives generate messages during builds. These directives can be nested inside **#if** messages:

```
#if TEST_BUILD
#warning Creating Test Build
#endif
```

The preceding code generates a warning message when **TEST_BUILD** is defined: The **#error** directive (shown in the following code) works the same but instead generates an error message:

```
#if (TEST_BUILD && RELEASE)
#error Creating Test Build with Release defined!
#endif
```

Editing Regions

You can use the **#region** and **#endregion** directives to create expanding/collapsing blocks when you use the Visual Studio .NET outlining features. The following snippet shows an example of this:

```
#region MemberVariables
   int i;
   double j;
#endregion
```

Visual Studio .NET creates regions when it creates your project. The regions encapsulate the code created and edited by the resource editor in Visual Studio .NET. You can create your own regions to make managing code blocks an easier process.

Modifying Line Numbers

I honestly can't figure out how useful this one usually is. It changes the line number, and optionally the filename, for error messages by the compiler.

```
// change errors to line 400, file InjectedCode.cs
#line 400 "InjectedCode.cs"
// code ..
// restore line number and filename.
#line default

// change line number:
#line 10000
// More code.
#line default
```

XML Documentation

As with the listing of the preprocessor directives in Appendix A, this appendix lists the XML tags you can use to document your C# code. Once again, this is a brief list that is organized based on the use of each tag. For more details on how each tag is used, consult the C# language documentation. You should use this appendix to see quickly which tags are applicable to the particular task you want to accomplish.

Remember that all tags must be preceded by /// comments.

General Tags

These tags can be used with any type in your source files. You will use these tags whenever you document your classes and methods.

Describing Types

The **<summary>** tag provides a brief description of the type:

```
/// <summary>
/// This class does the work of twenty men
/// in half the time.
/// </summary>
```

The **<remarks>** tag provides a longer description of the type:

```
/// <remarks>
/// This class creates many resources. It also does
/// a tremendous amount of work on our behalf.  If that
/// is not enough, this class can also determine when you
/// need a new cup of coffee.
/// </remarks>
```

Formatting Text

The **<para>** tag inserts a new paragraph inside another tag. Typically, it would be used with the remarks tag:

```
/// <remarks>
/// This class creates many resources. It also does
/// a tremendous amount of work on our behalf.  If that
/// is not enough, this class can also determine when you
/// need a new cup of coffee.
/// <para>
/// If it is too warm out, this class will tell you to get
/// a cola instead of a cup of coffee.
/// </para>
/// </remarks>
```

You can also create dictionary lists using the **<list>**, **<listheader>**, **<item>** and **<description>** tags to create a list in your documentation.

```
/// <list type="bullet">
///    <listheader>
///       <term>symbol</term>
///       <description>element</description>
///    </listheader>
///    <item>
///       <term>H</term>
///       <description>
///          Hydrogen
///       </description>
///    </item>
///    <item>
///       <term>He</term>
///       <description>
///          Helium
///       </description>
///    </item>
/// </list>
```

Creating Links

The **<seealso>** tag generates a cross reference:

```
/// <summary>
/// This class does the work of twenty men
/// in half the time.
/// <seealso cref="Class1.Main"/>
/// <seealso cref="Class1.Class1"/>
/// </summary>
```

At other times, you will want to place a link inline in the text you are creating, as follows:

```
/// <summary>
/// This class does the work of twenty men
/// in <see cref="half"/> the time.
/// <seealso cref="Class1.Main"/>
/// <seealso cref="Class1.Class1"/>
/// </summary>
```

You can also highlight a reference to a parameter by using the **<paramref>** tag:

```
/// <remarks>
/// This method waits for <paramref name="WaitTime"/> seconds.
/// </remarks>
public void Wait (int WaitTime) {
   // etc.
}
```

Using Tag Libraries

The **<include>** tag includes documentation from another file and lets you separate the code from the documentation, or it lets you reuse the documentation. Here is an example that loads an included file:

```
/// <include file='lib.doc'path='Lib/Member[@name="test"]/*' />
class C1
```

Here is a portion of lib.doc:

```
<Lib>
<Member name="test">
  <summary>The Test type </summary>
  <remarks>
    I am grabbing text from an included file
  </remarks>
</Member>
</Lib>
```

Code Samples

The **<c>** tag displays a single word as code, as shown in the following snippet:

```
/// <remarks>
/// Use the <c>Main</c> method to start
/// execution of the program.
/// </remarks>
```

You use the **<example>** tag to create an example. You nest the **<code>** tag inside the **<example>** tag to display the example code, as follows:

```
/// <example>
/// You construct the object giving it
/// the size of the cup of coffee you
/// want later:
/// <code>
/// HelpfulClass c = new HelpfulClass (16, oz);
/// </code>
/// </example>
```

Special Types

The **<exception>** tag, which is shown in the following example, describes an exception class:

```
/// <exception cref="System.Exception">
/// This exception is thrown when your
/// coffee spills.
/// </exception>
public class CoffeeSpilledException :
  System.Exception {
  // etc.
}
```

The **<value>** tag describes a property, as follows:

```
/// <value>This property returns the size
/// of your coffee.</value>
public Size {
  get {
    return CoffeeSize;
  }
}
```

Describing Methods

The **<param>** tag, shown in the following example, describes a method parameter:

```
/// <param name="coffeeSize">The size of the
/// cup of coffee.</param>
void MakeCoffee (int coffeeSize)
```

The **<returns>** tag describes a return value:

```
/// <returns>true if the coffee is done,
/// false if it is still brewing.</returns>
bool IsBrewing () {
 // etc.
```

The **<permission>** tag lets you specify the permission for a method. The **System.Security.PermissionSet** class describes the possible permissions:

```
/// <permission cref=>public</permission>
public static void Main () {
}
```

Index

A

Abort ( ) method, 298
Abstract classes, 25, 27, 170
  arrays, 326
  creating, 178–179
abstract keyword, 178
Abstract methods, 170
  creating, 179
  virtual, 170
Access modifiers
  defining properties, 74
  guidelines for use, 69
  list of, 70
  restricting data access with
    properties, 104
AcquireReaderLock ( ) method, 314
Addition operator, 31
Arithmetic operators, 31–32
  compound assignment, 63
  using, 63–64
ArrayList class, 329, 339–340
  enumerating collections, 340–341
  properties, 340
  searching, 343–344
  sorting, 341–342
  trimming, 340
Arrays. *See also* Collections.
  description of, 326
  jagged, 328
  length property, 13
  methods, 339
  multiple dimension, 328
  single dimension, 327–328, 335, 337
  string objects, 7

as keyword, 55
ASP.NET
  consuming a Web Service, 376–377
  creating WebForms, 349, 368–371
  creating Web Services, 371–372
  description of, 367
  files created for Web pages, 368
  testing Web Services, 373–376
Assemblies
  building strong names for, 400
  components of, 4–5
  global assembly installation, 400
  loading, 84
  locating types in, 386–387
  manifests, 4–5, 18
  metadata, 380, 384–386
  packaging, 4
  reviewing contents of, 14–15
  versions, 394
Assignment operators, 64–65
Attributes
  in assemblies, 211
  creating, 208–209, 219–220
  description of, 3, 206
  COM interoperability, 208
  conditional, 206–207, 212–213
  finding in a module, 220–221
  guidelines for creating, 209
  mandatory parameters, 210
  obsolete code, 208, 213–214
  properties as parameters, 210–211
  version number, 394
  Web Services, 207–208, 214–219
AttributeUsage attribute, 209

N

T

X